APR 2 0 2018

D0398290

The Rest of It

MARTIN DUBERMAN

The Rest of It:
Hustlers, Cocaine, Depression, and Then Some, 1976–1988

DUKE UNIVERSITY PRESS | DURHAM AND LONDON | 2018

© 2018 Duke University Press
All rights reserved
Printed in the United States of America
   on acid-free paper ∞
Designed by Amy Ruth Buchanan
Typeset in Arno Pro and Montserrat by
   Westchester Publishing Services

Library of Congress Cataloging-in-Publication Data
Names: Duberman, Martin B., author.
Title: The rest of it : hustlers, cocaine, depression,
   and then some, 1976–1988 / Martin Duberman.
Description: Durham : Duke University Press, 2018. |
   Includes bibliographical references and index.
Identifiers: LCCN 2017036324 (print)
LCCN 2017044097 (ebook)
ISBN 9780822371861 (ebook)
ISBN 9780822370703 (hardcover : alk. paper)
Subjects: LCSH: Duberman, Martin B. | Gay men—
   United States—Biography. | Gay liberation
   movement—United States—History.
Classification: LCC HQ75.8.D82 (ebook) |
   LCC HQ75.8.D82 A3 2018 (print) |
   DDC 306.76/62092—dc23
LC record available at https://lccn.loc.gov/2017036324

Cover art: Martin Duberman, 1981. Photo by Jill Fineberg.
Manuscripts and Archives Division, The New York Public Library,
Astor, Lenox, and Tilden Foundations.

To the memory of my mother

JOSEPHINE BAUML DUBERMAN

who saved my life but not her own

To break out of the structures of the arrogant eye we have to dare to rely on ourselves to make meaning and we have to imagine ourselves beings capable of that: capable of weaving the web of meaning which will hold us in some kind of intelligibility.

—Marilyn Frye, "In and Out of Harm's Way," in *Politics of Reality: Essays in Feminist Theory*

Contents

Preface

A number of people over the years have made a similar comment to me about my earlier autobiographical books: "How come you've never written about one whole decade, from the mid-seventies to the mid-eighties?"

When I stopped to think about it, the answer was obvious: "Those were the most painful years of my life. To stir them up again might be psychologically risky. They're better left alone." Avoidance and denial might well have worked forever, but having raised the question and answered it, I somehow felt the need to push ahead. Perhaps because it felt cowardly not to. Perhaps because I'd grown tired of late of writing about other people's lives. Perhaps—this is the hardest to admit—because I've long been aware that the general view of me is that I've had one of those rare charmed lives devoid of trauma, a view I understood and even thought reasonable, yet nonetheless resented. As I've grown older I've increasingly played the role assigned me of problem-free Super-Privileged White Man even as I silently grumbled about "not being understood." I wanted to yawp with the rest of them.

So here it is. And it isn't all pain and lamentation. Yes, it was a difficult decade, complete with heart attack, cocaine and hustler addictions, and confinement in a locked ward at Payne-Whitney. But it was also the decade in which I was able to publish a collection of my essays, coedit the anthology *Hidden from History: Exploring the Gay Past*, and, above all, complete my biography of Paul Robeson. Yes, it was a decade replete with repetitive angst over unresponsive lovers, one in which long-standing friendships and political alliances were broken, and one marked by depression and hospitalization. Yet it was also a decade that ended with meeting the man with whom I've lived ever since, which ultimately put me on a calmer, more sustainable path in life.

My Mother's Death

My mother had been operated on for a rectal tumor in 1976 that the surgeon, immediately following the operation, told me was benign; cancer, he said, could be ruled out. Then came the first pathology report, shocking us all with the diagnosis of malignant melanoma. Her doctor scheduled a series of tests to determine whether the melanoma was present anywhere else in her body; he was "hopeful"—though not "certain"—it was not.

The next month was a roller coaster of contradictory findings, raised hopes, sudden deflations. On October 28, my mother's seventy-fourth birthday, her doctors operated again: a "tiny recurrence," the surgeon said, adding that he'd "had to go pretty deep" and was keeping his fingers crossed that she wouldn't lose control of the sphincter muscle. She didn't, and was soon out of the hospital and back working every day in her tiny resale shop, Treasures and Trifles, while undergoing chemotherapy treatments.

A woman of bedrock courage (belied by the surface habit of petty complaint), she refused to let me or anyone else in the family accompany her to the treatments. She carefully worked out the logistics, timing the return leg of the car or bus trip (she'd impatiently dismissed the suggestion that she take a cab: "Why throw money out?") from the doctor's office to her apartment in Mount Vernon so that the vomiting that always followed a treatment would begin only after she'd safely reached home.

While the treatments were still ongoing she decided to cook one of her legendary family dinners: "my welcome back to life," she gamely called it. She outdid herself, preparing *two* sets of hors d'oeuvres, turkey, pot roast *and* tongue, strawberry *and* banana shortcakes. My sister proposed the right toast: "To a gallant lady." As evening came on and relatives started to leave, I caught the deep melancholy settling into

Ma's eyes, heard her unspoken thought: "The last time . . . the last . . ." I saw her firmly shake off the melancholy, determinedly rejoin the conversation. Who expects nobility in one's own mother? Having harbored for so long my youthful set of grievances against her, using up what compassion I had on myself, I got a belated glimpse into the stunningly brave woman who should have been—who was—so much more than Marty's "difficult" mother.

It did prove her last family dinner. By the summer of 1977 she'd developed swollen lymph nodes and—a woman who'd had insomnia all her adult life—began to spend an unnerving amount of time asleep. Her doctor told me on the phone (my mother allowed me to call him, if not go with her to see him) that "melanoma is fickle." He imperiously ticked off his ramifying and contradictory findings: yes, he was "virtually certain" the nodes are affected; no, chemotherapy is not "entirely useless" in combating the spread; yes, her endless sleeping "does suggest neurological complications"; yes, one could "just as logically" ascribe the sleeping to effects of the chemotherapy. He warned me against telling her the truth about her condition, which, as we moved into late summer, he spoke of as "hopeless": "Nothing more can be done medically, and she will not be able to handle the news."

I'd always thought of my mother as a person who could handle anything. In my own psychological arsenal she'd served as the super-concerned, omnipotent force that could make everything come out right. Her shamanistic power to chase away disappointment and fear remained with me even after my teen years, when I'd stopped telling her anything important about myself because I didn't want to risk getting near the subject of central importance: my homosexuality.

I already knew she could handle it. Five years earlier, when my essay review "The Literature on Homosexuality" was about to appear in the *New York Times*, I felt I had to give her advance warning. As I wrote in my diary, "This is nothing for a 70 year old woman to be reading in print." One night when I was befogged with fatigue, I "casually" blurted out on the phone that a review of mine was about to appear in which I mentioned my homosexuality. "Do you go into much detail?" she unhesitatingly asked. "No," I truthfully said, "it's just something I mention in passing." There was an audible sigh of relief, quickly followed by her saying, "Well, I'm very proud of you. It's a changing world, and nobody knows what normal means anymore. People who claim they do are stupid." I don't know what I stammered in reply—I was fighting back tears. Broaching the subject once proved quite enough for both of us; I knew it would make her sad and make me feel guilty. I was still too ashamed of being gay; "coming out," most people don't seem to realize, is often a *strategy* for greater self-acceptance, not the thing itself. I was bold enough in 1972 to declare my homosexuality publicly and had already become deeply engaged in the gay political movement, but I remained tongue-tied about the subject with my own mother.

I decided to go along with the doctor's advice and not tell her that her own condition was "hopeless." I'd never been convinced of the dictum that "a patient has the right to know." *I* wouldn't want to know: I'd want some hope to hang on to. My mother was more of a stoic, but I wasn't sure how much more. As for the touted right to face death directly and with dignity, that might be fine for those with a serene sense of completion—or a belief in an afterlife—but neither trait was part of the family heritage.

Besides, I knew my mother's minimal financial affairs were in order, and I couldn't bear to dwell on the disarray of her emotional ones. Ours had been a deeply conflicted, fumblingly potent bond, a connection achingly resonant with empathy yet encased in muted friction, profoundly entangled in issues of suffocating invasion and control. With the onset of puberty—and sexual awareness—I'd retreated into a monosyllabic silence when around her that became habitual: guilt about my sexual desires, in combination with an underlay of resentment over my mother's relentlessly intrusive personality, led me to build a protective fortress around myself. I couldn't stand the thought that in all likelihood she was going to die with so much—and especially so much tenderness—left unexpressed, nor that she was going to leave me bereft of what felt like my one true ally.

I decided to take my cue from her; if she pressed for more clarity about her condition, I'd *try* to provide it. But that decision wasn't easy to implement. I kept changing my mind about how much she already knew (or sensed) and about how much more she wanted to know. She'd sometimes whisper secretively to me that she knew she was dying, and now and then even threatened to kill herself. A day later she'd insist she was feeling much better, that her sleepiness must be due to the chemo treatments, and that she didn't need me "hovering" over her all the time.

Some of the family had planned to gather early in August 1977 in celebration of my forty-seventh birthday, at my cousin Ron's house in Saratoga. My mother insisted we proceed with the outing and, once we were there, insisted on going along with us to the race track. Her gallantry got her through five hours of muggy heat and engulfing crowds, but the following day she was noticeably more feeble—"all broken up," as she put it.

She propped herself up on the living-room sofa, shaky and weak, trying to stay awake, trying to maintain through sheer force of will some semblance of her usual place in the family tableau. The piercing high spirits of Ron's two young children as they dashed gleefully back and forth through the room provided some relief—as well as anguish at how their exuberance highlighted her own debilitated state. She smiled sadly as the shrieking two-year-old careened around the room, remembering (so I imagined) the antics of her own adored cherub forty-five years earlier.

In our few minutes alone she listlessly went over and over the advisability of continuing this or that medication, believing this or that diagnosis. She acted as if real decisions were at stake, but her tone confirmed a gut-level awareness that the debated options were nonexistent. Toward the end of the day she became nearly comatose. As I carried her to the car for the trip back home, she seemed angry at my touch, brushing away my arm with what little strength she had. ("So now, when it's too late," said her furious, unspoken words in my head, "you're willing to embrace me.")

That night I wrote in my diary, "I broke down at one point, but turned away before she could see. For all I know she wants to see, wants confirmation that someone cares, wants permission to mourn together. We don't trust ourselves. We can't comfort others. The family talks of the need to make her last days 'peaceful'—meaning easy on *us*. Our automatic response is evasion. We bicker over tactics, scapegoat each other, offer false support. All in the name of sparing *her*. What shit! *We* don't want pain. Bury it! Bury her! Quick, quick! Before anyone discovers anything. About being human."

Her doctor (as I wrote my close friend Barbara) was "a monster of arrogance and inhumanity"; we could rarely get him even to come to the phone, and when face to face in his office he alternately ignored and shouted at us. "I've been tempted," I wrote Barbara, "to punch him in the face—I mean literally." But my mother was terrified that he'd wash his hands of her case, and I felt he *was* entirely capable of throwing us out of his office, of refusing to continue as her doctor.

Following the trip to Saratoga, the melanoma spread into her abdomen and symptoms began to proliferate. For a time I think my sister and I managed (barely) to persuade her that the mounting pain and swelling were due to a combination of the chemo treatments, her "nerves," and an ulcer we invented. As the side effects from the chemo worsened, she shrank noticeably, but her mind remained sharp and her will fierce. The point came when her doctor finally decided to stop the chemo, though he told us he might begin radiation—even while admitting that it was unlikely to do any good, that the side effects were "unpleasant," and that it would then be impossible to keep her from knowing the worst. On one level I felt she already knew: she would increasingly tell me that she was "dying," but I chose to believe that she did so in the hope of being contradicted rather than because she believed her own statement.

My sister and I took turns staying with her during the day while her unmarried sister, "Tedda," with whom she'd long lived (my father having died some fifteen years earlier), was at work. Mostly we just sat in her apartment while she slept more and more. When I looked in at her asleep on the bed, her slight, thin body appeared almost girlish, and it would set me to thinking sorrowfully of how little happiness she'd ever found. Beautiful, smart, dynamic, she—like most women of her generation—had never had much of a chance. She'd gone to work in her teens, finishing high school at night, had made a mostly prudential marriage, had poured her prodigious energy into housewifely routines, and, when her marriage turned loveless, had poured it into contentious altercations with friends and driven devotion to my sister's three children—leavened, happily, by a resilient good-natured ability to make fun of herself.

When she was awake it was even harder. I could barely choke down tears while watching her hand tremble as she tried to raise a glass to her lips. In an apathetic, almost languid way, she'd go over and over the "mistake" she'd made in letting them do the original operation or, more energetically, would adamantly reject as a "waste of money" my suggestion that she let a housekeeper come in for at least one or two days a week. Sometimes she seemed so perky and rational that I'd start to wonder all over again—using *her* words—whether the original diagnosis had been right, whether her current weakness wasn't (as we'd kept assuring her) the byproduct of the accumulated chemo treatments, whether she hadn't entered a stage of remission.

Other family members felt she should be hospitalized, but I fought that decision, arguing that she should have the comfort of her own home, that there was nothing left to do medically that hadn't been done, and that at this terminal point in her illness the hospital doctors would only torture her, probing and testing solely for *their* information. But by mid-August she was sleeping almost continuously, refusing food, and, when awake, growing increasingly disoriented.

As her mind began to go, the day finally came when I agreed she needed to be in the hospital, and we took her by ambulance to Mount Sinai. Everything I feared would happen, did. She became instantly alert, terrified, angry; convinced that they would operate again and that she was dying, she began to tremble with anxiety, even as she energetically denounced the "needless expense" of a private room. The hospital staff seemed infuriatingly indifferent; her doctor never showed up that first day; she was refused sedation ("We have to have her clear for the brain scan"); and I couldn't get a nurse to even bring her a blanket. Choking with rage, I had to simultaneously invent rationales for calming her down: "Only a few days for tests"; "You need care and intravenous feeding to build back your strength."

When I finally got back to my apartment that first night, I felt, as I wrote brokenly in my diary, "helpless, defeated . . . *they've* got her now . . . couldn't spare her this final horror. . . . I think of her alone in that dark room, the needle in her arm, eyes glazed with fear . . . she would have managed to prevent that from happening to me. . . . I'm okay when I'm with her in the hospital, can't stop crying back here in the apartment . . . feel so fucking alone . . . the family keeps saying 'she's in better hands now.' Yeah, sure. We're better off, Ma's not."

When I arrived the next morning she seemed less fearful—or was too weak to express it, her voice so low I had to put my ear next to her lips to hear. She was mostly rational, except that she kept asking me whether "everyone has had lunch" and warning me to watch her pocketbook: the condensation of two lifetime obsessions. Her doctor finally appeared, said he'd begun "tests," thought the melanoma had reached her brain and that "the ballpark figure" was, "best guess," only a few weeks. But, he warned, "she could last five to six months. Your family had better start thinking of putting her in a nursing home."

They moved her that day into a two-bed room with another woman dying of cancer who kept screaming, "Marion! Marion! . . . Help, oh help! Get me out of here! . . . They've burnt my legs off! . . . We're stranded!" She went on screaming all that night. Next day I learned Ma had tried to get out of bed and had had a bad fall; they had then tied her down. When I arrived that morning, she was rattling the metal guards on the sides of her bed, moaning and tossing. As soon as she saw me, she cried out, "Take me home! Take me home!" Over and over she repeated the words, her glazed eyes forlornly appealing to me. Then, in a conspiratorial whisper, she told me to go to the closet and get her clothes: "Shush . . . not a word, they'll hear . . . get me dressed . . . we'll slip out . . . they won't see . . . into the car." She looked feverishly around the room for her dress, as her roommate took up the keening chorus, "Get us out! Get us out!"

In my shock, I tried to placate her: "Okay, Ma, yeah . . . I'll get your stockings . . . just be patient . . . just one minute." I dashed out to get a floor nurse. "I'm the only person on duty," the nurse at the desk responded coldly. "Your mother will just have to wait. She has private-duty nurses. Let them take care of her." I tried to explain that the private nurse hadn't shown up for her shift and that my mother needed attention *now*. I got a blank, hostile stare. She returned to her charts.

Racing back into the room, I discovered my mother had ripped the IV out of her arm and managed somehow to slide halfway down the bed, determined to escape. This time I tried admonition: "You *can't* go home now . . . two more tests . . . that's all . . . while you're here you must get the tests . . . try to be patient just a little longer, a little longer . . . I'll take you home *soon*."

"Not true," she responded angrily to each phony phrase. "Not true! . . . Not true!" Her voice sounded strangely fierce and adamant. Had she suddenly become rational again? Was she, in some bitter, final defiance, bent on a comprehensive unmasking of all the false blueprints that had been handed her for a "happy, meaningful" life. Two hours later the private-duty nurse finally arrived, and Ma subsided into mumbled agitation. I could hardly bear to look at her—my dynamo mother turned into a tiny, yellowing bag of bones, her voice gone, her eyes glazed.

But I couldn't stand not being in the hospital either.

Her doctor arrived to report that the brain scan was "negative," quickly adding, "It only picks up gross infiltration." He thought she would become increasingly and rapidly comatose yet doubted that she was approaching death. He urged me to proceed with my long-arranged plan to fly to Los Angeles for a few days, where my play, *Visions of Kerouac*, was in rehearsal at the Odyssey Theater and due to open soon. He said he could always call me back if her condition unexpectedly changed, though he didn't expect any dramatic developments over the next week or so. The family urged the same course, as did, more insistently, the play's producer, Lee Sankowich.

Lee had been phoning daily from L.A., begging me not to delay any longer. He'd already postponed opening night once, and to do it a second time would be taken as a sure sign that the play was in deep trouble. Lee was a soft-edged, decent man, but his latest call had been agitated: "The *Los Angeles Times* is offering to do a big spread on the opening, but that's contingent on your availability for a personal interview within the next several days. The article is *essential* to the play's success." He begged me to leave for L.A. at once.

Everyone insisted that I go, that there was nothing more to do for Ma, that she was no longer able to recognize anyone other than fleetingly, that it was now essentially a vigil. The doctor repeated that he expected no significant change for at least a week, other than her becoming increasingly comatose, and they could call me back if necessary. Ambition finally outweighing guilt, I decided to risk the trip. The night before I was due to leave, Ma's face lit up when I walked into the hospital room: she did momentarily recognize me, her beatific boy, her adored baby—then lapsed quickly back into vacancy, patting her hair distractedly, her blank eyes frantically searching the room for some unnamable, supremely precious object just out of reach. I broke down in tears.

The next morning the hospital called at 4:30. My mother had died, the nurse said, a few minutes before. How typical, I thought, between the tears: she didn't want to inconvenience me.

Attempted Therapies:
Theater, LSD, Bioenergetics

It would take a long while before I let myself experience the full impact of my mother's death. Immediately after her funeral I was in Los Angeles, the sharp edge of grief continually blunted by the typical hoopla of alarms and expectations that surround a theatrical opening. The awareness that she was gone, though, was never far off, the little boy's secure conviction of impregnable protection ripped away. It was as if a hostile force had shoved me out into a fierce thunderstorm, with no shelter in sight. A profound chasm had opened at my feet, and if I stared into it too fixedly, I'd lose my footing. My grief was all mixed up with a profound sense of guilt over how much that needed saying between us would never be said, the tensions never resolved, the love never expressed.

I sensed that it was too much to face all at once, and I tried to distance myself from the pain in whatever ways I could. In the first few weeks after returning to New York, it helped that I was absorbed with cleaning out my mother's personal possessions and with family fights of unexpected fury; my wretchedness got mercifully siphoned off into more manageable states of anger and gloom. The central family rift was between my sister, Lucile, and my mother's two sisters, Tedda and Flo. While Tedda was at work one day, my sister sold all the furnishings of the apartment my aunt had shared with my mother, leaving her—literally—with a cup and saucer and a bed. I considered it a heartless, appalling act and entirely sided with my aunts. Decades of accumulated (and largely concealed) grievances boiled over, and the breach between my sister and aunts was never healed—or for that matter, the breach between my sister and me, though there would be periodic interludes of reconciliation.

In going through my mother's personal possessions, I came across an album filled with photos of my parents on their honeymoon in 1923. My mother, then twenty-one, was stunning, her radiant vitality bursting through the picture frames. I flashed on her lying in the hospital bed, skin wrinkled and yellow, eyes vacant, a near skeleton. Where had the fifty years gone? The hope, the lively expectations, the radiance? Nothing left but bric-a-brac and the frenzied anger of relatives fighting over it. The tears came pouring out.

In the weeks and months that followed I came up with various strategies, half-consciously formed, to defend against feeling engulfed. One was to stop writing in the diary I'd been keeping on a near daily basis since 1970. I'd used it less to record events than to probe my psyche, filling it—dutiful creature of a culture that equated homosexuality with disease and depravity—with repetitive, lacerating probes into my inadequacies, laments over my assorted failings and ill fortune. It was a habit less cathartic than self-punitive. I badly needed a rest from it—from recording, and reinscribing, my character defects, real though magnified. What I needed instead was compassion and forgiveness—of my mother *and* myself, symbiotically entwined.

I stopped the diary habit on a dime, but I could only dimly perceive what else needed altering. I felt a cycle was ending, with malaise and dislocation the symptoms, yet with only a fuzzy sense of how to strike out in a new direction. I did seriously think of abandoning academia, of resigning my professorship at the City University of New York. The appeal of making a clean sweep, adopting a whole new persona, was in certain moods romantically intense. Had the thirty-year detour into academia, I asked myself, been a mistake all along? Was it possible in my late forties to retrace my steps, get back to what I was all along "meant" to be doing? The questions seemed on their face absurd, the odds forbidding. As I continued to flounder around, I even let my involvement with the gay political movement, which had become central to my life—I'd been on the founding boards of the National Gay Task Force and Lambda Legal Defense—deteriorate into more occasional spasms of activity. (The shift in the movement itself, from radicalism to reformism, made its own large contribution to my decreasing commitment.)

One way of distancing myself from the present was to turn back to the past, to paths not taken but possibly still open. Most prominently that meant making, or remaking, a life in the theater, reinhabiting my previous roles as a playwright (*In White America*) and critic (for *Partisan Review* and *Harper's*), and maybe even *way* back to age seventeen, when I'd spent the summer touring Vermont and New Hampshire acting the role of George in Thornton Wilder's *Our Town*. I'd never understood why or how the firm decision I made that summer to skip college and pursue an acting career had found me that fall enrolled as a freshman at Yale heading toward a major in history. An invisible dirt mover had somehow scooped out my confident teenage path, the driver seen, or sensed, but nameable only now, in guilty retrospect: my mother. (She'd given firm instructions to the tour leaders to *stop* praising my acting talent.)

The option of returning to the theater wasn't entirely a pipe dream. Throughout the seventies I'd had considerable encouragement and exposure, so a life in the theater didn't seem utterly far-fetched. In 1969 the Actors Studio had invited me to join its playwrights unit (though a single exposure to Lee Strasberg's smothering arrogance was enough to make me quit). In 1970 an evening of my one-acters, *The Memory Bank*, had opened off-Broadway to mostly good reviews. But the producers had been neophytes, lacked the moxie to capitalize on the favorable press, and the plays had closed after a brief run. The production probably wouldn't have happened at all had not a friend of mine, Lew Lehrman, provided most of the financing.

Lew and I had met ten years earlier at Yale and become intensely close. For a time he pursued a doctorate in history, but then decided to enter his family's business, Rite Aid, which he built into a corporate monolith. After he married and converted to Catholicism, his politics shifted from radical left to conservative right (though as defined by supply-side economics, not by Birch Society bigotry). Our relationship gradually cooled, though as late as 1982, when he ran for governor on the Republican ticket against Mario Cuomo (and lost by a mere 2 percent), he asked for, as he put it, my "counsel and help." I assumed that he meant my help with the gay vote, which I explained was strongly Democratic; if he had any hope of attracting a significant segment of it, I advised him, he should announce his support for a gay civil rights bill and his intention of appointing openly gay people to his administration. He didn't. I voted for Cuomo, and my contact with Lew thereafter was negligible.

As for *The Memory Bank*, it got a second life when Edward Albee and Richard Barr produced the one-acters that same summer of 1970 at the John Drew Theater in Easthampton (where the homosexual subtext of the plays scandalized the natives, who stayed away in droves); later they were workshopped at the Manhattan Theater Club, and two of the three were subsequently chosen for the annual volume *Best Short Plays*. Soon after, PBS commissioned me to write what became *Mother Earth*, a play about Emma Goldman, the intrepid anarchist—which PBS then turned down as "too radical." Warner Brothers sounded me out about writing the book for a new Broadway play, CBS about doing the inaugural script for a thirteen-part TV series called *The American Parade*, and the City of Philadelphia commissioned me to write a film to celebrate the Bicentennial in 1976. I focused the script on the Quaker refusal to wage war against the Delaware Indians; it too was refused as "too radical."

The Kennedy Center in Washington also made plans to celebrate the Bicentennial: it announced a season of ten American plays, six of them revivals and four newly commissioned works. I was offered one of the commissions and duly produced *Visions of Kerouac*, centered on the homoerotic relationship between Jack Kerouac and Neal Cassady. Of course I should have known better: Roger Stevens, head of the Kennedy Center, was the man who had denounced *One Flew Over the Cuckoo's Nest* as "disgusting." Predictably he wanted nothing to do with *Visions of Kerouac* (though later, after the L.A. production, it was performed both in New York and in London). Finally, there was the duo of Jules Irving and Alan Mandell, who at the time ran the Lincoln Center theater; they asked me to submit a new play to them, and when I did, they turned it down—in "dismay" over "the turn" my work had taken, over its new focus on homosexuality. Everyone, apparently, wanted "Son of In White America." (The original had had a long run off-Broadway, two national tours, and several foreign productions.)

Still, as I looked over the varied inquiries and commissions I'd had during the seventies, there seemed grounds enough to believe that a life in the theater (and the concomitant abandonment of academia) was plausible. Confirmation arrived as if on cue. Some months after my mother's death, when I was still in a state of immobility, Elaine Gold, the head of the Corner Loft Theater, a well-respected operation at the time, asked if I'd let them do a reading of a short play of mine that she'd somehow come across. Would I! The offer seemed like nothing less than a message from on high. I discovered that some surprising heavies were in regular attendance at the Loft, and José Ferrer directed the reading of my play, which was rapturously received. Jolted out of my lethargy, I started hanging out at the Loft and was soon signing up for an acting class with the noted director Frank Corsaro. I loved the process of rehearsing, had a renewed sense of purpose, felt importantly busy, and found considerable encouragement for my fantasy of a dramatic (in both senses) midlife career shift.

The notion seemed on the verge of becoming a reality when Elaine repeated to me Corsaro's opinion that I had "the makings of a great leading man." Good Lord! Did I *really*? Was the pipe dream a genuine possibility? Could I actually make a successful career change this late in life? Was everything I'd hoped for about to come true? Well, yes— except my hand was now being forced and I had to recall a few rock-bottom facts about myself. What I'd forgotten while entertaining my fantasy of rebirth was how deeply wedded I'd become to security and routine. Nearing fifty, even a malcontent like me had learned that life's most distinguishing feature was its precariousness—which a life in the theater exemplified.

I wasn't a migratory spirit. Even vacations—the chance to plunge into a new environment—filled me with foreboding, not delight. The unmoored acting life was the very definition of instability, of never feeling settled and safe. The Loft performances and praise had done temporary wonders for a psyche sunk in gloom, but *im*permanence, the touchstone of a life in the theater, held no allure for me. I lacked the temperament, the courage to live in limbo. Despite all my discontent with academia, as a tenured professor I had a secure, cushy life; it seemed madness—yet another spasm of grief—to forsake academia for a pie-in-the-sky apprenticeship in a profession notorious for its precariousness. I lingered for a few months more at the Loft before reluctantly retreating.

What I moved on to wasn't much safer. A former student of mine who'd become a friend was a devout adherent of countercultural norms and nostrums and scorned security and safety as unworthy states. Appalled at my apathy, he guilt-tripped me into trying LSD therapy as a "surefire" way to "dynamite" my entrenched immobility. The experience proved terrifying and misguided (I describe it in detail in *Midlife Queer*), yet when the same friend next waxed rhapsodic about the wonders of bioenergetics, I again agreed, almost indifferently, to give it a try. I spent several months doing individual sessions, then graduated to a week-long "intensive" at the Center for the Living Force, a mountain retreat in Phoenicia, New York. During it I *did* "break up," poured out my sorrow, and reveled in the attention I got for going, as one communard strenuously put it, "straight up to the abyss and looking in." I was declared a hero, an emotional daredevil, a spiritual avatar.

All of which—but especially the daily contact and intimacy—*did* help. I did feel reawakened, had an authentic surge of renewed energy. I decided to invest it, though, not in further explorations of my depleted psyche but in a return to a particular kind of activist scholarship that I'd embarked on some five years before and had put aside when my mother fell ill. *Any* kind of scholarship—exploring *other* people's lives—is, I've long felt, one of the ultimate forms of self-distancing, but at this point that was precisely what I needed. That might be called cowardice, a retreat from facing pain directly. Fine. I never claimed to be a stoic. Besides, when feeling guilty over numbing my feelings with affectless research, I reminded myself that *this* kind of research was at least politically essential.

A New Kind of History:
Gay Scholarship

Between 1972 and 1976 I'd been crisscrossing the country, visiting various manuscript libraries—the Kinsey Institute, the Massachusetts Historical Society, the Countway Medical Library, the Lilly Library, and others—in search of buried or overlooked material that might inform the newly emerging history of sexuality in general and queer lives in particular. The activist component seemed to me obvious: by exploring earlier patterns of same-gender relationships, we'd be better able to understand the parochial, and mutable, nature of our own—as well as society's shifting judgments of them through time. The field of gay studies was still in its infancy in the seventies, and too little evidence had accumulated to allow for any comprehensive history. Yet the time was ripe for initiating the inquiry. What was needed was a succession of archaeological digs, preferably by an army of patient scholars, that would begin to turn up the necessary building blocks for mapping the vast unexplored terrain of queer history.

During my five years of hopscotching through manuscript archives, I'd already come across some fascinating, if often fragmentary, material. Among the more startling discoveries were the handwritten notes that an early (1910) prominent American psychotherapist had taken down about his sessions with a gay patient; a petition for divorce from the early eighteenth century on grounds of impotence, along with confirming medical testimony; manuscript letters relating to Walt Whitman's sexuality; and the diary a prominent New England woman kept during her analysis with Jung in Zurich.

Given the paucity of information then available and the growing demand for a historical framework with which to understand homosexuality in its current guises, I decided to try to get at least some of the documents I'd discovered into print. At that time few scholarly journals were likely to prove receptive to such material. But there were a few. One of them was *Signs*, the new feminist journal; its editor, Catharine Stimpson, was delighted with the early divorce petition and published it forthwith. The *Radical History Review* likewise was much taken with extensive ethnographic data (affidavits, interviews, and depositions) on Hopi and Zuni ritual sexual practices that had been recorded between 1914 and 1921 in New Mexico and Arizona and which I discovered at the Smithsonian Institute. The *Review* published two substantial excerpts from the material, along with my commentary, itself extensive.

As a nonspecialist in Pueblo culture, I'd embarked—when I discovered the documents—on a course of intense reading in the literature to try to make sense of the material, which on its face was startling. Hopi rituals and ceremonial dances included cross-dressing, public urination, the flogging of children, and exaggerated displays of representations of the male penis. I learned from my reading that the Hopi were profoundly suspicious of outsiders attempting to probe the "meaning" of their rituals; historically outsiders had been associated (accurately) with misrepresenting Pueblo life even as they forcibly attempted to alter it. I showed the Smithsonian material to several anthropologists I knew, and their uniform response had been to "explain" it in terms of "symbolic rituals" designed to produce rain and metaphorical "mini-dramas" designed to enforce social mores.

I wasn't satisfied with their response. I distrusted the overwhelming emphasis they placed on the *symbolic* (the representational, figurative) dimension of behavior to the possible exclusion of its full reality. Several of the affidavits seemed to describe sexual behavior ("I seen a squaw suck a buck's prick") that seemed explicitly to license a range of nonmarital, promiscuous activity—perhaps to amuse, perhaps to instruct, perhaps both. The anthropologists' stress on "dramatic simulation" as a sufficient explanation for the sexual content of the dances struck me as possibly a function of their own sex-negative bias, a resort to the abstract in order to avoid the embarrassingly concrete. Like most historians, I'm fascinated with particularity, with detail, wary of static models, and alert to the variations over time in the meaning of seemingly unchanging behavior. Our Western value structure, with its Neoplatonic penchant for abstracting experience, inculcates in us a zeal for classification that can nullify what is most special—enrichingly eccentric—in a given event or gesture.

What did cross-dressing mean *for the Hopi*? Did it take place only during ceremonial dances, and was it wholly a male phenomenon? What does the practice tell us about the differing socioreligious roles played by males and females in Pueblo culture? What interrelationship, if any, existed between cross-dressing and bisexuality or homosexuality? Did flogging children occur only during initiatory rites, and what significance—religious or otherwise—was attached to the practice? Was the whipping as severe and the children as stoic as the affidavits suggest, or was some degree of play-acting involved—and if so, by whom and for what purpose? Was there any analogous inflicting of pain between Hopi *adults* (biting and slapping during sex, for example)? Did the floggings carry sexual overtones, bear any of the emotional or symbolic weight (dominance/submission, etc.) that in our culture we connect with "sadomasochism"?

These were some of the questions I raised when writing my commentary on the affidavits for the *Radical History Review*. Its editors then came up with the creative idea of asking two specialists on Pueblo culture, Richard Clemmer of Cal State and Fred Eggan of the University of Chicago, to try their hands at a response. They did, stating categorically that all significant questions about Hopi rituals had long since been satisfactorily answered by specialists in the field. (In other words, no border-crossing allowed.) They accused me—a mere historian—of harboring "some very erroneous impressions concerning anthropology, anthropologists, and Hopi culture" and "corrected" them at considerable length. To my illiterate ears their corrections sounded implausible, irrelevant, and downright rude, and I said so in my lengthy response.

In regard to cross-dressing Professor Eggan did acknowledge that some "meager" evidence existed of "occasional transvestites in Pueblo society," though he reassured us that "none has been present in recent history." Yet I subsequently came across material on the Hopi dating from 1965 that contained specific references to cross-gender dressing and behavior, though I had no idea whether it could be linked or equated to our own cultural reference points and practices. In recent decades a younger generation of anthropologists has been more interested than their predecessors in addressing questions relating to human sexuality—and less inclined to base their assessments on patriarchal assumptions.

EXCEPT FOR THE *Journal of Homosexuality*, founded in 1976, there were no scholarly journals in these years devoted primarily to LGBTQ concerns, and although at least two influential publications, *Gay Sunshine* in San Francisco and *Fag Rag* in Boston, were decidedly radical, neither had the needed space nor, arguably, the interested readership to warrant the inclusion of extensive documentary material. But then, in 1980, the gay bimonthly *New York Native* began publication in New York City and invited me to do a regular column, which I called "About Time" and which ran for more than two years; it served as a tailor-made outlet for some of the shorter manuscripts I'd unearthed.

Preparing them for publication—choosing excerpts and writing explanatory notes—provided a valuable distraction from my ongoing bouts of dejection, adding a bit of voltage to my undercharged mood. On occasion I even managed to inject some campy humor into my commentary on the documents. One example was the previously unpublished pocket diary kept by James Wilson, a Founding Father of considerable eminence, that I found at the American Philosophical Society in Philadelphia.

In 1774 Wilson had published his seminal "Considerations," in which he argued that because the colonies had no representation in the British Parliament, that august body had no legitimate authority to pass laws for them; power derived from the people. Further, as a member of the Continental Congress in 1776, Wilson played an influential role in pressing for a declaration of independence, subsequently helped to prepare the first draft of the 1787 Constitution, and two years later became a member of the Supreme Court. Wilson's biographers describe his personality and private life as "enigmatic," with little more said. Yet the contents of his pocket diary suggest that his "restless energy and an almost frightening vitality" (as one contemporary described him) were qualities that leaked over, as it were, from his public to his personal life. There was one problem with publishing the diary: its inconsistencies in handwriting, along with some internal contradictions, led me to question its authenticity. I said as much to members of the Philosophical Society's staff. They reacted indignantly: the diary, I was sternly admonished, is "indisputably, authentically by James Wilson."

Fine by me. When introducing excerpts in my *Native* column, I dutifully noted my doubts about the document's reliability, then announced tongue-in-cheek, "It is my privilege to present a glimpse into the private life of one of the few individuals about whom it can legitimately be said, 'he laid the cornerstone of our liberty.'" Herewith a sample of the excerpts I printed:

> January 1773 [Wilson had married two years earlier]: "I promise in the coming year to avoid lewd women—they are the bane of our life. Last year I topped six and thirty wenches."
> January 13: "As usual lay with . . . cook at night."
> April 26: "One testicle much swollen . . . Poulticed it—with flax seed."
> May 6: "In a house of Joy on Docks."
> June 7: "A great itching in my parts . . . Dr. Physic says Clapp. Oh my, again—I must have had it from the Parson's wife?"
> November 24: "Maria, chamber woman. I could not resist her charms. I cried God help me as I thrust her."
> December 22: "Clapp—Much itching in my flopper—Must keep away from my wife."

The Wilson diary was one of the few documents I published in the *Native* that related to heterosexuality. I did so while campily claiming that I was offering it in response to the demand from straight readers for "equal time"; the poor things, I wrote, longed for a sexual history of their own. The straight readers of course were mythical, and my archival search and the *Native* columns that resulted from it focused on same, not opposite, gender love and lust.

Some of those finds were substantial. At the Massachusetts Historical Society in Boston, where I'd spent years researching two of my early books, I knew the staff well, and they gave me free run of the stacks—that is, unrestricted access to a considerable amount of mostly uncatalogued (sometimes even unwrapped) material. My most astonishing discovery was a recently acquired and voluminous diary kept by a minor writer named F. S. Ryman—some forty folio volumes, each folio three times the size of a typical hardcover book today—with those dating from the 1880s the most intriguing for researchers into sexual behavior. Ryman flooded his diary with details of his heterosexual exploits, yet it also contains a number of entries dealing with same-gender relations that are immensely suggestive, especially in regard to the history of male-male friendship.

Ryman lived in upstate New York during most of the 1880s, and a number of his diary entries from that time recount his close friendship with Rob Luke, a hotel clerk, and raise some fundamental contrasts with the way we view male friendship today. Here's one of Ryman's entries (written in August 1886) about Rob:

> Rob came over to stay with me last night. . . . I confess I like the oriental custom of men embracing & kissing each other if they are indeed dear friends. When we went to bed Rob put his arms around me & lay his head down by my right shoulder in the most loving way & then I put my arms around his neck & thus clasped in each other's arms we talked for a long time till we were ready to go to sleep & then we separated as I cannot sleep good with anyone near me. This a.m. Rob got up to go at 5 o'clock & as he was starting he came to the bed & threw his arms around my neck & we kissed each other good bye though I expect to see him again to-day. Now in all this I am certain there was no sexual sentiment on the part of either of us. We both have our mistresses whom we see with reasonable regularity & I am certain that the thought of the least demonstration of unmanly & abnormal passion would have been as revolting to him as it is & ever has been to me.

I used to read that entry and other similar ones from Ryman's journal to my classes on the history of sexual behavior—invariably to hoots of disbelief: "He's as queer as a ten dollar bill!," et cetera. An understandable reaction. When was the last time any of us—some gay men excepted—cuddled and kissed a close friend, or even fantasized about doing so? Gay men can be more given than straight men to certain standardized physical expressions of affection, like hugs and pecks on the cheek, but through ritualized overusage, even those gestures have become all but empty of emotional content—seriously *under*expressing, perhaps, the actual extent of our attachment.

In any case, both gay and straight men would today be likely to equate the *passionate* embraces that Ryman and Rob exchanged with erotic arousal. That's not to suggest that they necessarily *were* sexually attracted or involved (though Ryman's denial in his diary is *so* strenuous as to raise our suspicion). No, their physical (as contrasted with genital) contact can probably best be explained as the function of a different set of conventions from ours about what are or aren't "appropriate," permissible expressions of affection between two close male friends. As I commented when I published excerpts from Ryman's diary in the *Native*, "It would seem that comparable gestures can decisively shift their symbolic meaning in the course of a hundred years, can 'signify' quite different emotions during different eras."

As I also wrote, the Ryman diary inevitably poses the question of just how "prudish" the Victorians in fact were—and just how "liberated" we are. I put my own tentative conclusion this way:

> On the basis of the Ryman diary we're now able at least to say that *some* nineteenth-century men were (contrary to the standard view) remarkably full and unself-conscious in physically expressing affection for each other. By contrast, today many gay men seem able to give freely of their loins to strangers but are far more chary than Ryman and Rob of giving freely of their affection to friends. Perhaps what's been involved is a trade-off, not (as some glib liberationists would have it) an advance. It's possible we're sexually "freer" than ever before with members of our own gender—but more emotionally constricted. I'm still not one to see sexual lust and emotional commitment as necessarily at odds, but there seems a disquieting lack of evidence that they're mutually reinforcing. As "hooking up" roars round the land, the capacity (even the wish) for intimacy seems progressively to wither. No causal connection has been shown, but I could do with a little reassurance that the correlation is merely coincidental.

If we go back in time yet another half-century, we come across two previously unknown and unpublished 1826 letters between "Jeff" and "Jim" that reveal a male-male relationship that, unlike Ryman and Rob's, is apparently overtly and unapologetically sexual, yet without either man claiming what we'd today call a "gay" identity. The two letters in question are in the James Henry Hammond manuscript collection in the South Caroliniana Library in Columbia, and the retrieval of the letters is itself a tale of cautionary intrigue worth recounting. But first to the letters themselves.

At the time they were written both "Jim" and "Jeff" were untried, inconsequential young men, yet within a few years both would become significant public figures, Jim—James Hammond, the recipient of the letters—rising to become one of the antebellum South's "great men," a U.S. senator and the governor of South Carolina, a noted agricultural reformer, and a prominent defender of black slavery whose writings served as a cornerstone of the South's "Pro-Slavery Argument." Jeff Withers never achieved such problematic heights, but while still in his twenties he became editor of the influential *Columbia Telescope*, then helped lead the nullification (of federal statutes) struggle, and later became a judge and prominent secessionist.

In 1826 twenty-two-year-old Jeff was studying law at South Carolina College. In a letter to Jim dated May 15, 1826, his tone is playfully sardonic:

> I feel some inclination to learn whether you yet sleep in your
> Shirt-tail, and whether you yet have the extravagant delight
> of poking and punching a writhing Bedfellow with your long
> fleshen pole—the exquisite touches of which I have often had the
> honor of feeling? Let me say unto thee that unless thou changest
> former habits in this particular, thou wilt be represented by every
> future Chum as a nuisance. And, I pronounce it, with good reason
> too. Sir, you roughen the downy Slumbers of your Bedfellow—by
> such hostile—furious lunges as you are in the habit of making at
> him—when he is least prepared for defence against the crushing
> force of a Battering Ram.

As we learn from a second letter from Jeff, Jim did respond to the first on June 13, 1826, but his letter, if extant, is not in the South Caroliniana archives. Judging from Jeff's second letter, Jim must have made some sort of jocular response, for which Jeff sportively upbraids him in his reply: "I fancy, Jim, that your *elongated protuberance*—your fleshen pole—has captured complete mastery over you—and I really believe, that you are charging over the pine barrens of your locality, braying, like an ass, at every she-male you can discover."

What to make of these astonishing two letters, quite without parallel in the known correspondence of the period? We have enough information about James Hammond to put his sexual history in some sort of context. His contemporaries often described him as mercurial, impetuous—and lustful. Though he haughtily rejected the abolition-ists' charge that white masters exploited their female slaves sexually, Hammond himself had a slave mistress, and when he tired of her, he forcibly substituted her twelve-year-old daughter. That much, it can be argued, was within the conventional limits of permissible behavior of the day. What lay outside it was Hammond's attempt in the 1840s to se-duce the teenage daughters of Wade Hampton, another of the South's "great men." Hampton read Hammond the riot act and blocked his candidacy (for a time) for a Senate seat; Hammond gave up his family mansion in Columbia and retired to his country estate. He described all this in his diary in a tone of willful, aggrieved petulance: *he* was the wounded party, and merely for "a little dalliance." Public figures of his eminence, Hammond suggested, should be entitled to indulge their amorous appetites without having to suffer censure or retribution. The arrogantly assertive master class didn't take kindly to any questioning of its prerogatives.

Returning to the two earlier letters from Jeff Withers, the criti-cal issue that arises from their references to same-gender eroticism is whether such behavior should be regarded as anomalous or rep-resentative. "Was Withers and Hammond's behavior unique," I wrote in the *Native*, "or does it reveal and illustrate a wider pattern of male-male relationships—till now unsuspected and undocumented, yet in some sense 'typical' of their time, region, race, and class?" The answer: we don't know. There's no comparable evidence in the correspondence of the period—or perhaps it hasn't yet surfaced, which is precisely why the field of scholarly inquiry (call it the "history of intimacy," if that makes you less anxious than the "history of homoeroticism") is needed and necessary.

And it *does* make people anxious. When a scholarly edition of Hammond's diaries (titled *Secret and Sacred*) did finally appear in 1988, the editor, Carol Bleser, dismissed my discussion in *Radical History Re-view* of the two letters from Withers as "a rather tortured reading." In her interpretation the letters "can more easily be viewed as deriving from the fact that Hammond and Withers shared a bed, the norm for those times, and from the fact that young men . . . are frequently tumescent without any specific sexual stimulation." Well aware of both facts—that is, sharing beds and youthful tumescence—I still fail to see how they explain "furious lunges" at one's bed partner or disturbing his slumber by "poking and punching" him with one's "long fleshen pole." Perhaps Professor Bleser believes that the youth and nighttime proximity of two males will *automatically* produce sexual contact—put another way, that we're all "situational bisexuals." An intriguing theory, even an appealing one. I only wish Bleser had argued the case and provided some semblance of evidence for it.

If the Withers letters produced an unpersuasively anxious rejoinder from Bleser, they produced a muted version of apoplexy from the director of the South Caroliniana Library. As I learned while traveling around the country exploring various archives, in the mid-seventies the history of sexual behavior was still a long way from being an acceptable topic of scholarly inquiry. I did come across some archivists, such as Richard J. Wolfe at the Countway Medical Library, who felt that such research was long overdue, that it was of potentially large importance for understanding our national character, and who ransacked their collections for material that might feed my inquiry.

But they were in a decided minority. Even at Indiana's Kinsey Institute—which bore Alfred Kinsey's name but had misplaced his inquisitive spirit—Paul Gebhard, then its head, first stonewalled and then reprimanded me when I asked to see materials relating to homosexuality that C. A. Tripp, author of *The Homosexual Matrix* and a man who'd worked at the Institute for nine years, had tipped me off about. To show me the material, Gebhard sternly admonished, would be to indulge in a serious breach of confidentiality. Tripp had predicted as much: Gebhard was not a homophobe, Tripp had warned me, but he lacked audacity and was averse to risk-taking—the very qualities Kinsey exemplified.

Tripp had told me that the Institute had a good deal of uncatalogued historical material relating to homosexual behavior, and specifically mentioned the correspondence, running to some four hundred typed pages, between Kinsey and a European businessman with the curious name Sixt Kapff. In his letters Kapff recounted his remarkable sexual adventures during his travels, along with acute general observations about varying cultural practices. When Kinsey was in Europe in 1955, Kapff offered himself as a personal guide and, according to Tripp, put to rest any lingering doubts Kinsey might have had about Kapff's veracity—and sophistication. (Following Kinsey's death in 1956, Tripp himself continued the correspondence with Kapff.)

When I repeated all this to Gebhard on my arrival at the Institute, specifically mentioning the Kapff-Kinsey correspondence, he looked blank; he said he'd "have a look" but doubted if they had much "that would interest me." In the interim, he suggested I plow through the catalogue file, which I dutifully did, finding next to nothing, while awaiting the results of Gebhard's "look." Finally, after three full days had gone by, Gebhard managed to come up with a single uncatalogued collection, most of it concerning the 1950s. It did have some valuable reminiscences about gay activity in the Civilian Conservation Corps camps during the thirties, but when I requested copies of them, Gebhard limited me to an absurd *three* pages and added that if I wanted to take additional notes, it would have to be by hand.

That seemed to me gratuitously hostile (or needlessly timid). If he was willing for me to take notes at all, why not allow me to do so in the most expeditious way: by making photocopies? When I protested his policy, Gebhard remained blandly, pleasantly immovable. As the last holdover from the Institute staff of the forties, only Gebhard knew the actual extent and location of the historical materials, and he resolutely withheld them. What he didn't know was that Kapff had earlier given Tripp a photocopied set of his entire correspondence with Kinsey, which Tripp—with Kapff's explicit permission—turned over to me when I returned to New York. I included a sizable chunk of it in my 1986 book, *About Time: Exploring the Gay Past*.

GEBHARD WAS DOWNRIGHT audacious when compared to the head—"Archer," I'll call him—of the South Caroliniana Library. I sent him a formal request for permission to publish the two Withers letters early in March 1979. Two weeks passed. Then four, then six. In mid-April, having still gotten no response, I wrote again, the second letter a near duplicate of the first. April passed into May, May into June. Still no word. I started to get angry and fired off a third letter—by certified mail—telling Archer that his silence could be interpreted either as giving consent or as an attempt at censorship. Should I opt for the first interpretation, I wrote, I'd simply proceed forthwith to publication; if I decided on the second, I'd feel the obligation to other scholars to report the matter to the Joint Committee of Historians and Archivists, the prestigious arbiter of matters relating to academic censorship.

That did it. Within the week I had a reply. Dr. Archer expressed regret that I'd "found it necessary" to write him "such a sharp letter"; surely I might have understood that he was a busy man and had to "await a convenient opportunity" to seek counsel regarding my request. He was now able to report (that was quick!) that the original donor of the Hammond papers had "asked"—that is, *requested*, not required, as my own set of consultants would subsequently point out to me—that none of the manuscripts be used in such a way as to "result in embarrassment to descendants." The donor, Archer acknowledged, was deceased, but he considered the obligation "still in force." In other words, no, I could not publish the two letters.

I wasn't about to drop the matter. When I turned to various friends, scholars, and legal experts for advice, the concurrence was that I was within my rights, legally and morally, to proceed straightaway to publication, and without explicit permission. They based that conclusion on the doctrine of fair usage (*Meeropol v. Nizer*), which established an author's right to quote without permission an "appropriate" amount of copyrighted material. This wasn't an airtight ruling, my expert in copyright law pointed out, since "appropriate" had been variously interpreted by the courts. But if fair usage should fail to sustain my right to publish, he said, I could fall back on other justifications, in particular the fact that the South Caroliniana Library had not sealed the Hammond papers from scholarly scrutiny and had catalogued and provided photocopies of the two Withers letters. Clearly the Library had not acted in a way suggesting that it regarded the donor's request as a binding stipulation.

Taking my expert's advice, I did proceed directly to publication (in the *Journal of Homosexuality*), and Archer never raised a peep—though he might have if I'd actually mailed the final letter that had been dancing around in my head: "I can't imagine why you could view publication as a potential 'embarrassment to descendants.' For two men like Hammond and Withers, who've gone down in history as among the country's staunchest defenders of human slavery, I should think their reputations could only be enhanced by the playful, raucous—the humanizing—revelations contained in the two letters."

I never sent that letter, and I never heard again from Archer. But if I had, I would have responded that much of the current scholarship issuing from our universities functioned primarily to rationalize existing arrangements of power and that the time had come for a genuinely *un-harnessed* scholarship that could uncover the data needed for challenging antiquated values and for nurturing alternative visions of the good society. As regards gay people, moreover, as well as the broad history of sexuality and intimacy, I would have argued that the prevailing and dangerously narrow view of what is acceptable historical inquiry, and, by implication, permissible norms of behavior, had to be busted open. The heterosexist world had long held a monopoly on defining legal and ethical propriety, imposing its definitions on the rest of us. To continue to accept and abide by anachronistic definitions of what constitutes "sensitive material" and "acceptable" areas of historical inquiry would be tantamount to collaborating in sustaining "things as they are"—to be complicit in our own oppression.

The bottom line, obviously, is that in the wake of my mother's death I hadn't jumped ship, hadn't abandoned academia or run off to join the circus. "Sensible," I told myself. "Mature." I also told myself that although I was reinhabiting my historian's role, I was doing it in a new way, helping to foster a field of inquiry—gender and sexuality studies—of more than academic interest: the archival materials being unearthed could provide the gay and feminist movements with fresh data for challenging old assumptions and stereotypes.

Reading My Circadian Chart

I couldn't find much comparable balm when I began to renew some other old habits. Within a year of my mother's death, I could finally feel some sexual energy returning, and I began employing it in familiar, inauspicious ways: periodic visits to hustler bars, serial affairs with much younger men of strenuous charm and sly unavailability.

Some of them even pursued *me*. There was Brad, who I first met at the Loft, where, like me, he was an aspiring actor. He told me he was a good friend and occasional bed partner of Allen Ginsberg's, and he lovingly wooed me with a low-key Buddhist vocabulary of core simplicities. Ours was a meeting, Brad announced, of miraculous synchronicity. I agreed—for a full three weeks. Then came his psychotic break in my living room at 5:00 a.m., the flower child turning into Manson, accusing me of "evil," of having become available to him too soon, thereby making myself "unworthy of pursuit." By being "open and vulnerable," I'd "*compounded* my formidability" under the illusion I was diluting it. My readiness to let him see my "weaknesses and fears," Brad stormed, was a "form of sadism" since it made him "feel still more inferior": I should have come off my pedestal "slowly." Somehow I managed to get Brad out of the apartment and thereafter kept him at arm's length.

Then there was David, a dashing assistant curator at the Met who dressed in double-breasted suits and who, like Alexander, was always on the lookout for new worlds to conquer. I had first caught David's eye, he later told me, when I spoke at the 1975 memorial service for Howard Brown, who'd been New York City's commissioner of health, had subsequently come out, and had then spearheaded the group (myself included) who formed the National Gay Task Force—later belatedly changed to Lesbian and Gay Task Force. Howard and I quickly became good friends—close enough for him to describe to me the pleasure he took in prancing around his townhouse in high heels. As a result I decided to introduce him to the Gilded Grape, a Midtown bar known as a hangout for what we then called "drag queens" and their often macho Hispanic boyfriends. The place delighted Howard; he fervently announced, "Not to appear in drag is elitist!" (Forty years later that sounds like a line from *Transparent*.)

At any rate, as David later told me, he'd been "impressed" with my speech at Howard's memorial and had decided that the easiest way to meet me was to invite me to give a lecture at the Met. When he called, I initially put him off; I'd been doing a surfeit of lectures lately and wasn't interested in meeting what I assumed would be another overly articulate, *faux* elegant art curator. I offhandedly said he could try me again in the spring, if he wanted. Tenacity, I would rapidly learn, was David's middle name. When he next called he suggested a lecture topic: "Two Hundred Years of Hidden Homosexual History." That struck a missionary chord, and I agreed to hear more at lunch.

Out to greet me came not the prissy, affected stereotype I'd expected but a dramatically handsome, engaging, and bright twenty-five-year-old. He looked like a *sexual* Nureyev. Over lunch David pointedly filled in his vita: a Summa from the University of Texas, a First in Classics from Cambridge. What dazzled me, though, wasn't his credentials but his physical prepossession, the forceful self-confidence readily visible behind the veneer of boyish bravado. This superstar-in-training, it quickly became clear, wanted to be seen as super-nice as well, yet I was left in no doubt that beneath his offerings of pleasantries and flattery, David was used to getting what he wanted when he wanted it.

Smitten, I began to see him with some regularity, and it wasn't long before the dancing courtier role I'd been easing into as appropriate to middle age had me prematurely committing to an ivy-covered cottage in the Cotswolds. David reacted to my intensity with his own ingrained mix of foxy enticement and monumental evasiveness. Having initially wooed me with vigor and easily broken down my guard, he now became the seductive veiled virgin, available for occasional viewing but no sustained touching. It turned out he had a boyfriend in Washington, feared he was "falling in love" with me and didn't want to—fearful, he said, of being "pulled apart."

David's self-presentation as a Prince of the Realm coexisted with his twin self-image as a Porcelain Princess, one prone to suicide if pushed or pressured. His feelings for me, he insisted, were "intense," but he feared releasing them. As weeks passed into months, he returned just enough phone calls and made just enough dates to deliver a thoroughly muddied message: "I'll be devastated if you decide to stop seeing me, *but* essential to my emotional well-being is an insistence on 'simplification.'" Translation: "The circuits are plugged in, but I won't flip the switch."

His willful constraint drove me nuts. Never particularly patient, when David was in one of his aloof, uncommunicative moods instead of retreating I redoubled my pursuit, apparently convinced that my powers of persuasion would ultimately prove irresistible. I was even willing to consider what I called "the Sackville-West Solution": minimizing or even avoiding genital sex, with its disruptive anxieties, in the name of intensifying our emotional bond. Ever steadfast in pursuit of unavailability, I was in some ways the dumbest kid on the block, the one who could never learn basic semaphore.

I finally gave up only when David moved out of the city, a move he announced in fatally distancing (though he thought them comforting) words: "I don't think you'll ever know how much you've done for me." I consoled myself with the knowledge that David *did* care but couldn't take his finger off the "hold" button; besides, forty-eight was a bit old for romantic love, especially since, ideologically, I didn't believe in it. Years later I got a dispirited phone call from him; he was living in the Midwest, working for a textbook firm, had gotten married (to a woman), had a young child—and suggested a get-together in New York. I took contemptible satisfaction in turning him down cold.

Brad and David were mere novices in the arts of seduction and duplicity when compared to Chris, who in the fall of 1978 followed directly in the line of succession. Surpassing his junior associates, Chris announced his certainty, soon after we'd met, that he'd found in me the "life partner" he'd long sought, and he wanted us "to commit to a life together of monogamous devotion." The religious overtones of "devotion" weren't incidental. Chris was a devout Catholic, taught in a parochial school, and had gone uncertainly back and forth about whether he had a strong enough "calling" to enter a seminary.

That alone should have sent me straight to a Jewish dating service. Chris wasn't the first gay Catholic I'd known, and more often than not, they were tortured with guilt about their "problem." Yet Chris assured me that I'd "revolutionized" his outlook on life, that he'd put the notion of entering a seminary permanently behind him, that he was profoundly committed to making our relationship work, and, though we were bound to go through some rough patches, that he had every confidence we'd weather them. From the beginning the relationship was stormy, but I told myself the squalls mostly arose from the inevitable difficulties in understanding and accommodating the other person's differentness.

Nor did I feel in my familiar position of obsessively pursuing an invulnerable narcissist. If anything, Chris remained the more persistent and the more certain (so he kept saying) of his commitment. When misunderstandings arose, I was encouraged by the straightforward way I handled them: I spoke my mind cleanly; I was willing to risk a break rather than conceal my feelings and needs. Chris too held his ground. Which I liked. He was stubbornly insistent on his individuality, though unsure, as we all are, about some of its components. Now and then I caught a whiff of smugness or furtive concealment, but the scent didn't linger (and I dutifully told myself that nobody is perfect).

It wasn't long before I'd fallen hard. Chris fit my specifications for an ideal partner: deeply serious, uneasy in the world, disgruntled over "things as they are," disdainful of mere material goals, powerfully, conflictedly sexual—and drop-dead gorgeous. Besides, approaching thirty and with a master's degree (nonsensically that somehow mattered), Chris seemed far more adult than Brad or David, and I managed to convince myself that he could sustain his vows to me, forgetting that they were merely secular.

When we had a run-in or a misunderstanding, I began to find myself—it was now a year and a half since my mother's death—scribbling down a thought, a resolution, an insight on a scrap of paper. That led in short order to getting out my old diary and occasionally writing a more extensive entry. Soon after that I was back to scribbling more regularly, though not with the frequency that had once been the case. One of the longest entries I made was, in essence, "What to do about Chris?"

The "answer" was tortuously elaborate, went on for pages. Today I can hardly decipher it, given all the crossings out and scribbled "on the other hands." This seems to be the gist of it:

> What seems an irrevocable commitment on Chris's part becomes suddenly, mysteriously clogged with fears he claims unable to

locate or name. . . . I press the value of "let's look at it" even as I know how little understanding and support that finally offers, given the frightened sense on both our parts that, after all, our worlds can't be bridged . . . given the hurt and anger I feel at his furtiveness, sexual prudery, emotional constriction, and *my* inability to let anything go by without comment (usually aggrieved), my perfectionism, my determined effort to make him more like me—which if he did would kill my interest in him, not because he'd yielded but because he was no longer *Chris*. . . . I need to give up the foolish insistence that the secret of any deep connection can be unlocked. I need to live more by the realization that it's the whole of Chris that engrosses me, not this or that attribute; that the "rearrangements" I persistently seek (and he persistently resists) are misguided—and their failure triumphant good fortune. . . . If only the oscillations weren't so wild and exhausting—wilder than I've ever known and more unyielding, and fuller in range, from deep tenderness to profound rage.

Fierce and furious, month after month, on we went. Sex, as per usual, soon revealed some of the deeper fissures and set off more alarm bells. Chris's preferred self-image as a self-sufficient anchorite wanting nothing for himself or of this world, was strongly contradicted by his behavior in bed. The focus was *all* on him, his needs, his fantasies, his orgasms. I was assigned the role of performing assistant—sadistic assistant: "Grab my ass! Pinch my nipples! *Squeeze* my cock!" All of which was pleasant enough as—so I thought—preliminary experiments. But for him they were closer to final parameters, the only shifts being in amplitude. His professions of loving me bore—in the great Catholic tradition—no necessary or desirable connection to pleasuring me. More accurately, they were inversely related: the extent of his love was gauged and validated (in his mind) by the amount of steadfastness he showed in refusing to complicate—sully—it with sexual need, physical urgency. *Mine*, that is. Satisfying *his* sexual needs somehow left our love untainted.

Oh, we had some lovely nights together of cuddly noncombativeness, but by the time our relationship had hit the six-month mark, Chris had uncorked a set of sexual demands that, after one go-round, I refused to repeat. His masochism, it turned out, ran deep; his guilt and his aspiration to sainthood required flagellation—literal. I did, at his insistence, take a belt to his ass, then to his body—did it once and told him I'd never do it again, that it repulsed me, made me feel awful, that raising welts on someone I cared about wasn't my idea of love, however unhip that made me. He said nothing at the time but apparently felt confident that he could continue to control the scene. When drunk a few weeks later, he again demanded that I use the belt on him. I refused absolutely. This time he believed me. How did I know? Because he began almost immediately to withdraw, to disentangle from the relationship.

The process was swift. He announced in June 1979 that he'd be spending the summer studying Latin at a language school on Long Island and would only occasionally be coming into the city. When he did, it was to tell me that "our closeness" had become "too frightening" for him. He had (again) rethought his priorities: it now felt to him, he said, like he had to make a choice between "spending my life with one person *or* devoting it to the church."

"Why does it have to be either/or?" I foolishly asked.

"I'm going to apply for admittance to the seminary" was his indirect but decisive answer. "The language school is attached to a seminary."

"I see."

"I've met somebody. A seminarian. His name is Rob. We've had sex together—once. He won't do it again. Says it's against his vows. I can and will honor that."

"A celibate relationship *at age thirty*? *I* can't—and I'm forty-eight." I didn't mean to, but I'd just confirmed that his choice *was* either/or—and he'd made it.

"I'm glad you understand. I won't be coming into the city again. Thanks for everything, Marty."

And no more said. That was that. The parting was brutal and painful. I unfairly told myself that Chris had managed to find the brute *within* and had played the card, as they say, masterfully. I felt bereft and helpless. I'd long since said everything possible to persuade him that we belonged together, all to no avail. With Rob he'd found a celibate lover who was also a true believer; he didn't have to choose between the two after all, since giving up sex (not love) was for Chris a trifle compared with defying the Church.

For weeks I was in a terrible state, wracked with crying jags, filled with rage. I felt torn apart, immobilized. I was never going to find steady companionship, I told myself—let alone in combination with satisfying sex. I felt so desperate that I let a friend of mine who'd never retreated from the glory days of the counterculture arrange for me to have my chart read by Gregge Tiffen, the famed California guru trained in Tibetan numerology and astrology—which my friend described as "a body of knowledge accumulated over thousands of years, a system of celestial mathematics based on a ten-month calendar, unintelligible to a Westerner, but not to Tiffen, who'd studied for ten years with Bhim Prasad Gauchan, the great Tibetan master."

Christ, I thought, why not? I've tried every other goddamn thing—LSD therapy, bioenergetics, aikido, transcendental meditation, not to mention those Western staples, drugs and psychotherapy. Tiffen, it turned out, was on a rare visit to New York. "Clearly," my friend gravely said, "he's here because you need him to be. Don't pass up this opportunity." Tiffen, with "great difficulty" (so he informed me), managed to find an available time for a reading of my past life and future prospects. Profoundly skeptical though I was, I felt desperate enough to clutch at any straw—eager, not merely willing, to believe the future might prove different from the past.

Tiffen spread out my circadian chart between us on a desk in his hotel room, turned on the tape recorder, and began to explain my "background" life. I had come into this incarnation, he told me, with unresolved anger from having failed to successfully rebel against my tyrannical father, with the result that in my current life I was still "tangling with authority, muscling up to do battle." The "learning lesson" for *this* life, Tiffen forcefully said, is to "use your energy for yourself, turn it inward. Stop jousting at windmills. There'll always be windmills. Forget about them! It's butting your head against a stone wall."

I politely protested that much of my political activity in the past had been directed against real social evils that *needed* to be resisted. Tiffen frowned disapprovingly but said nothing. When I followed up with the guilty confession that for the past year or two I'd been much less active politically, he smiled approvingly.

"Look at your chart," Tiffen said. "These celestial plots are given numerical values on the outside rim, which we call rulers—but never mind: you won't understand the mathematics. I'll simply give you the results. One striking finding is that close personal relationships give you *a lot* of problems and sometimes go very, very badly. The woman in your life wants more of you than you're willing to give because you've got too many other things going on."

"You're right about the problems," I said, "but as I see it I usually give too much too quickly. As for the 'woman in my life,' " I added, in as neutral a tone as I could muster, "I need to throw something in here which may be important, which I'm *sure* is important: I'm gay."

Tiffen looked blank—after a noticeable flinch. "It doesn't make any difference. The gender is irrelevant. The karmic problem is from your background life. You must find a mate much like yourself if there's any hope of settling down. . . . But more of that later. First, I need to give you some very unfortunate news. Before meeting today, I did a numerological analysis of your name and found to my horror that it contains a ten. With a ten sitting in your chart," he solemnly warned, "you are courting disaster. You *must* change your name. The most logical solution would be to change the spelling of your last name to Dubermanne—that way, the phonetics would stay as close to the original as possible."

"My last name," I said, trying not to sound too grandiose, "is, er, somewhat known. Maybe I could do something with my first name?"

"No, no!" Tiffen was vehement. "The problem is with your *last* name! Sooner or later this is going to cause an explosion. I'll guarantee it. I'll stake my professional life on it!"

"Would it help," I timidly asked, "if I resumed using my middle name, Bauml, my mother's maiden name?" Tiffen lit up, quickly did the numbers (or rolled the wheels or did whatever it was he did). The result? "Yes, that would be an improvement. It's workable. It would avoid disaster at least." In retrospect I can hardly believe it, but I decided on the spot to restore my middle name. It would honor my mother *and* appease the (circadian) gods. And so it was that my full birth name would appear on my next three books (*About Time, Paul Robeson,* and *Hidden from History*). Finally, in 1991, with my memoir *Cures*—by then the trauma over my mother's death having receded and my literary agent having risen in revolt over the "absurd mouthful" of using three names—I reverted to "Martin Duberman."

The problem of the ten solved, Tiffen turned back to the issue of a soul mate. He pointed dramatically to a spot on my chart and announced with a gasp, "Look at this! Just look at it! *Your sixth ruler goes*

OFF *the chart!* You have a *profound* need for 'home'—for rooted domesticity. But—*but*—the antipical retardant of the second ruler stands firmly in the way. I fear you will never achieve that goal."

I must have visibly slumped in my chair, because Tiffen instantly sounded a more positive note. "There is one way, only one, and the odds are not good. You must find a mate with your same conflicted needs, someone who, like you, strongly wants a home but also needs a wide variety of outside outlets and events, a person who doesn't like being tied down. That's the only kind of person you could achieve any permanence with. It's a tall order." You're telling me, I thought, thoroughly unnerved, not dreaming that a decade later I would meet a man with whom I've been happily settled for some thirty years. (And who, *like* me, shies away from "a wide variety of outside outlets and events.")

In 1979, wretched and depressed, I would have joined a gypsy caravan if one had hovered into view. I was well aware that the exercise with Tiffen bordered on the absurd, yet I did take some momentary comfort—for a whole day—in being encouraged to blame the stars rather than my peculiar character ("disorders," I want to add) for the serial nightmare I'd been undergoing with potential candidates for matehood.

I soon turned back to troubling deaf heaven—and to taxing the patience of my closest friend of many years, Dick Poirier, the literary critic. Dick and I, along with Leo Bersani, had been a tight trio of friends since meeting in graduate school some twenty-five years earlier; when Leo moved to Berkeley, Dick and I had drawn closer still. In the weeks following Chris's abrupt departure, I poured out my grief to Dick, endlessly analyzed the reasons for the relationship falling apart, vowed that in future I'd look to friends for closeness and hustlers for sex: "Bifurcation is the path to salvation."

"I think I must be deeply masochistic," I announced at one point.

"You think?" Dick said, risking only the trace of a smile.

"Why? You don't?"

"I don't believe in pigeonholes. I simply think you have a *tendency*"— here Dick allowed himself a chuckle—"to convert fairly run-of-the-mill infatuations into some sort of Wagnerian *Weltschmerz*" ("world sorrow," a word we'd picked up in graduate school while preparing for our German proficiency exam and used campily ever since). "As I see it, you have a rather large capacity for self-castigation. But technically you're *not* a masochist—you don't associate sexual pleasure with pain."

"Do I detect a lack of sympathy? You sometimes over-defend me—unless, of course, I'm being pushy about defending myself."

"There's nothing *wrong* with being a masochist! It's just that you're not *it*. Sorry, dear, you'll have to find other grounds for self-reproach. Even a change in vocabulary would be an improvement." Dick's tone was a mix of high camp and simmering impatience. "All this insistent, obsessive, self-scrutiny—it isn't congenial to social relations."

I got the message but couldn't help another bleat or two. "Chris has hurt me deeply, the abrupt way he broke it off after he'd been the one who—"

"You're a veritable hero of suffering. *There*—will that do?"

Dick had called a firm halt to lamentation. He could be tender and empathic, but he was also formidably, famously impatient with self-pity. It wasn't a quality in his own makeup, and he grew testy when others indulged it. It made him grumpy and intractable. His own tolerance for emotional pain was far more pronounced than most people's—certainly more than mine. When Dick grieved he neither denied it nor wallowed in it; it was *there*, a fact to be lived with. He believed in the *non*-talking cure.

"You need to move on," he said evenly. "Close the book on Chris. You've got a lot—an awful lot—in your life to be thankful for. *That's* what you need to focus on."

Resentful, I knew better than to express it. I wanted to tell Dick he was being harsh. *Perhaps* he had a point, but it seemed cruelly premature to be making it now. Why couldn't he understand that I missed Chris terribly and that I needed to talk about it? I did mumble something like "At my advanced age I'll never be able to replace him, even if I—"

Dick lost patience. "Stop it, Marty. *Stop* it! Chris was never right for you, never a good match. Too tortured, difficult, *Catholic*—as you've known from the beginning, or should have. But would you listen? No, of course not. Look at your recent record, for God's sake: Brad, David, Chris! Has it ever crossed your mind that maybe you don't *want* a lifetime partner?"

"Yes, often." I could hear the sulkiness in my voice. "I need privacy, a lot of it. I'm a writer, for Chrissake. I need to be alone, I know that.

I *prefer* to be alone—as long as I'm in constant demand sexually and socially." My stab at humor fell flat.

"Plus," Dick added, unsmiling, "you enjoy sexual variety. As do I. We don't buy the stereotypic formula that defines happiness as settling down with one person. *There*, I've said it."

Dick smiled. He usually sensed when he was on the verge of getting *too* tough and would back off. "Would you care to have me itemize just a short list of all the wonderful elements in your life, *aside* from Chris—Jesus, I almost said *Christ*!—that ought to make you one of God's most grateful creatures?"

I couldn't help but laugh. "Please do. And don't make it too short."

"A. You've got a job. B. You're in good health. C. You don't look your age. D. You're white. Is that enough? No? Okay—and E. You've got a full head of hair."

We both laughed. "Yes, but it's graying."

"Oh, poor baby!" Dick reached over and stroked my check. "*Such* a wretched ingrate. Fortunately, you know it. Now: as your senior, I'm prepared to offer some practical advice."

"Oh good. I'm sure it's worthless, but I'll follow it to the letter."

"It's very simple. Very basic: Start going back to Rounds—not *every* night, but now and then. I was there Wednesday. Some lovely young things wandering about. Plus Vladimir Horowitz, ensconced alone, as always, in one of the banquettes, silently watchful. I wonder when he gets a chance to practice. No wonder he only gives one concert a year."

Hustlers

Rounds was one of the current hustling hot spots, a scene that had changed little since my libido took a hike after my mother's death. Two very different bars served as two very different backdrops. The climate and clientele in Rounds, the elegant, handsomely designed and softly lit bar in the East Fifties, was light years away from the other central emporium, the down-and-dirty West Forties hangout, Haymarket. Urban renewal hadn't yet hit the Times Square area—its shaky start would begin in 1981—and Haymarket, compared to Rounds, had a tenser ambience, terser conversations, tougher young men—and lower prices. Even some of the Bloomingdale regulars who frequented Rounds would now and then drop in—"in a fit of madness," they liked to say—to savor Haymarket's "adventurous" climate. Haymarket in turn seemed a fortress of safety when compared with Forty-Second Street itself, which, pre-"renewal," still retained its ancient character as a hub of illicit activity, ranging from high-risk street pickups and drug deals to a cornucopia of peep shows and porn theaters.

One evening some years earlier, when Dick and I were due to rendezvous at Haymarket, he arrived with Gore Vidal in tow, along with Gore's amiable, unassuming companion Howard Austen. Dick had known Gore rather well for some time, but (my memory's shaky here) that night may have been my first encounter with him—though thereafter our paths occasionally crossed. At the time I was working on my play about the Beats, *Visions of Kerouac* (one of six plays the Kennedy Center had commissioned for its Bicentennial celebration), and knew that Gore and Kerouac had hopped into bed at some point. Always the diligent historian, I promptly asked Gore how big Kerouac's cock was. "Average size," he urbanely replied, not missing a beat. "But what surprised me was that he was circumcised—the Lowell working class isn't supposed to do that."

When I pushed for more details, Gore—with trademark hauteur and no apparent irony—obliged: "I felt he and I owed it to American Literature to go to bed together." A look of mild disgust passed over his face: "We only 'belly-rubbed.'" (Dick later told me, true or not, "Vidal is almost never interested in anything else.") Perhaps inspired by the cash-and-carry atmosphere of Haymarket, Gore then proceeded to claim that "a man named Kelly used to pay Kerouac and Cassady to have sex together while he watched and jerked off. As you must know," he loftily concluded, "Kerouac was mostly homosexual, Cassady mostly trade."

The conversational gambits at Rounds were in general more mannerly and indirect. Assured young college students (for which substitute incipient filmmakers, struggling actors, aspiring rock stars) mingled with unembarrassed ease among snottily elegant, conspicuously successful older men. Hustlers and Johns were often indistinguishably fashionable in dress and indistinguishably glib at banter. To be sure, some traditional gauges still prevailed to separate youth from age: skin texture, hairline, muscle tone (tightness of buns being *the* critical differentiation). Yet not even these distinctions were any longer infallible, thanks to the ubiquitous use of Nautilus machines and the marvels of modern cosmetology.

The tight young look-alike bodies poured into designer jeans and open-neck Armani shirts that came in and out of Rounds concealed far more diversity than was immediately apparent. Yes, there were college students and out-of-work actors aplenty, many of whom, on cue, would subject you to some variation of "I don't regard hustling as any big deal. I simply decided it made much more sense to sell my body for a few hours every week and spend my time working on my craft rather than doing some stupefying nine-to-five."

But there were many others who might dress the part of upwardly mobile youth but disdained its class manner. On my very first foray to Rounds following Dick's stern directive, I ended up talking for several hours not with an aspiring artist attentive to safeguarding his "instrument" but to a full-time locksmith from the Bronx who was also a part-time auxiliary cop. After several drinks Tony confided in me that he was currently letting a sixteen-year-old Puerto Rican kid—whom he'd met in a gay bar—stay in his apartment. He was doing it as a favor for a friend, another cop, who'd fallen for the lad but had no place to house him.

That night Tony and I exchanged phone numbers. He called the next day, came down for another three hours of talk, told me he wasn't interested in hustling me, acknowledged that he was carrying a gun, gave me a big hug at the door, expressed the hope that we could get together again later in the week, and promised—as one might an older brother or duenna—to call me later that night to let me know he'd "gotten back to the Bronx safely." At this late date I've lost all memory of what followed, but not much of anything, I think. What I wrote in my re-inaugurated diary that night was that I thought he was an "enticing package of nonconformities, though so muted and underplayed as to seem the essence of normality—New York normality. My interest more cerebral than chemical. His, too, I suspect."

I didn't return for a while to Rounds, but Dick's instincts had been right: chatting up an enjoyable storm with Tony—the hustling context irrelevant—did help push me to going out more, to start accepting invitations that I'd been almost automatically turning down. A few of the parties were even fun. At a shindig hosted by Joe McCrindle, founder of the *Transatlantic Review*, for Denis Lemon, editor of the *London Gay News*, I ran into some old political comrades, Betty (now Achebe) Powell and Ginny Apuzzo, and we got happily high on two joints I'd brought along. I didn't care for either McCrindle or Lemon, but the novelist Bertha Harris (*Lovers*) was also at the party, and every time I saw her I liked her more—tough integrity, smartass funny.

Less fun, and a good deal stranger, was the party Susan Brownmiller threw for Jane Alpert. "The Alpert Case" was a cause célèbre at the time, especially within feminist circles. In 1969 Alpert had been involved in planting bombs in eight separate government installations to protest the war in Vietnam. Arrested, she'd skipped bail and gone underground; resurfacing after four and a half years, she'd served twenty-seven months in jail and had recently been released. While still underground, Alpert had written *Mother Right: A New Feminist Theory*, in which she stressed the "unique consciousness" of women, emphasized the innate, biologically grounded differences between the two traditional genders, and politically broke with the radical male left.

Her history and her views polarized the women's movement; some leading feminists, including Ti-Grace Atkinson and Flo Kennedy, accused Alpert of having given the FBI information that had jeopardized the safety of a number of women still in hiding, in particular

Pat Swinton ("Shoshana Ryan"). Ironically I'd earlier been in an acting class with the renamed Ryan, had found her powerfully empathic, warm, and real, and had grown very fond of her.

I hadn't met Alpert before, though Susan and I had been on-and-off friendly for more than a decade. Given my penchant for theatrics, I thought the Alpert evening sounded promising; Susan's invitation had specified "dinner," which I took as code for an intimate gathering and the prospect of some engrossing conversation. Not at all. I arrived to find Susan's glamorous Village penthouse awash in an exuberant, flashy, voluble flow of people. (Susan later told me that Alpert had been so fearful no one would show up that an additional last-minute batch of invitations had gone out.) From my vantage point, the evening proved a near-total bust—a typically fractured Manhattan side show in which everyone got their glancing half-sentence of recognition.

Alpert herself seemed more bewildered than anything else. I got to talk with her for a grand total of three minutes, broken into segments. She seemed like a sweet, shy Sarah Lawrence girl, circa 1960, harmless and decent, the tiny rhinestone glitters pasted on her eyelids and cheeks a crucial indication that she had no idea whether she'd been dropped into a nest of drag queens or a sorority reunion in Scarsdale. When I ran into a longtime acquaintance, the journalist Jack Newfield, he pronounced *Mother Right* (Jack always pronounced, always with a heavy dose of patronization) "brave and honest." Not having read it, I had no reason to doubt him. In any case, I told myself, neither the Janes nor the Jacks were true representatives of the idealistic young I'd so much admired during the sixties—though they might represent the survivors. I didn't linger. I needed grounding and headed straight up to Rounds.

A few nights later I went to yet another party, this one for the feminist academic Catharine Stimpson, to celebrate the publication of her new book. I hadn't seen Catharine in a while and enjoyed reconnecting with several other people at the party. That was especially true of the historian Marilyn Young, as trenchant and direct as ever, and Kate Millett, with whom I had a prolonged shared *holler* about the "Homophobic Philistines" who controlled the publishing world. The only reason her book *Flying* had finally gotten published, Kate told me, was because Doris Lessing "read the manuscript and *told* Bob Gottlieb at Knopf that he *had* to take it on." That sounded a trifle pat, but who cared: I was back out in the world and enjoying myself. My wise friend Dick had been right: "Get your ass off the pity pot." I had to remind myself that grieving needn't be unrelenting to prove its authenticity, nor was experiencing relief from it evidence of shallowness. I was relearning the ancient truth that sadness and pleasure seamlessly coexist, one easily giving way to the other even in the worst of times—the shift jagged yet persistent.

Dick and Leo were still the two friends I saw far more often than any others and still felt closest to, though neither was traditionally (vote, lobby, agitate) political in the way Betty Powell and Ginny Apuzzo— or, for that matter, still older friends like Jesse Lemisch and Naomi Weisstein were. (Twenty years later, with *Homos*, Leo would become a leading *non*traditionalist "queer theorist.") I remember one particularly vivid dinner with Dick and Leo during which I urged them, with more than a touch of self-righteousness, to become at least somewhat active in the fledgling gay movement, which in this pre-AIDS period was making only painfully slow progress; foolishly I cited Sartre's insistence that intellectuals have to put themselves on the line. "Absurd!" Dick predictably shouted, growing belligerently red in the face. Leo was less vehement, though also annoyed. (Whenever an argument between us got heated, Dick would growl, Leo sputter.)

Dick loved contention. He had an intransigent, imperious side that surfaced rather rapidly. On that particular evening he grandly proclaimed, "Each of us has his work to do. Men like Sartre are far too valuable to be risking jail or injury!" When I tactlessly suggested that what was *really* at risk was their own comfort, Dick's wrath visibly gathered force—though that evening, anyway, we somehow ended up exploding in laughter, not anger. (I think it was when Dick did one of his wicked end runs and archly inquired if I was planning to add a roof garden to my duplex.)

Dick was in fact far less cowardly—after all, he remained a close friend of the ferocious Lillian Hellman—than either Leo or me; under pressure I trusted Dick's instinctive generosity, his willingness to put himself on the line for a friend (but not a "cause"), though he'd scowlingly deny the compliment as "sentimental" and would insist we get back to his real pleasure: playing the contrarian. Leo was less theatrical and full-throated, more emotionally guarded. I lurched between the two temperaments, my impulse often emphatic, my action often truncated.

I placed myself politically, sometimes noisily, on Dick's left yet over the long haul was a good deal more self-protective than he.

On another evening, with neither Dick nor Leo present, a dinner party *did* turn explosive when the subject became Castro's Cuba. One of the other guests was the distinguished cinematographer Néstor Almendros (he won an Oscar for *Days of Heaven* and was nominated three other times), who'd been exiled by both Batista and Castro. With an air of imperious moral superiority, Almendros launched into a bitter vilification of the revolution. I'd read widely in the literature on Cuba a few years before, while preparing an introduction to the published version of Hans Magnus Enzensberger's play *The Havana Inquiry*, and I took the position that Castro had made considerable strides in eliminating the island's vast inequalities in health care, diet, and education that had characterized the preceding Batista regime—greater strides, proportionate to its resources, than we in the United States could claim.

It felt good to be engaged in political argument again, though in truth I prolonged the contest mostly in a futile effort to impress Almendros's scrumptiously stunning boyfriend Wally (who'd earlier been, it was whispered, Nureyev's lover). Political disputation, in the upshot, proved *not* the way to Wally's heart, though he did invite me to a screening a few nights later of his porn film in progress. I found the cinematic elements surprisingly impressive—too much so for commercial success: the opulent staging and narrative sophistication ran counter to the haphazard erotics of the day.

That second night Almendros and I managed to avoid a repeat argument about Cuba, but the point I'd earlier made between the revolution's accomplishments and our own country's lagging concern for the plight of its poor wasn't, in the mid-seventies, preposterous on its face. The prosperity that had marked the U.S. economy for nearly three decades after World War II—the most prolonged boom on record—gave way in the early seventies to the Arab oil embargo, stagflation, high rates of unemployment, and a decline in real wages. The stock market lost nearly half its value between 1973 and 1980, and the Great Society's safety net took on the look of a ripped parachute hanging ghost-like from the tree branches.

Nor was there much else that felt positive to those of us on the left. The growth in globalization and the rapid disappearance of industrial jobs had led to a sharp decline in union membership—and, as a result, in working-class bargaining power. Residential racial segregation remained stubbornly in place, as did, following like the night the day, entrenched school segregation. "Free market" capitalism had a resurgence in financial circles that took the premium off compassion and placed it heavily on the "rightness" of greed and consumerism. ("If you're not doing well, it's your own laziness or lack of ability.") The installation of Jimmy Carter as president in 1976 marked an era of deregulation that saw government services further weakened or gutted and the gap between the haves and have-nots widening disastrously. Like the two ends of a seesaw, as more and more Americans fell below the poverty line, the number of prisons and a renewed emphasis on capital punishment rose higher. The general upsurge in right-wing ideology would lead to Ronald Reagan's election to the presidency in 1980.

Manhattan was at a particular low point in the mid- and late seventies. Basic services were curtailed to the point where garbage went uncollected for days, the foul stench wafting through the streets; unemployment stood at 11 percent in 1976, with 14 percent of New Yorkers on welfare; and the crime rate rose to a level not seen in any American city since the 1930s. In the summer of 1977, when a citywide blackout—during a heat wave, no less—produced rampant looting and hundreds of fires, the city seemed on the verge of bankruptcy and collapse, with fear and malaise endemic.

The best that could be said of the pervasive atmosphere of decay was that it was possible to be poor and still live in Manhattan—including in the low-rent Downtown area, where cultural experimentation blossomed and the demimonde gathered at CBGB and Max's Kansas City. The cultural revolution had survived the demise of the antiwar movement and the New Left's critique of inequality, and in the midst of widespread dislocation the decade saw the simultaneous emergence of feminism, the beginnings of a gay protest movement, the rise of the American Indian Movement, and an ongoing, if painfully slow, increase in the number of African Americans entering universities and elected to public office.

The small, struggling gay political movement of the late seventies was no match for the explosion of libidinal energy that characterized the burgeoning gay male disco scene. As early as the mid-sixties

Manhattan had boasted more than a dozen dancing emporiums—including Arthur, the celebrity hangout—but the gay version that now came into its own (as Alice Echols has brilliantly described in *Hot Stuff: Disco and the Remaking of American Culture*) far outstripped the earlier clubs in erotic display. Among the now-legendary dance palaces (many of them membership only) that had mainstream magazines hailing the new "gay chic" was the Flamingo, the Tenth Floor, the Paradise Garage, 12 West, the Sanctuary, and—among the last to open (in 1980) and the most notorious—the Saint.

The emphasis was on "lumberjack masculine" bodies, fueled by drugs and poppers, writhing in sweaty ecstasy to the dance floor's throbbing beat—and to sexual release on the balcony and in alcoves. I vaguely recall one nondancing visit to the Sanctuary and a dozen dancing ones to the less flamboyant Ice Palace on West Fifty-Seventh Street, but gay men in their late forties like me—there were always a few dazzling exceptions—knew better than to look for conviviality and comradeship among the perfectly formed pecs of the disco palaces.

Many of the chic gay dancing clubs excluded women and people of color; sexual abandon and political awareness were poles apart in these years. The long-haired, androgynous gay men of the sixties and early seventies, attuned to gentle pacifism, bent on displacing, not duplicating macho posturing, had slid *way* out of sight by the mid-seventies. Putting daffodils into the gun barrels of the National Guard had given way to less delicate gestures: fist-fucking in hammocks, licking (if granted permission) leather studded jock straps. Labelle, Donna Summer, and Grace Jones—not Joan Baez—now held center stage. In disgust at current gay male preoccupations and frustrated at the lack of concern with women's issues, many lesbian feminists separated from the national political movements and formed their own organizations.

Still, the contrast between the early and late seventies can be overdrawn. Yes, the radical exuberance once typified by the Gay Liberation Front or the public "zaps" of the Gay Activists Alliance had largely petered out by the end of the decade. Yet the notion that "gay is good" (not pathological, not criminal), that it was "okay to be different," had resonated widely, quietly spreading across the land. The proof came when Anita Bryant launched her crusade to "save the children" in 1977 and John Briggs, the following year, introduced Proposition 6 in California to ban gays from teaching—and met with a massive outpouring of anger and mobilized resistance that defeated both campaigns and culminated in the 100,000-strong 1979 March on Washington. The moralistic publicity glare that focused in the urban centers on the discos and the sexual emporiums missed the main story: more and more of the mainstream young were leaving their closets, embracing their differentness, and beginning to let their voices be heard.

A Heart Attack

With grief over my mother's death now less acute, I started to write again, but only short articles and reviews; I wasn't feeling focused enough to take on a book-length project—or even to come up with an appealing topic for one. The bulk of my psychic energy was still centered on keeping my head above water. I could have dinner with a friend or even enjoy myself at a party, but out of nowhere an unwanted haunting memory could suddenly throw me off balance, disrupt my shaky equilibrium.

Two things made matters worse: I was on leave from teaching in 1979, which meant too much free time for brooding, and Chris unexpectedly reentered my life, though indirectly. He wrote to me from San Francisco, where he'd moved—entering a seminary had once again lost its appeal—asking me to forgive his "fearful egocentric" behavior, acknowledging that he hadn't been able to "see or understand" himself very well, and suggesting we "renew contact" on his next trip back East. I didn't believe in his (or anybody's) core transformation and evaded a meeting. Yet even the indirect contact of a letter stirred up an unexpected amount of turmoil. ("Maybe he really has changed? Maybe this time around we might be able to . . .") Emotionally the turbulence over Chris fed into and got entangled with the lingering pain over the loss of my mother. The combination became explosive when I added one more ingredient to the mix: cocaine.

I'd been smoking pot off and on (sometimes mixed with hash) for some time, usually in connection with sex, and found it a benign, pleasant stimulant. I first tried cocaine in the early seventies, when a trick (to use a then-current term) offered me some, promising an endless night of erotic bliss. I didn't much like it, nor could I figure out why it was touted as "the world's greatest aphrodisiac." It did clear my sinuses and made me briefly euphoric, but it turned me *off* sexually. On a second try the result was similar: the coke neither heightened my lust nor freed up my inhibitions; instead it focused and distanced me. "A strange drug," I concluded in my diary. "My reaction is negative."

It must have been lousy coke because after those two false starts, I had no trouble seeing it as a powerful adjunct to sex. Not that I sought it out in the early seventies or became reliant on it, but when it was offered I happily accepted. I no longer doubted that it enflamed sexual desire (and imagination)—though sometimes frustrating my ability to satisfy it (the limp cock syndrome). I also found it useful for concentrating my attention when writing, though it didn't provide me with anything brilliant to write about. If coke was a mixed blessing for both sex and writing, it was infallible as a numbing agent—and numbing was what I most needed at this point in my life.

As the anguish over my mother's death and Chris's abandonment moderated, I could see more clearly that not all of the dejection that continued to mark my life could be neatly assigned to losing them. Ma and Chris were the nameable, proximate causes of the acute desolation of recent years, but the pain of their disappearance fell on fallow ground, confirmed the unease and anxiety that had long underlain my surface affability. Mine was a family background, bluntly put, of muted unhappiness, of a vibrant, unfulfilled, invasive mother and a disaffected, distant father, that combined, as I entered adolescence and sexual awareness, with a homophobic cultural climate that engendered shame and self-distrust. A hundred episodes in my past that I can barely recall even in outline, let alone rank in terms of affect, administered a steady dose of humiliation ("You're so pretty you should be a girl"), seeding rivers of self-doubt. That backdrop of unhappiness prowled deep in my being, consciously stilled with activity and "accomplishment" yet always lurking, awaiting an outlet, an opening through which it could pour, legitimately pour, because now nameable: Ma; Chris. My grief over them was real and full, yet what got unleashed in their name had a much earlier origin, a far deeper current, all the more brackish for having been pushed underground, mutely forceful, eager for the chance to burst through.

BY THE LATE seventies I'd stopped seeing coke as a serendipitous additive now and then and started to actively seek it out. A journalist friend introduced me to a dealer named Ronnie, touting him as "New York's finest." For once a reputation proved deserved. I'd never had better stuff, never basked in such sure-footed euphoria. Yet I still had the brakes on: I hated the aftereffects, the black moods when coming down that could be offset only with Valium. That, plus not having a lot of extra cash to spend, kept me from becoming a regular. I continued to use, but no more than once in a while, and for most of the seventies I don't remember ever buying more than a gram at a time.

When high, though, I did love the stuff and couldn't for the life of me understand why anyone would prefer liquor. Booze, at best, loosened you up at a party you didn't want to be at; coke was for intensely pleasurable isolation or unhinged sex. Used in moderation, and for specific occasions only, I told myself, coke confirmed the countercultural cliché about better living through chemistry.

But then came the night when, alone on a street in the Village on my way home from dinner with a friend, I was suddenly hit with chest pain so excruciating that it nearly knocked me to the pavement. Somehow I managed to get myself to the nearby emergency room at St. Vincent's, where I was given an EKG, pronounced fine, and sent home. Hours later, the pain having failed to subside, I called my sister, who in turn called an ambulance. St. Vincent's did another EKG, again pronounced me fine, and again tried to send me home. They hadn't counted on my tiny sister's formidable will; she threw a calculated tantrum, screamed that I *wasn't* fine—by then I was incontinent—and threatened to sue the hospital unless a specialist was called in *at once*. A cardiologist duly appeared and within minutes had me transferred to the intensive care unit. He was in no doubt: I'd had a massive heart attack.

What followed was a frightening month-long stay in the hospital, replete with an endless procession of tests, doctors (and their entourages), and varying edicts about the need to "reshape" my life, undergo bypass surgery, accept semi-invalidism. When I pressed for an explanation as to why a forty-nine-year-old man in excellent shape—I'd had a full physical the very week of the attack and been told I was in "splendid" health—should have had a heart attack, the doctors hemmed and hawed, referred vaguely to genetics and "excessive stress," and pronounced me a "medical anomaly."

I'm the one who brought up cocaine. My lead physician, a Dr. Hawley, asked me how often I used it. I told him, truthfully, "a couple of times a month. I'm more like a binger—an occasional blast." Cocaine, he replied, "is essentially a benign drug"—yes, he really did say that; it was apparently a common medical view at the time. Cocaine becomes "problematic," Hawley went on, "only in large doses." His conclusion: "I do not believe, from what you're telling me, that cocaine was a factor in your heart attack." Though that *was* the standard medical opinion in the seventies, I never entirely believed it: I had no other significant risk factors for a heart attack (and down to the present day no further symptomatology).

In my memoir *Midlife Queer* I've written at length about the assorted horrors of St. Vincent's, where incompetence marched hand in hand with compassionate expertise, as well as the frightening period immediately following my discharge, when every symptom reminded me of the prediction one hospital intern had so kindly made to my face—that I "was a time bomb waiting to go off again"—and that made Hawley's injunction to "reduce stress" in my life seem like a bad joke. Rather than repeat all the misery of that year, I'll pick up the story about six months in, after I'd been allowed to resume moderate activity, including exercise on a stationary bike.

A medical milestone in my recovery was a thallium stress test that revealed "some additional ischemia" in the same area as the heart attack that "might portend some future trouble," but, more important, *no* ischemia on the left side. My new doctor, James Horowitz—I'd left Hawley in the dust the second I exited St. Vincent's—called that "a good result." He took me off medication and said he saw no reason to contemplate either an angiogram or bypass surgery.

By the fall of 1980, a year after the attack, I'd regained considerable optimism about the future and more buoyancy than I'd felt for some time. In October I bought myself a notebook and on the first page wrote, "I'm going to force myself to keep a journal again. I have to activate *some* form of writing, and this seems the easiest for starters. . . . The heart attack gave my life meaning. Symptoms, alarms, self-attentions absorbed what minimal energies I had, diverting me from stale broodings over the loss of Ma & Chris, allowing me respite from the nagging pressure to continue writing even as I knew I'd lost any genuine urgency to do so." Hopeful that a normal life span lay ahead, one that "sensibly" excluded drugs, I gave up as well on maintaining my defiantly youthful appearance—which before the heart attack had been marked by challenging twenty-year-olds on the squash court and working out on the Nautilus machines at the health club. ("What?! You can't be in your forties!" "Ah yes"—head tilted modestly to the side—"I can and am, *fifty*, to be precise.") Now that I was "no longer absorbed by the routines of recovery," I wrote, "I have to look elsewhere for renewed meaning to end the death-dealing staleness that's marked the past few years."

I'd been on leave from the university on a fellowship but now returned with relief to teaching; I'd always enjoyed working with students, and it was good to discover that I still did. I also decided to go back into therapy, despite the destructive mistreatment I'd received earlier (which I've recounted in *Cures*). I liked the new guy, Bill Trevor: he wasn't doctrinaire and told me early on that if I had any problem it wasn't homosexuality, it was "unrequited tenderness." "It's difficult for you," Bill said, "to get the love you need when you're giving out signals that you don't need it, when you don't let people see your vulnerability and pain." I had my doubts about that; it seemed to me people *wanted* to see me as invulnerable, as somebody who easily navigated the world; in my opinion they delighted in having an excuse for not taking my problems seriously—since their own were quite enough to cope with.

Bill also thought we needed to work on formulating a new set of emotional priorities that put my "long-standing need for intimacy" clearly above my "short-term pursuit of fantasy 'cowboys.'" That sounded like the right goal, and I tried hard to reduce my skepticism as to whether the "talking cure" had the needed instrumentalities to help me reach it. After all, I'd spent more than my share of time devoted to self-scrutiny, in and out of therapy; I'd garnered a cornucopia of "insights" into why I did this and not that, yet they seemed to lead me only to finer—subtler, more contradictory—insights, not to any significant change in my feelings or behavior. Maybe the core doesn't change once the personality essentials have been indelibly imprinted (by age two?). Maybe, I gloomily, giddily thought, what really needs redoing is my childhood—or perhaps a resplicing of my genes.

Bill thought all that was "premature pessimism," an avoidance mechanism designed to evade what might well prove a painful search for what he called my "emotional DNA," the tumbler lock that would allow me to find closeness with others without being "jerked around by them" (Chris), to stop being misled by reluctance—justifying its appeal by conflating it with "depth"—treating unavailability as the sign of an "interestingly complicated personality," as a challenge, a mystery that, with sufficient devotion and persistence, I could solve, could convert into tender, blissful togetherness. Hmm, yes, all that did ring a bell. Okay, I'd give therapy yet another shot, a last one.

I gradually increased my socializing, seeing old friends more and meeting some new ones, like Tom Stoddard and Ken Dawson, two young standouts in the new generation of gay activists—both of whom would die of AIDS. Another new friend, Helen Whitney, I first met when she interviewed me for her pathbreaking documentary film *Homosexuals* and was immediately drawn to her passionate intensity. We quickly became, and remain, close friends. Ever the moralist, I generalized in my diary about how my friendships with women—my longtime friends Barbara Hart Weiss and Rosalyn Higgins were two others—seemed much more able to survive "more than garden-variety stress, disagreement, and separation. The capacity for sustained commitment," I wrote, "may not be functionally related to chromosomes, but they surely are sorely devastated by culture."

One balmy afternoon I even took a leisurely walk by myself— previously an unthinkable indulgence—down Christopher Street. "*Tout gay New York*," I later wrote in my diary, "seemed on festive parade. I actually saw several couples *kissing*! Can affection be back in fashion? Construction worker/cowboy/leather outfits were notable by their absence. Could macho finally be on the way out? Or is it that tough guys don't go out till nightfall?" I ran into several people I knew. Arthur Bell, the *Village Voice* columnist, looked ravaged, paper thin and limping badly. Rumors about him ranged from drunkenness to arthritis to diabetes. (It was diabetes; Arthur died of it in 1984, age forty-four). I stopped and talked to Rich Schmiechen (coproducer of the 1984 Academy Award–winning film *The Times of Harvey Milk*). "Sweet man," I wrote in my diary. "His graying hair becomes him. I can scarcely remember our brief mini-affair a half dozen years ago, only that his unyielding blandness and deference quickly turned me off. Meaning, perhaps, that he was *available*." (Rich died of AIDS in 1992 at age forty-five.)

I had Christmas dinner that year, 1981, at Naomi Weisstein and Jesse Lemisch's apartment. We'd been close friends for more than fifteen years. Jesse, a fellow historian, had long been radically outspoken in his politics and had lost several academic jobs as a result. Naomi, at forty, was already recognized as both a brilliant scientist and a pioneering feminist; in the sixties she'd cofounded the Chicago All Women's Liberation Rock Band and written one of the iconic texts ("Psychology Constructs the Female") of the second wave of feminism. She was also an electric personality—iconoclastic, irrepressibly daring, a joyful mischief-maker.

Recently she'd come down with a mysterious virus and that Christmas Eve was already showing signs of reduced energy. Before long she'd be confined to bed with severe vertigo and debilitation that required round-the-clock nursing. She would never recover, but nor would she ever lose her miraculous spirit. "To the most courageous person I know" is how I put it in 2009, when I dedicated *Waiting to Land* to her. Never able to leave her bed, Naomi died in 2015. She was "a brazen cheerleader for audacity," I said at her memorial service, and her loss was "unimaginably awful."

The Reagan Years Begin

I slowly began to reengage in politics, both gay and otherwise, though not to the extent I had earlier. With the landslide election of Ronald Reagan in November 1980 and the defeat of one liberal senator after the other, the country lurched to the right with a vengeance. "No one can sensibly call the results an 'anti-Carter' vote," I wrote in my diary.

> Americans are notorious ticket-splitters, and when they *don't*, when they machine-gun down progressives on local, state and federal levels alike, something more, something a great deal more frightening, is involved than fear and anger over an inflationary economy or a determination to send the peanut farmer back to Plains. Something like a Carrie Nation fury at what was widely being called "the decay of traditional moral values." The right wing has tied together a neat bundle of scapegoat "issues"—from abortion to busing to ERA to gay rights—and persuaded the electorate to believe that *it*, rather than corporate greed, is the chief villain.

Given the size of Reagan's victory, in combination with the Republican capture of the Senate, our new president could, I felt, claim a popular mandate for "cleaning up" the entire array of moral misfits that "disfigured" the public landscape. The Moral Majority, I feared, might well represent the country's mainstream. A fundamentalist drift had been under way for some time, but combative born-again Christians, led by Jerry Falwell, Pat Robertson, and Jesse Helms, now proceeded to up the ante, to denounce the secular Satanism of American life with a brush broad enough to include the absence of prayer in public schools, sex outside of marriage, abortion, feminism, and homosexuality. Equating economic success, as the right (Calvinist to the core) did, with evidence of spiritual salvation, the corollary followed that any individual failing to thrive under the benign system of laissez-faire capitalism had only themselves to blame. The growing maldistribution of wealth, according to these true believers, was the result not of existing class, race, and gender barriers to advancement but rather to an individual's lack of ability or drive—or, more simply, to "immorality."

My friend Vivian Gornick decided that the ideal balm for sagging political spirits was to attend a reading by the eighty-year-old proletarian writer Meridel Le Sueur at the School of Marxist Studies. I reluctantly agreed to go, and was glad I did. Le Sueur had recently published what is probably her best known work, *The Girl*, and the place was packed with some 150 or so twenty-five- to thirty-five-year-old women dressed in expensive "worker" outfits and filled with noisy adoration for Le Sueur's "proto-feminism." We recognized a few other "oldies" in the crowd, including Barbara Garson (best known for her provocative 1967 political play, *MacBird!*), who took one look at Le Sueur's formidable proportions and what Barbara called her "clear pool" eyes and moaned, "Oh God, she looks like she can—and will—talk forever!"

To our surprise, Le Sueur turned out to be a wonderful speaker, her voice strong and sonorous, her anecdotal bridges warm, unselfconscious, and moving. Still, the rhetoric (as I wrote in my diary that night) was "pure Mike Gold preserved in formaldehyde circa 1931. Examples: 'The violence of the hatching of the world egg [sic] is terrible to see right now, but also wonderful, for out of the stinking corpse, the living is being born.' Or: 'Radicals never have nervous breakdowns.' Or: 'The patriarchy invented linear time.'"

The leaden litany destroyed whatever lyricism there was in the poetry but didn't destroy the overarching impressiveness of the woman herself. Looking much like an ancient Indian, her yellow-gray straw hair parted down the middle and wrapped up in a severe bun on top, her body covered with a huge striped poncho, colorful strips of beads and emblems adorning her neck and chest, she seemed a force of nature— enduring, unflappable, whole. As Annette Rubinstein, who was also present and was herself a left-wing icon, put it, Le Sueur is "an integer, not a fraction."

Integer or not, Vivian and I had occasional fits of the giggles at some of Le Sueur's pickled views and prose ("We must go for our wisdom to the people, our great revolutionary people"). Yet (as I wrote in my diary), "like all great naifs, her passionate authenticity silenced, even awed us. To be that full, strong—and optimistic!—at 80!! [She lived to be ninety-six.] Who could not be stunned by the sheer tenacity? We were restored to reality by an announcement from the floor that 'next week Ernie Brill will read from his short stories on occupational health and safety.' "

IN JANUARY 1981 I moved from the Village to a new apartment in Chelsea on West Twenty-Second Street (where I still live). It was at the top of an 1850s brownstone, with terraces and wonderful light, and I felt terribly happy about the change of scene. The move felt emblematic: I was putting a harrowing period in my life behind me, or so I believed and hoped. I was leaving an apartment haunted by illness and old griefs and shifting to a warm, sunlit home that offered a genuine opportunity, if hardly a guarantee ("Everywhere I go, I go too—and ruin everything"), for quieter, deeper pleasures, less luxuriant miseries.

As if to remind me that I was still vulnerable, another letter from Chris arrived. He wanted me to know that he included me "in what some people call 'prayers'" and added, "I learned honesty from you, M.D." He suggested that we get together during his upcoming trip East. I knew I couldn't see him without upheaval; "he's still in my marrow," I wrote in my diary. Before I could overthink it and end up inviting turmoil back into my life, I sent him a brief note saying that I'd be glad to stay in touch and wished him well but thought an actual meeting still premature. Nope, early to bed, early to rise makes a man healthy, wealthy—etcetera. How sensible! How praiseworthy! How mature!

Euphoria being among the least reliable emotions, once I was settled in the new apartment I was soon looking around again for an absorbing writing project and in general feeling "soggy," stalemated. I couldn't even manage more than a very occasional journal entry, though I now and then willed the pen across the page. Yet I was more footloose than depressed, was mindful of my manifold blessings, grateful for having survived several forms of heart attack, pleased at resurrecting personal and political contacts—and at not hanging out at my old hustler haunt, Rounds.

David Kalstone, the warm-hearted, super-social literary critic, moved in next door to me, our two terraces abutting. We'd wave "Good morning" and sometimes exchange a bit of gossip—or rather, I'd listen to his, since my own circle was too narrow to yield up many tidbits. Now and then someone would appear on David's terrace who I knew or had known, and across-the-fence conversation grew more animated. Often it was the writer Ed White, David's closest friend, who I'd known casually for many years and whose warmth and wit I'd always enjoyed. One evening Ed appeared with a young man—I'll call him Matt—who gave me a start. "They're having a semi-mini," David managed to whisper. What I didn't reply was that Matt and I had had our own "semi-mini" some time earlier, though I barely recognized my outdoorsy jogger of yesteryear in the thin, bespectacled young garret scholar who stared mutely at me.

I fully expected that one day the specter from my earlier life who would appear on David's terrace would be Dick Poirier, since they both taught in the English Department at Rutgers. My heart attack had produced a rupture in our close friendship of many years that I kept hoping would be repaired but never was. Even as I write this, some thirty-five years later, I still feel anguish over the loss. What happened was that Dick had greeted the news of my heart attack not by rushing to the hospital but by taking off for Italy, from where he sent me exactly two postcards; they attested to the wonders of the climate—and the availability for cash of squadrons of gorgeous young men.

This wasn't a new pattern with Dick. Way back in 1972 I was complaining in my diary about his disappearance when I was going through a tough time: Dick "bitterly denies and resents" the common view among those who know him best

> that he runs from friends in trouble. When I have seen him, he's been grumpy, argumentative, almost reproachful—as if I have no right to be needy. Some of that severity I produce: I'm vocal and relentless in my suffering. . . . I can't figure out what makes him guarded and aloof when close friends get upset. Maybe he doesn't want his own pain about the loneliness of our lives activated. Maybe it's some New England hangover about the shamefulness of not settling private griefs privately. Paradoxically, Dick is a generous man and friend—though he tends to stifle the quality if he senses any demand.

Months after my release from the hospital, I tried to tell Dick about the astonishment and hurt I'd felt at his disappearance. He responded, with some heat, that what I failed to understand was that when someone he cared about deeply was in serious trouble *that he couldn't fix* he had to remove himself from the scene. Sorry, I responded, that just isn't good enough. In any adult relationship worthy of the name, you swallow your discomfort and go to the aid of a friend in need—you don't disappear. Dick didn't see it that way and ended the friendship. I kept hoping we could repair it, but the only times I ever saw him again were when we accidentally ran into each other at Rounds or some other bar on the circuit.

I noted three such occasions in my diary during 1981. Twice, I wrote, Dick "glared through me, or so I imagined." The third time, when he happened to lean over the stool next to mine at the bar, I said "Hello." He "seemed only slightly startled," I wrote that night, "not as if taken unaware by a close friend but as if glancingly annoyed at the intrusion of someone he couldn't quite place & didn't want to trouble having to (how often I've seen Dick give that haughty/befuddled glance to others in the past!). He quickly moved off."

I painfully remember Dick "once saying to me," the diary entry continues, "after one of our periodic quarrels, that our friendship was so long-standing and deep that it could weather any disagreement or misunderstanding. And now it's been nearly two years of frozen silence. I wouldn't have believed it possible, though I should have, knowing his history of abruptly deciding that he no longer had any interest in ever again seeing—whoever; and having heard him for months (just before our break) saying that he was 'fed up' with Leo [Bersani] & intended to stop seeing him, other than at most casually & infrequently" (and he doubtless told Leo the same about me). I would have settled for that much. In the years that have followed, I've never formed as deep a friendship with another man, let alone one I so much admired and cared for. I believe Dick did have several good male friendships—he died a half dozen years ago—which probably says something about where the merits of the case actually lie.

Our friendship had been going through a troubled patch in the period preceding my heart attack, with Dick growing more and more deaf (or mordantly disdainful) of the "bad news" I kept conveying about this or that. He'd become off-handedly dismissive of my "childish whining," and I imagined him implicitly contrasting it with his own superior stoicism—a contrast I felt accurate enough. Still, I didn't like being patronized and felt subtly dismissed—felt I'd become a stand-in for the mistreatment meant for his lover but which he didn't dare vent directly for fear of losing him.

I'd been making an effort of late not to report any news to Dick that wasn't (as related to me) sunny and self-deprecating or (as related to others) amusingly malicious: the court jester currying favor with monarchy bored. My own self-betrayal in the role did as much to breed anger in me as Dick's withdrawal of warmth and empathy brought grief. In any case the bonfire had been stacked for some time and only awaited an event, which the heart attack provided, dramatic enough to ignite it. I don't know how Dick would have named and ranked the combustibles. I do know that I continue to this day to mourn the loss of our friendship; it's a long-standing sorrow, and doubtless the reason I write about it at such length.

The New York Civil Liberties Union and the Gay Movement

At the fiftieth birthday party of a friend, I had a sharp, extended exchange with one of the other guests that made it clearer than ever to me that politics was back on my mind—and needed to be. It was a large, hectic party, and she and I—until then complete strangers to each other—sat down on one of the couches almost simultaneously, both breathing sighs of relief at the respite. We laughed at our shared reaction, which got us to talking despite ourselves. I have no idea how Martin Luther King Jr.'s name came up, but when it did "Sally" scowled and pronounced him "a simply awful man," referring, it turned out, to the revelations subsequent to his death of what she called "his philanderings—his awful exploitation of women."

That took my breath away, but only briefly. I told her that I was gay, did quite a bit of "philandering" myself, sometimes paying cash, and didn't believe that such activity automatically cast me into the outer circles of Hell. (In truth I'd never fully resolved the ethics of paying for sex and would periodically experience a spasm of guilt about it, but I wasn't about to admit that to Sally.) It turned out that she was a lawyer and a self-declared "liberal," and she smoothly finessed my revelation of being gay. "Perhaps," she said, "the power relationship between heterosexual men and women is different—more overwhelming than that between older gay men and younger ones." If so, apparently the charge of immorality might to that degree be mitigated.

That was Sally's notion of a "concession." Otherwise she held her ground—tenaciously, and for two bloody hours. We soon focused not on the cash issue but on promiscuity, with Sally denouncing King as "a *thoroughly* worthless human being." Jesus, I thought, if Sally's at all representative, liberals are as disgustingly archaic as reactionaries; she sounded like Jesse Helms, not Allard Lowenstein. Sally insisted that she was primarily speaking as a feminist, one who had strong views about both prostitution and pornography. Her underlying conviction, she went on, was that monogamy is a morally superior way of life, carrying as a corollary the belief that sexual "infidelity" is *inherently* a "betrayal of trust."

Acknowledging no "extenuating" circumstances, Sally convicted King (and me, by implication) as a "monster" (her actual word). No amount of courage and moral rectitude in other areas of his life could compensate one iota for his "exploitation of women." Is it possible, I asked, tongue in cheek, that at least some of King's bedmates "had put the make on *him*, had enjoyed their encounters, whether or not cash was involved?"

So secure was Sally in her views that she refused me even the crumb of raising her voice. "No," she firmly replied, "it is not possible—other than in the damning sense of a woman deluded into false consciousness by King's formidable presence and reputation." "You should know," she added, "that I speak as an ex-Marxist"—said with a smug smile, as if assuming that I would regard Marx as the ultimate moral authority.

Not being ex- or current myself, my jaw did not drop open in surrender. Nor did I think that Marx's attack on economic exploitation, with which I agreed, could automatically be transferred point for point to hustling: the shifts in power, the options available to both parties, the quality of the human exchange, were all variables. It had come out earlier in the conversation that Sally and her husband lived in a townhouse that they owned, and she'd let me know, without a trace of irony, that she could not abide people "who *on a daily basis* failed to treat their servants well." She was unresponsive to my suggestion that her and her husband's ability to acquire property and to employ others to do menial tasks suggested they'd had opportunities in life not widely available and thereby threw some moral doubt on the purity of their lifestyle.

Rubbish, was the gist of her reply. She reminded me again that she was an *ex*-Marxist and further insisted that the "success" of the civil rights movement had made it possible for anyone with ability and drive to get ahead. Even if true—which it wasn't—had society no responsibility, I asked, for the well-being of those who "lacked" ability and drive? "Yes, of course," Sally responded. "A safety net. A minimal one, so as not to sap motivation and support laziness." I said I thought we could rely on racism to "sap motivation."

On and on we went. The breaking point came when Sally slapped down her trump card: "I suppose one has to see a child growing up to understand these . . . matters"—matters, that is, of "innate" morality. I gagged at the smug patronization but was too flustered to deliver the line I thought of later: "The experience of parenting doesn't guarantee and isn't the equivalent of an ethical life." Instead I sputtered something about how ugly I found the superior virtue of American liberalism—and bid a hasty good-night. In my diary that evening I berated myself for not having "swatted the smug bitch" and ascribed my hesitation to "the decades of self-doubt and guilty apologetics engendered by homophobia that had swept over me yet again (and now and then always will, I suppose, however much I like to believe that these days self-acceptance is firmly rooted)."

Perhaps it was my self-lacerating mood, but I was flooded that night with thoughts about Chris. He was more palpably with me than in months. I could *feel* the hold his "faith" exerted over him, could feel my failure to make the necessary leap of imagination: "That I am not Chris, nor he, me." It wasn't enough simply to have acknowledged his difference and to have refrained from comment on his religious commitment; he *knew* I didn't honor the commitment, however much I enjoyed the differences it created between us in perspective and attitude. I was filled with sadness, with self-blame at how much I had failed in understanding. Yet I sensed, at the same time, that I was overdoing it, attempting to anchor the floating guilt (exploitative, childless wretch!) awakened in me by Sally's cool indictments.

But self-recrimination no longer had the hold on me it once did. I felt I was at least *beginning* to live the life of an everyday mortal: "due" nothing, not even a long life; susceptible to the usual number of "unwarranted" disappointments, jolts, and denials; myself responsible for steering clear of people and occasions that called out my overdeveloped penchant for self-assault. I would never fully learn to "settle"—my privileged upbringing guaranteed an abnormally high set of expectations— despite future defeats waiting in the wings. Yet I *was* less sanguine about prospects and outcomes, less optimistic about my ability to produce a desired result. Reduced expectations were expressed in how I socialized: I was going out more, but the processional had become more sedate: *one* party; dinner with *one* friend; two to three beers at most; in bed by midnight (sometimes 9:00); rare (like once a month) forays to the old hustler haunts in search of the Ideal Hero; sex just as rare.

Happily I didn't much miss the lack of amplitude—the perfervid hunt, the miscued sexual adventure, the overload of coke and pot, the next day's fog of exhaustion and loss. Now and then I felt the old-time urge for excess—for obliterating, late-night orgies of poppers, coke, and sex—and once or twice I even indulged it, though I kept the heat at least a few degrees below heart attack level: "No, you can't have the fourth beer, the fifth snort of coke, the tenth popper, the third—or fourth—hour of uninterrupted lapping and pumping."

I even had an occasional mini-affair, but nobody came close to stirring up the agonizing passion I'd felt for Chris—no intense confrontations, no bottom-line probes for the "truth of our relationship," no lamentations at the inability to maintain a consistent level of fierce intimacy. Casual evenings with pleasant acquaintances had become the new norm, surface chatting about the latest movies, what shade of cerulean to use on the living-room walls, the charms and drawbacks of living in Chelsea, whether or not I should offer my apartment for a fund-raiser for Lambda Legal Defense Fund, the organization that litigated issues relating to gay civil rights. (I'd been a member of its founding advisory board.)

The only evening that came close to the old amplitude was a small gathering at Naomi and Jesse's place that included Susan Brownmiller and Sean, a friend she'd brought along, who was well into his cups on arrival. Naomi's impish spirit—I used to call us the twin drama queens—saw an opportunity and gleefully seized it. She announced, with a mischievous twinkle, that she wanted to discuss "the most important issue currently dividing the feminist and gay male movements: NAMBLA."

"Here she goes," I thought, half amused, half alarmed at her daredevilry, while the four or five others present looked merely mystified, never having heard of NAMBLA. With a wink of complicity in my direction, Naomi proceeded to explain that NAMBLA was the man-boy love organization that argued for the revitalization of the cross-generational pattern once commonplace in Periclean Athens.

She elaborated her own position a bit more. It was a foundational mistake, Naomi said, to conflate children with teenagers. Equating the two hopelessly confused the issue. There was no case to be made, in her view, for sex with children, but she thought there *was* some merit to the NAMBLA argument that a postpubescent body is Nature's way of announcing a readiness for sex. And as long as no force was involved, why not?

"Teenagers aren't mature enough," somebody said, "to make a real choice. Their hormones may be raging, but their brain cells haven't kept pace."

"Nonsense!" exclaimed Naomi, herself a pioneering scientist of the brain. "We don't know nearly enough about the brain to make that assertion. I could just as easily argue that when the brain sends out a signal of sexual availability—menstruation, say, or body hair—it requires that the signal be heeded, otherwise continuing maturation will be obstructed."

"Besides," I threw in, "how many adults do we know who are 'ready,' mature enough, to make genuine choices about bed partners? Excluding this crowd, of course, of astoundingly evolved human beings." Everybody laughed on cue, and Naomi flashed me a broad smile.

"This business of 'choice,'" Naomi said. "It's that old chestnut, free will versus conditioning. How many of *our* so-called choices are 'freely' made instead of automatic reflexes dictated by our past socialization? How many forty-year-old women, schooled since birth to defer to men, will simply comply, as trained, with their wishes—"

"Quite unlike," I piped in, "a tough-minded fifteen-year-old boy taught to defend his independent manliness by any means necessary."

"Bullshit!" Sean yelled, right on cue. He'd gone on drinking after arriving, and I'd been noticing his mounting flush of anger. To my surprise, Sean was yelling at me, not Naomi. "You wanna fuck young kids!" he shouted, jabbing his finger in my direction. "I know your kind. You're a goddamn child molester!"

Naomi sighed contentedly and sat back to watch the fireworks she'd so expertly stacked up explode.

"I have *zero* interest," I yelled back, "in having sex with children. A nineteen-year-old? Sure, maybe, if he's hot enough. You do know, I assume, that teenagers *are* having sex, right? Whether you like it or not."

"They're not having sex with fifty-year-olds," somebody else interjected. "They're having sex with *each other.*"

"Oh, so that's okay?" I responded. "So they *are* old enough to make 'genuine choices' about that, about using protection and so forth?

Do they suddenly lose that ability when dealing with somebody older? Some teenagers *are* physically attracted to people older than themselves. Okay, maybe not fifty, but—"

Sean exploded. "See, see! You *do* wanna fuck kids! Don't tell me, I can tell, I can tell! You're a fucking bullshitter, a fucking faggot! *You wanna fuck boys, don't tell me*—"

At this point Sean jumped up, but Susan quickly reached out and grabbed him, for which I was grateful. (Sean was *big*.) "Sean, Sean!" she admonished. "It isn't productive to call someone a *bullshitter*."

"Well, he is, goddamn it! He is!" Susan's intervention had helped: Sean sounded slightly less volcanic.

Everyone did gradually simmer down, and soon afterward Susan told Sean they were due at so-and-so's party, or some such, and had to leave. No sooner did the door close behind them than *Susan*—not Sean—came under gossipy attack. "He's her type," one of the women said. "Nonsense!" Naomi piped up. "She hasn't seen him in seven years, I know for a fact. He happened to drop by her place today. She asked if she could bring him along."

"If she *is* attracted to him, I can understand it," I said.

"Really?" Even Naomi looked puzzled.

"Yeah, sure. Working-class brutes, the booted, macho construction worker—it's a fantasy staple for many gay men, including some of the most politically active ones, though we officially descry the 'macho enemy.' "

"Yes, yes," Naomi eagerly agreed. "It doesn't happen to be *my* taste"— she gave Jesse an affectionate glance—"but part of our anger at the macho man is a reflection of our guilty sexual attraction to him."

"Excuse me!" one of the other women said. "The anger comes from being abused and raped!"

"Oh wow, that reminds me," Naomi said, "have you read Masters and Johnson's new study of straight men's sexual fantasies? No? Well it turns out their third most common fantasy is to be raped by a *gang* of women!"

Various guffaws and disclaimers followed, and from there we branched off for the rest of the evening into low-key discord about the reliability of Masters and Johnson's data and whether or not fantasy life can be measured at all. No one said it openly, but we sort of missed Sean's volatility. The rest of us were essentially like-minded, and our marginal disagreements were a bit boring in contrast to the hot-blooded clash with Sean. There I was again: lamenting the lack of amplitude, longing for excess.

The predictable (from both the clash and the boredom) outcome was a two-week round robin of hustlers and coke, but then I did manage to call a halt, and by midsummer—we're still in 1981—I'd returned to my sensible, somnambulant routines. What's more, I congratulated myself in my diary at having successfully aborted the "childish" need for excitement and restored a placid state of grace: "The ability to accept & enjoy what *is* has been integrated into my life more than ever before. . . . I'm aware these days of my manifold good fortune and able to enjoy—a friend, a movie, a walk—infinitely more than when I remained fixated on past griefs and future aspirations."

Well, sort of. The fact is, my agent, Frances Goldin, was in the process of sending out a new manuscript of mine that interwove portions of some of my essays with psychosexual excerpts from my diary. I'd reworked the manuscript several times and felt that I'd finally found an appropriate form. So did Frances. She was high on the manuscript and confident of placing it quickly with a publisher; her assurance had a lot to do with my upsurge in confidence. Frances was a dynamo—she'd recently had the guts, at age fifty-seven, to start her own agency and to represent only those books—feminist, socialist, gay—that aligned with her own left-wing politics. With an amplitude to match my own, she decided on the simultaneous submission of my manuscript to the editors in chief of three houses: Bob Gottlieb at Knopf, Michael di Capua at Farrar, Straus, and Michael Korda at Simon and Shuster.

The response was swift—and negative. Gottlieb sent a curt note: "I'll tell Marty my reasons if he *doesn't* get it published," which I took to mean that I *shouldn't* publish it. Michael di Capua was more formulaically diplomatic: "The manuscript confirms my long-standing view that Marty is an exceptional person and writer—but it's not the sort of work we could make a success of." Korda didn't immediately weigh in. I asked Naomi to read the manuscript, counting on her passion for the unconventional. She came through with flying colors, regaling me with enthusiasm: "Oh wow, Marty! Do I envy and admire you! Do you realize what those rejections say about the book? The fact that it *offends* the sexual fascists who control publishing is *proof* of the book's effectiveness and importance! Don't you dare withdraw it!" Frances too chalked up the rejections to "bottom-line fear of the material"—to homophobia. I wasn't so sure; not every manuscript turned down, I nervously thought, is because of its iconoclasm—but I chalked that up to my general loss of confidence and kept it to myself. Their responses were much too comforting to tamper with.

Despite having two such savvy cheerleaders in my corner, my mood began to deflate. Frances soon heard from Korda (a one-line note: "I am not the most compatible editor for this work"). Undaunted, she turned to less lofty personages, but they greeted the manuscript similarly: "Not for us"; "Wouldn't know how to market it"; "The public isn't ready." I tried turning to something new—maybe a play, I thought, about the heart attack—but couldn't make much headway. I got a temporary boost in spirits when told I'd been elected to a three-year term on the board of the New York Civil Liberties Union, glad for the opportunity (as I wrote in my diary) "to try and make some of those needed political connections (& alliances) between the gay community & other left-of-center groups."

But I didn't feel at all confident about just how "left" the gay mainstream was these days: discos, drugs, and sex still maintained their primacy in urban, privileged, gay, white male circles, preempting political activity. The National Gay Task Force, on whose board I'd sat for some half-dozen years, had usefully used traditionally liberal means (like curtailing police harassment) to modestly productive ends (like getting antigay legislation rescinded). Modest but meaningful: by 1980 nearly half the states had repealed their sodomy laws, and more than two dozen municipalities had rescinded discriminatory statutes. Other organizations, such as the Gay Liberation Front, the Gay Activists Alliance, and Radicalesbians, had earlier conducted daring "zaps" and street actions that not only raised public awareness of our mistreatment but had also produced some important concrete results. The American Psychiatric Association had removed homosexuality from the category of "mental disorder," and the Civil Service Commission had lifted its ban on hiring gay people. The symbolic high point was probably the passage of a gay rights plank during the 1980 Democratic National Convention.

Yet the countercultural élan that had characterized gay political groups in the immediate aftermath of the Stonewall riots, which had called for an alliance of all oppressed minorities in the struggle to sweep away entrenched structural inequalities ("intersectionality," they call it today, often assuming the concept is brand-new), had all but disappeared by 1980. Zaps had given way to law briefs, sit-ins to petitions, marches to lobbying, radicalism to reformism. The building of a network of viable community institutions *had* been successfully begun—but they were primarily in service to the needs of a privileged white male constituency. Few women and people of color sat on the boards of national LGBTQ organizations or felt that their concerns were part of the agenda.

Gay male sexism played a key role in driving any number of lesbian activists into forming separate organizations, thereby diluting the potential force of a unified community. I saw that sexism firsthand on the Task Force Board, where an outraged Frank Kameny would periodically infuriate the women on the board (and a few of the men) with his fierce polemics against "contaminating" the gay movement with feminist concerns. Disunity, to be sure, can to some extent be viewed as constructive, the expression of a diverse constituency insisting that its special needs be met—yet not when internal friction becomes so pronounced that the umbrella organization breaks apart into opposing and hostile units. On top of all this, the vast majority of gay men and lesbians during the seventies remained in the closet, so the membership rolls and financial resources of the national movement were woefully inadequate to meet even its modest agenda; the annual budget for the Task Force in 1980 was a measly $260,000.

Nor was it clear during the seventies that a "gay" identity should take automatic precedence over the varied, sometimes competing loyalties deriving from class, ethnicity, gender, or race. A movement that stressed nongay aspects of identity to such an extent that no collective action was possible was no more desirable than a movement that ignored them. What was nowhere on the horizon—what is even today only somewhat visible—is a national movement broad enough to address issues that relate not solely to matters of gender and sexuality but also to those associated with poverty, homelessness, gross economic inequality, unjust criminal justice and immigration policies, and a lack of educational opportunities and jobs, to the array of discriminatory practices that confront those who are not white, male, and middle (or upper) class.

In the seventies the organized national movement, such as it was, centered (and to a considerable degree still does) on demands for equality before the law (the right to marry, etc.). What was and still is needed is a movement infused with the recognition that (to quote James Baldwin) our top priority isn't "to rent a room in a house that's burning down" but to build a new house. The radical cutting edge of the current generation of gay activists has today finally shifted the goal from equality to liberation. They express disinterest in—scorn for, even— the "equal" right to kill people in war or to rely on church and state to legitimize our unions. No, they want to interrogate the institutions themselves, to challenge structural racism and class privilege, national- istic claims to superiority, and relational arrangements that do not hold up lifetime monogamy as the gold standard.

After attending a number of New York Civil Liberties Union board meetings, it seemed to me questionable whether the ACLU's stated mission—the defense of civil liberties (itself no small task in the face of Reaganesque intolerance for "deviation" of every kind)—could ac- commodate itself to the more radical social vision being articulated on the barely visible fringes of the gay movement, the one being tenta- tively constructed by a few gay men and a few more lesbian feminists. (Most gay people continue to aspire to mainstream acceptance, not disruption.)

In an effort to make my position on the NYCLU board as effective a springboard for change as possible, I consulted with two longtime friends who'd had considerable experience with the Civil Liberties Union: the openly lesbian lawyer Nan Hunter, who'd been a project director with the ACLU's national legal staff for nine years, and Ron Gold, who'd ed- ited the NYCLU newsletter during the 1960s and was a cofounder of the National Gay Task Force. Both Nan and Ron had essentially the same advice for me: Take it slow; don't come across as a single-issue person; and recognize from the start that the Civil Liberties Union does *not* consider gay rights a leading—or even significant—priority.

Ron briefed me in considerable detail on the recent record of both the national and local ACLU boards in regard to gay issues. The ACLU, he told me, still thinks that gay rights is a sexual privacy issue—the right of consensual adults to act as they please in their own homes. The ACLU didn't generally regard gay rights as a free speech issue, let alone legitimate grounds for protesting job, housing, or immigration discrimination. The case of *Gaylord v. Tacoma* in the 1970s was an indi- cation of the ACLU's limited awareness and the extent it might be willing to intervene in pressing for even minimal protections for gay people. Jim Gaylord, a social studies teacher in Tacoma, Washington, had been summarily fired from his job simply for responding with a truthful yes when asked by the school superintendant if he was gay. The Washington State Supreme Court turned down Gaylord's appeal, and the U.S. Supreme Court refused to hear the case. The ACLU did not intervene.

There were currently any number of instances and issues, Ron went on, about which the ACLU had done absolutely nothing, not even offering an amicus brief. In 1981 a congressional statute was on the books excluding "sexual deviants or psychopathic persons" from entry into the country, even though Congress had neither the knowledge nor the power to legislate "illness." In Oklahoma it was still against the law in 1981 even to *speak* about homosexuality, let alone about the viability of a gay lifestyle. In three other states—Arkansas, Texas, and Kansas— antisodomy statutes applied *only* to homosexuals, though the "sodomitical" acts of oral and anal sex were not exactly unknown among committed heterosexuals. It seemed obvious—though apparently not to the ACLU—that if certain specific acts are crimes, they cannot legitimately be crimes for only certain people. That point had been made in a model penal code that some states had of late been adopting but—due to strenuous opposition from the Catholic Church—not "liberal" New York State. Yet the New York Civil Liberties Union had made no move to protest the situation.

Ron suggested that I focus my energy on getting the NYCLU board to recognize that a gay dimension was inherently present in a wide variety of issues. For example, he said, when enunciating principles that must be safeguarded in the treatment of mental patients, the Civil Liberties Union needed to recognize that some parents were hospitalizing or institutionalizing their gay children. On the federal level, the Housing and Urban Development Act excluded gay people from eligibility— and to date the ACLU had failed to protest the exclusion. Nor had it taken on the differential treatment being meted out to gay people in prison, where they were being routinely denied privileges, like exercising in the yard, extended to other prisoners. "Above all," Ron urged, "be active in regard to nongay issues. That will convince the board's liberals that you're not a single-issue person—and can therefore be trusted!"

A tall order. I was the only openly gay person on the large (some three dozen) NYCLU board, and as I was to discover during my five-year tenure, liberal allies (forget radical) were somewhat hard to come by—even after I followed Ron's advice and frequently got involved in discussions of nongay issues.

In 1982 Tom Stoddard, who was openly gay and whom I knew, became the legislative director for the NYCLU. We talked over some possible pegs on which I could hang a political consciousness-raising session for the board. Soon after, Tom himself would provide the peg when he became one of two finalists for the post of executive director. The board's day-long debate on the two candidates shocked me with its sly homophobia ("Tom's a bit of a 'magical creature,' don't you think?"; "In these difficult times we need to steer clear of an 'unsafe' choice"). The board members who uttered those remarks (and there were others) would have angrily rejected my characterization of them as "homophobic." And that, as I wrote in my diary, is exactly the trouble with "sophisticated" liberals: "their rhetoric avoids the grosser forms of bigotry, assuming a guise subtle enough to allow them to disguise *from themselves* the nature of their feelings"—a feature of liberalism with which blacks had long been familiar.

In the end Tom lost out in the balloting to the other—and, from my point of view, far less qualified—candidate. I stayed on the board for several more years but no longer regarded the NYCLU as a potentially significant ally in the struggle for gay rights. When I did resign, I got a touching letter from one of only two African American board members at the time, telling me how much he regretted my departure. In reply I said I'd often felt a strong kinship between the two of us on values and priorities but had "gradually become aware that those values are not—to my considerable and probably naive surprise—wildly popular (ha!) on the board as a whole. Where I'd expected virtual consensus on certain 'self-evident' principles I'd found sharp divergence, with centrist/conservative views more often than not dominant. 'Lordy,' I'd sometimes thought in dismay, 'is this a Civil Liberties Union meeting—or the Chamber of Commerce?!'"

Tom himself went on to become executive director of Lambda Legal Defense Fund, building up its staff from six to twenty-two people during his tenure; he also coauthored the gay civil rights bill that the New York City Council—having turned down umpteen previous bills—finally passed in 1986. Tom died of AIDS in 1997 at age forty-eight; he lived to see the life-saving introduction of protease inhibitors, but he was among those for whom the miracle pills failed to work.

I USED WHAT other opportunities came my way to let my views be known. In 1981 the *Nation* organized an American Writers Conference, a massive three-day gathering of some three thousand writers held in New York at the Roosevelt Hotel. I was on a panel with Bertha Harris (who I adored), Marilyn Hacker, Richard Howard, Cherríe Moraga, and Ed White, and we were asked to address the question "How and when will gay and lesbian writers be taken seriously?"

When my turn came I began with a one-line answer, "When we live in a serious culture," which I went on to define as "a culture that doesn't merely tolerate differences or make pro forma accommodations to them, but which is genuinely *appreciative* of differences." In my opinion, I continued, we were further away from such a climate than we were fifteen years ago. "Today differences tend to get translated as deficiencies, and from deficiencies it's a hair's breadth to 'deformities.'"

A comparable disdain, I added, was nearly as apparent within the gay male community itself—I didn't feel qualified, I said, to speak about the lesbian community—as within mainstream heterosexist culture. Most gay men, I suggested, were less than supportive of writers in their midst who were attempting to explore and express aspects of gay life "that don't merely imitate or mimic traditional models of behavior." To take it a step further, I wondered aloud how many gay male writers were themselves attempting such depictions of our valid and valuable differentness. A few—here I singled out my fellow panelist Ed White— *were* struggling "to give voice to the texture of lives long buried beneath the masks and armor we've had to cultivate over generations in order to avoid detection and denunciation—in order to survive."

Only a few gay publications, I argued, were devoted to exploring that differentness from the mainstream—here I named *Gay Sunshine*, *Fag Rag*, and Toronto's *The Body Politic*—and they were struggling to stay alive, an exhausting, probably futile struggle. (All have long since gone belly-up.) Until the recent advent of the *New York Native*, I added, Manhattan—purportedly the "gay center of the world"—couldn't even support a single serious biweekly news journal. The *Native*'s press run of roughly ten thousand didn't begin to approach the sales figures of publications primarily devoted to male erotica—magazines like *Blueboy*, *After Dark*, and *Honcho*. I made a point of describing myself as a fan of *Honcho*'s wondrous raunchiness but felt I was nearly alone in also reading the politically incisive *The Body Politic*. (When I cohosted a fund-raiser for TBP, fewer than two dozen people showed up.)

It felt to me increasingly true, I said, that mainstream gay male values were closely, and it seemed increasingly, identified with and indistinguishable from centrist, white, middle-class values. It's hypocrisy, I argued—worse, it's self-deception—"to pretend that gay writers aren't being taken seriously solely because *they*—those Others, the Enemy—insist on stifling our voices. They *do*—indisputably. But we are ourselves in collusion, stifling our own left-of-center voices." Which wasn't to suggest, I went on, that the heterosexist white male establishment *doesn't* control the media and *doesn't* refuse to air other than ancient stereotypes of gay people on TV, film, and radio or to publish gay writing that departs too radically from those preconceptions.

Why *would* they encourage new and challenging images? I asked. What power elite has ever *willingly* opened the gates to outsiders? I mean, *real* outsiders. Why would those in the driver's seat deliberately set about to sabotage its ownership of the road, to dilute its power, share in its wealth? Publishers, I argued, were increasingly owned by corporate conglomerates that recoil in terror from printing subversive works by serious *heterosexual* writers, works that, in Reaganite America, might overstep the ever more narrowly defined parameters of "acceptable" dissent. Corporate giants have always defined success in terms of dollars accumulated, not in terms of thoughts provoked or values challenged.

Nor was any obvious avenue available, I went on, for increasing our society's openness to change or to speed up the tempo. "When the odds aren't good—and they aren't—two choices remain and only two: to toss in the towel or to dig in your heels." I summoned up the well-known advice of Joe Hill, the labor leader murdered by the state: "Don't mourn me, *organize*!" Don't mourn mainstream America's hostility, cultivate and support *each other*—which currently wasn't happening often enough. "Let's concentrate on ending the indifference within our *own* community. Let's celebrate our differentness, end the petty backbiting that continues to fragment our ranks and dilute our strength, making outside suppression, real as it is, all but redundant. Even *if* we could do all that, there was no guarantee we wouldn't still be squashed by the reflexive repression of our tenaciously conformist culture."

When a group of us adjourned to a coffee shop for postmortems, the talk was desultory and dispiriting. "Maybe it's simply a case," I wrote in my diary that night, "of having sat through too many panels over the last decade—with so little notable advance in insight, or human connectedness; as Rita Mae [Brown] said during the *Kaffeeklatch*, "it's long since begun to sound like an echo chamber."" I myself didn't feel that cynical or disdainful. I shared the view that the gay male community was currently at its most apolitical point since Stonewall, but I felt that the energy and commitment of some of the younger men at our coffee shop postmortem—in particular Scott Tucker, Brett Averill, the political columnist Larry Bush, and the French queer theorist Guy Hocquenghem (author of *Homosexual Desire*)—represented a promising new guard that might dig us out of the doldrums. Finally, though, it wouldn't be a panel of earnest writers that would revivify the movement but a deadly virus poised to make its gruesome presence known.

For the *Village Voice*, Arthur Bell wrote a caustic piece about the Writers Conference as a whole but singled out our panel as a standout for "insights" that "held the audience spellbound." The exception, according to Arthur, was Cherríe Moraga, whom he blasted for her guilt-tripping third world "clichés." I thought Arthur dead wrong. I'd sat next to Cherríe during the panel, could feel her intense uneasiness, and was therefore all the more moved at her gutsy, impassioned cri de coeur about the movement's ignorance of third world gays—moved enough to buy her book *This Bridge Called My Back* the next day.

If anyone on the panel performed under par, it was the poet and translator Richard Howard, who flashed his neon-blue tie, tossed off a few glib comments—and was gone ("another pressing engagement"). Nor did I think Ed White, who I had always liked and admired, was up to par that day; clearly winging it, he delivered a few breathy, irrelevant remarks and then lapsed into an abrupt, uncharacteristic silence. Marilyn Hacker offered more substance, but in a singsong monotone that made it difficult to stay focused on her words. And dear Bertha, whose remarks were mostly smart and witty, caused a furor when she let slip the comment "Beethoven's Ninth is worth a hundred *Uncle Tom's Cabins*"—a bit of borderline racism that led one woman of color to shout out from the audience, "I'd like to come up there and *throttle* you, Bertha!" None of which Arthur Bell seemed to have noticed or thought worthy of comment.

A week later another gay political event, the Lambda Awards dinner, gave my spirits a boost, thanks mostly to the number of old comrades-in-arms I ran into, including Charlotte Bunch, Ginny Apuzzo, and Morty Manford. Charlotte pointed out the (uncomfortable) irony of our presence: "Ten years ago most of us were busy denying our existence, now we're celebrating it—in the Hotel Roosevelt ballroom no less," and with assorted City Council representatives and New York State legislators in attendance. In her keynote speech Charlotte made the crucial point "Too many of us are too far out of the closet now for our existence to be denied." The next item on the political agenda, she argued, "is what the quality and dignity of our existence will be; our own wishes in the matter won't likely automatically carry weight—we have to fight and fight, as the Moral Majority's favorite scapegoat, to have our voices heard."

The very next day, as scheduled, I taped a session for the TV program *The Open Mind*. I didn't wholly botch the assignment, but—with Charlotte's words still ringing in my ears—nor did I do the scintillating job I would have liked. I left feeling deeply frustrated at not having been more effective, since in 1981 it was rare for the national media—especially television—to provide a forum for any of us to respond to our critics.

The weakness of the gay political movement in the period immediately preceding the onset of AIDS, and its overriding conformism to mainstream values (far more true of gay men than lesbians), was again confirmed for me when, soon after the Writers Conference, the Lambda Legal Defense Fund asked me to present a "certificate of merit" at their annual fund-raising dinner to the two-year-old organization Black and White Men Together, a group devoted to confronting and combating racism in the gay male world.

I took the occasion to restate my conviction that racism—"along with its kissing cousins, sexism and classism"—was nearly as rampant in the gay world as in the straight, though almost never openly discussed. I pointed out that the political groups that had emerged immediately after the 1969 Stonewall riots—the Gay Liberation Front and the Gay Activists Alliance—had formulated a radical agenda for the movement which over the past dozen years had gotten diluted or discarded. We *had* gained greater visibility and protection by making ourselves more "acceptable" to the mainstream, but the bargain amounted to a form of self-betrayal. We'd bent our energies and image to conform more closely to middle-class mores than our actual lifestyles, implicitly—and rightly—challenged. Our subcultural differentness from mainstream values—which the Gay Liberation Front and the Gay Activists Alliance had proudly proclaimed—had in recent years been steadily downplayed, and in the process, I argued, we'd largely discarded the radical social analysis that mainstream society stood most in need of.

I congratulated Black and White Men Together for puncturing the reigning complacency and facing up to the serious problems dividing and disfiguring our community. Against a tide of apathy and timidity, I said, they'd set a new agenda, encouraging those of us on the left to reclaim our radical roots and to rechart our course. Throughout my speech I saw a number of white males in the audience angrily get up and leave. (In its write-up of the event, the *Native* referred to the "palpable wave of animosity" that greeted my remarks.) In the next few days I received several hostile phone calls and letters, including one from a friend who I thought shared my politics; he characterized my remarks as "inappropriate and offensive."

AND THEN—BOOM!—out of nowhere, so it seemed, I was suddenly hit with the worst depression in a year. "In bed, in tears," I scrawled in my diary, "trying to hold back full-scale flood. Worst day in a long, long time." What the hell triggered it? Surely not the BWMT event: opposition usually enlivens me. I managed to get myself over to Bill Trevor's office, where I alternated between hyperventilating and hyperanalyzing, and later boiled down the session in a spotty, ambiguous diary entry: "The elusive mystery of who connects with whom, why, & for how long, & on what basis. My *deepest* despair is that I never will—I'll only keep connecting with the deep despair. Bill [Trevor]: 'You have to experience this desperation, but don't have to linger over it, in order to break the recent logjam.' . . . He thinks my characteristic reaction is 'What did I do wrong? How did I fail (in friendship, etc.)?'—which can tip over to self-destruction."

After the session I still felt shaky, had occasional sweats, got into bed at 5:00, stared at the tube, went back on Dalmane, and slept fitfully. Next day I had another session with Bill. We tried again, for the umpteenth time, to figure out what had caused the panic attack, the sudden onslaught of desolation—the more unexpected because it erupted during a period of renewed writing (though sketchy) and political engagement (though marginal), and the improved sense of well-being they'd brought.

In Bill's view, I *had* made progress in regard to not *automatically* assigning blame for any failed or unsatisfying relationship to what he called my own "inadequacies of character, harrowing myself with bitter self-recrimination." He felt too that I'd come to the realization over the past year in therapy that life without companionable love isn't a life without rewards and pleasures; I had renewed appreciation for my manifold blessings, and despite the bruising experience with Chris and repeated rejections of my new manuscript, of late I'd managed to maintain a workable equilibrium.

The remaining conundrum, in Bill's view, was the discrepancy between my capacity for closeness—which he felt was "not in doubt"—and my inability to achieve it on any consistent level. "Mysteriously," I *had* achieved it when in my twenties; my five-year relationship with Dick Buckley had been stormy, yet we'd formed a deep connection and had broken apart only when I completed my doctorate and had to leave Boston to take up my first job in academia. Since then I'd had several short-term affairs, but in the past decade I'd become "an impossibilist" for some reason, spending my energy in pursuit of variously unavailable people, most recently Chris.

And now, suddenly, the equilibrium I'd worked so hard to achieve (according to Bill) had blown sky high. Why? We canvassed a full spectrum of logical explanations, all equally plausible, equally unprovable. Perhaps it was a case of unconscious self-sabotage: I couldn't tolerate a life of truncated expectations. Perhaps I was "temperamentally" (biologically?) a defiant malcontent who preferred periodic onslaughts of emotional turmoil to the dull routines of a peaceable life. Perhaps I was (physiologically?) bipolar. (Bill vetoed that one: "You're *not* manic: some people trigger in you a kind of high-spirited banter"—Yes, I thought: Naomi—"that shuts off as soon as the social situation ends.")

Perhaps it was an issue of "territoriality" (Bill's word). Come again? "It's a close cousin, a subcategory perhaps, of the need to control." "Control *what*?" I petulantly asked. Bill's even-tempered response: "You don't like people hanging around for indefinite periods. You want a well-defined timetable for contact." No, no, no, I insisted. "That applies only to surface socializing. From my point of view, Chris could have hung around indefinitely." That produced another "perhaps" from Bill: "Perhaps because you sensed there was no chance he would."

I sighed deeply. We could go on with the explaining game indefinitely, I thought. Maybe logic has nothing to do with it. Maybe Gregge Tiffen, the Tibetan astrologer, had put his finger on it: "Your circadian chart shows a clear conflict between your deep need for domesticity and your wide-ranging need for variable contacts." Maybe, maybe. Each explanation seemed as valid as every other. Maybe I just wasn't built to sustain equilibrium for very long and had to dynamite it periodically. Yet now, post–heart attack, uneasy about my health, I couldn't physically afford to wallow in turmoil for *too* long. Bill reassured me: "You're also unusually resilient, so you're able to bounce back from a period of turbulence with comparative ease."

Bill finally seemed content to settle for the diagnosis of "a low-grade but steady underlay of depression." Yes, I countered, but what's caused the low-grade depression? Maybe—this was *my* last contribution—the answer lay in "growing up gay in a homophobic culture" that instilled an unyielding amount of self-hatred. Bill and I crept to our neutral corners. The hell with it, I thought. At age fifty it's time to settle: you are who you are, for better or worse. Instantly a voice whispered back: "fifty" is merely your latest excuse—as was the heart attack—for not trying to push on. Sure, go ahead and "settle," if that's the best you can do, but the ground you're resting on looks pretty parched.

It was then that yet another "maybe" crept insidiously into my head: *maybe* psychoanalysis had become as old-fashioned as putting oil on canvas.

Within weeks—just as Bill was about to prescribe an antidepressant—the stalemate broke: *I had hepatitis*—a clear-cut, nonpsychological condition. The diagnosis had finally emerged after I started having headaches, attacks of nausea, dizziness, and exhaustion. When I thought to take my temperature, it was 102. I didn't call Bill; I called my new heart specialist, Dr. Downey, whom my longtime friend Joe Chaikin, the Open Theater director, had recommended. Downey ordered a blood test, which confirmed Type A hepatitis, which in turn, Downey thought, might well explain why I'd also been experiencing skipped beats of late. My "sick liver," he said (sounding much like Philip Roth), needed "rest."

"Is hepatitis potentially dangerous, given my heart condition?" I asked.

"The only time I'd be concerned," Downey curtly replied, "is if you'd entirely lost your appetite and—"

"But I *have!*"

"Oh. Well, just relax and stop worrying."

So here we are again, I thought, a different route to the same conclusion: change your personality.

"Leave it to you to be in fashion," Leo wrote me from Europe. "*I've never had hepatitis (I'm not even sure I can spell it), but it's by now practically the experience of a generation (and a half).*" He meant, of course, a gay male generation. Fortunately I made a pretty rapid recovery. I was soon free of nausea, and my appetite quickly rebounded. My friend Barbara Hart and her husband, John Weiss, camped out in my apartment for the first few days, cooking for me and providing good company, and after they departed, my dear Aunt Tedda came down often with food and called me twice daily. (So much, I thought, for my purported issues with territoriality.) Within ten days I was celebrating my fifty-first birthday in a restaurant with Vivian Gornick, and we chatted up a storm for nearly five hours. A month after that my blood tests returned to normal and all hands pronounced my recovery "remarkable." Downey gave me permission to resume exercise and sex—"mildly." Whatever that meant. I defined it as a slow return to using a stationary bike and running some errands. As for sex, I jerked off a few times and left it at that.

The sole remaining cause for concern was the continuing skipped beats I kept getting. Downey decided on another thallium stress test, and the results were mixed. The good news, according to the lab technician, is that "the heart muscle is very strong"; I "tested out like a sedentary, normal twenty-five-year-old" (normal, no less). The fly in the ointment was that after ten minutes on the treadmill, with my pulse up to 172, the technician picked up several "pairings"—double skipped beats. The meaning? "We don't know," he said; he was the rare technician willing to broach protocol and actually communicate. "Pairings up to one year following a heart attack are considered a decidedly negative finding, and medication is always prescribed. But in your case—*two* years from the attack, the finding is 'mysterious,' especially since you otherwise test out so well, throw off no symptoms of additional disease."

Ah, that word again: "mysterious." In some matters I had no wish to be atypical. The heart attack itself had been called a "medical anomaly"; I was one of those people who seem at low risk for an MI and yet have one. The technician said, "It's people like you who most baffle cardiology" and whose "atypical presentation is currently on the frontier of cardiology research," which he then defined—the explanation increasing my level of anxiety—as "the frontier of cellular deficiency, beta blocks, conduction, electrolyte, and enzyme failures, and so forth." It was up to Dr. Downey, he said, to decide what to do next.

I prepared a list of questions to ask the good doctor. Is my "condition" a deteriorating one—will double skips inevitably become triplets, and so on, until one unfine day the border is crossed into fibrillation? Is there a choice between medications—indeed *are* there relevant medications? Does the arrhythmia suggest "something is cooking," another MI waiting in the wings? Since my heart *is* getting enough blood and oxygenation— is "normal"—what's causing the arrhythmia in the first place? All questions, I felt sure, for which evidence was scanty and conclusions unlikely. Yet questions that needed asking nonetheless—if for no other reason than to assert my own agency in any decisions that had to be made.

Downey didn't agree. His secretary managed to get him to come to the phone, but he wasn't about to stand still for a long string of questions. That wasn't his notion of how to deal with a patient (i.e., a nuisance). Before I could even begin to read off my long list, he disdainfully barked out his usual begrudging, monosyllabic orders: "I'm putting you on Procan SR. Among its possible side effects are fever, chills, and pleurisy, so you must arrange for weekly blood counts. Goodbye." That was it. No questions answered, no reassurance given, no doubts tolerated. His secretary whispered—as if in the presence of the pope—"He's been called to Iran to consult about the shah." Good luck, Doc—maybe we can arrange a prisoner's exchange.

It was time, obviously, for a second opinion. My friend Penny, a nurse, got me the name of a respected research cardiologist at Einstein, a Dr. Friedman, and Bill Trevor started to look into finding someone at New York's prestigious University Hospital. I wasn't confident. I *did* want to leave Downey, but from what I'd seen of the surly arrogance that seemed to typify the cardiology profession at St. Vincent's, finding someone with Downey's skill in combination with a less abrupt, patronizing manner would be highly problematic.

It took a while to get an appointment with Dr. Friedman, but it was worth the wait. He looked over all the documents and test results I brought with me and then told me that he saw little in them to cause concern. It was exactly what I wanted to hear of course; I hardly cared whether his opinion was more or less accurate than Downey's. Procan, Friedman told me, was an experimental and probably useless drug. (It was later taken off the market.) Besides, my arrhythmia might well be a benign secondary effect from the combination of hepatitis and the low-grade anxiety that I'd been feeling for months. The sum of his advice? "Try leading a happier life. Try accepting the fact that you *are* in the clear medically."

"What you need to do now," Friedman went on, "is to get on with living. Forget the arrhythmia, forget the Procan. Forget measuring out pleasure in cautious little thimblefuls. *Enjoy your life!*" Uh-oh, I thought, I don't think he quite gets the picture, hasn't a clue about my penchant for excess—the likelihood that I'll convert thimblefuls into quart bottles in a flash. And so I told him that one of the ways I some-times "enjoyed life" was to mix sex and coke, or coke and writing. "I don't endorse the use of cocaine for anyone," he responded. "But *some* coke—some anything—is okay. *You're in the clear!*"

It was as if—serving a life sentence and headed for the gallows—a pardon had suddenly come down from the governor. The prison gates had been thrown open, and I dashed through them. Two years earlier, in the period immediately following my heart attack, I'd yearned to recover a *modicum* of my earlier energy and activity and swore that, if given a second chance, I'd do nothing to jeopardize my health; I'd find a way to live contentedly on a less intense level. But persuading myself that the "simple" life, without love or engaging work, could be satisfy-ing, even pleasurable, was tantamount to claiming that a tree could look just grand without any leaves.

A glassine envelope appeared as if by magic on my desk. Oh well, I swore in my diary, "*this* coke, but *no more!*" After all, I'm not suicidal, and Dr. Friedman *has* endorsed a *moderate* use of cocaine. Mmm, I probably should have asked him for a definition of "moderate," but no matter—I'm just going to have a snort or two to start me writing. My sensible side wasn't fooled. "If I heard of anyone else acting with such stupid bravado," I wrote in my diary, "my response would be angry and moralistic—'the damned fool will get what he deserves!'"

I had my first snort at 4:00 one afternoon in early November 1981. My fingers flew over the typewriter keys—what a joy to feel the words, the right words—flow out. By 10:00 I'd gone through the gram, and I had a twenty-page scene on the "heart attack" play that I'd been desultorily working on for months. That night I slept fitfully; during periods of wakefulness I angrily denounced my foolishness and swore "Never again!" Next day I felt decidedly under par, with vague pressure and congestion in my chest.

I had a session scheduled that day with Bill and nervously confessed—though making sure to tell him first what Friedman had said about cocaine use. Bill's reaction was temperate. He wanted to know first of all where I'd gotten the coke—had I been involved in any dangerous street dealings? No, a few nights ago I'd gone back to Rounds, and quite by chance had run into David Paul, a filmmaker in L.A. whom I hadn't seen in years. I'd been the first man David, at nineteen, had ever had sex with—which he promptly ran around the bar telling people. My onetime sweet puppy dog, full of energetic infatuation, was now a slick, double-breasted film executive. We hadn't been reminiscing more than a few minutes when he brought up cocaine, telling me that he (and most of his crowd, it seemed) had a "splendid connection" who provided them with only the "finest" stuff. "Why, are you into it?" "Well, I've tried it now and then," I vaguely replied. That was all David needed: "I'll call L.A. and have a gram sent to your home address; you'll have it by tomorrow." "You're kidding! Aren't the mails dangerous?" "Nonsense, I mail the stuff all the time." And thus it was, I told Bill, that I'd "found" that glassine envelope on my desk.

In response Bill focused on the coke, not David. "I don't know Dr. Friedman, but if he did say that you show no evidence of residual heart disease, then I suppose his opinion that *moderate* use now and then is okay can be trusted. I'm glad to hear you've finally had some sort of creative breakthrough. But you shouldn't be under any illusion that no risk is involved."

"I'm not, I'm not. I think the risk is worth it. Anyway, Friedman didn't sound like the risk is significant. It's no big deal, just a mild break from my boring routine. Financially I couldn't afford to do coke often if I wanted to."

During the next two weeks—David supplying—I went through another three grams and completed not only several more scenes of the play but also a proposal for a new book, "On Being Gay: A Modern Appraisal." Arnold Dolin at New American Library expressed immediate, enthusiastic interest in it and was awaiting an okay from the higher-ups to officially offer me a contract. With that nearly under my belt, I'd gotten the authorities at CUNY's Lehman campus (where I taught) to let me offer a seminar for the spring 1982 semester entitled Sexual Deviance: Historical and Contemporary. The book and course in combination seemed like a whole new start.

By this point David had returned to L.A. When I asked if he could somehow get me a few more grams until I'd "solidified" my writing breakthrough, he laughed, said "Sure," and mailed them by Federal Express! "If only coke wasn't so damned sure-fire," I told my diary. "What I enjoy most is the total absorption, the illusion that I'm importantly engaged." I loved the *state* coke put me in: ice-cold frenzy and isolation, obsessional focus, utter confidence that the flow of words was unstoppable. Snug in my rooftop aerie, a line or two snorted every half-hour or so, I plowed along wholly engrossed in the writing, oblivious to the passage of time, resenting even the interruption (ordinarily eagerly awaited) of a phone call, oblivious to the usual pressing fantasy of the Ideal Other pleading for sex, for romance, for permanent togetherness. Fortunately I had exactly $316 in the bank, which might force me to call an abrupt halt. Then again, why? Maybe I could take out a bank loan? Or borrow from Aunt Tedda?

Bill continued to acquiesce, reluctantly. As he put it, "It comes down to a choice of risks: the prolonged stress and anxiety of your current stalemate could do you as much—or more—harm than trying to break the stalemate through coke. And the stalemate has gotten firmly entrenched and seems fiercely resistant. Coke guarantees that you'll write—content and quality probably irrelevant for now."

Writing the Paul Robeson Biography

The offer came out of the blue. Frances Goldin, my agent, called to say that Paul Robeson Jr. had just left her office, and their conversation had taken a wildly unexpected turn. She'd recently taken Paul on as a client, helping him search for the right person to do his father's biography—a search on which he'd already spent five years. That particular day the two had just returned to Frances's office after asking the left-wing publisher Alan Rinzler for advice. In his twenty years in the business Rinzler had made a notable mark, publishing Hunter Thompson, Dee Brown's *Bury My Heart at Wounded Knee*, and giving Toni Morrison her first break with *The Bluest Eye*. Rinzler had urged Frances and Paul to think big, and the names of Morrison and Alice Walker came up; Paul wasn't enthusiastic about either.

Frances had to cut the meeting short and get back to her office for some pressing business, and she suggested that Paul come with her and browse through her living-room bookshelves while she tended to a conference call. What followed, as Frances later told me, was that Paul took down my biographies of Charles Francis Adams (which had won the Bancroft Prize) and James Russell Lowell (a finalist for the National Book Award), and then browsed through *The Uncompleted Past*, a collection of my essays, nearly half of them relating to the black struggle. After she finished her conference call, Paul asked her, "Tell me more about this Duberman guy. How come you never suggested *him*?" "Because," Frances replied, "you once said that you hated his plays."

I assume Paul was referring to what was by far my best known play, *In White America*, a documentary theater piece about being black "in white America" that had opened off-Broadway in 1963 and been a considerable hit—it won the Vernon Rice/Drama Desk Award, had two national tours, and had been produced in London and Paris as well. My guess is that Paul hated the play because it doesn't include his father's story—an omission I'd now agree was egregious, but back when I wrote *In White America* the government had succeeded in making Paul Sr. a nonperson, either absent from the history books altogether or treated as a pro-Soviet traitor. Still, as a professional historian and left-winger, I should have dug deeper and known better. (When the fiftieth-anniversary production of *In White America* opened in New York City in 2015, I added a new scene that encapsulates Robeson's defiant spirit in facing down—at the cost of his career—the right-wing bigots of the House Un-American Activities Committee.)

Anyway, according to Frances, Paul went on to say (as I recorded in my diary) that he "didn't know Duberman had written *these* books. They have all the qualities I've been looking for in a writer: an understanding of the complexity of people and events; a prose style alive with nuance; left-wing but not dogmatic political views—*plus* a bent for theater." Frances confirmed his judgment and asked Paul if he wanted her to set up a preliminary meeting. He did, and within the week the three of us were sitting in Frances's living room discussing prospects.

We talked for six hours, at the end of which (as I wrote in my diary that night) "Paul said he didn't need any further meetings—he was now *sure* he wanted me—and I said I was enthusiastically prepared to accept on the spot." He offered me exclusive access for seven years to the previously closed—and vast—Robeson archives, currently housed in a nondescript Manhattan office building. Those terms were immensely generous—ideal in fact. Yet there was one outstanding issue, I said, that we hadn't addressed.

Frances had warned me in advance that Paul might well ask for "final approval" of the manuscript in any contract we drew up. If true, I told her, I wouldn't be able to accept the offer—I couldn't have the son of my subject, with his own emotional investment, constantly looking over my shoulder, protesting my interpretations, demanding changes. That would work against my responsibility to do as objective a job as possible—even while fully aware that the goal of objectivity could only be approached, never achieved.

I made all that clear to Paul during that first meeting. I told him that final say over what did or did not go into the book had to be mine alone—that if he was offering me something less than full control over what I wrote, I would, reluctantly, have to turn down his offer. To my (and Frances's) surprise, he conceded the point at once, without any discussion, heated or otherwise. It turned out that before our meeting he'd consulted with his friend Herb Gutman, the labor historian and expert on American slavery (*The Black Family in Slavery and Freedom, 1750–1925*), who I also knew. Paul told us that Herb had said "Duberman is the *perfect* choice—inspired," but had added, "He'll never accept the assignment unless given exclusive rights to the archives"—they were enormous in scope and had never before been open to scholars—as well as "total artistic freedom."

And so, Paul now told us, he'd already resolved the issue in his own mind before I'd even brought it up. He then went on to say, "I have to give my father up—turn him over to you, to history. It hasn't been easy for me to accept this, but I know I must—though as we move ahead, I'll doubtless backslide." He movingly described his "long struggle to hold on," and the difficulty he'd had "in letting go," and he acknowledged that his "possessiveness and distrust are bound to resurface." (Indeed they would—and in a sometimes fierce and bruising way.)

The issue of final approval resolved, I had one other agenda item for that first meeting. "I have to say," I told Paul, "that when I heard you wanted me to do your father's biography, I was stunned. You can see that I'm white. But do you also know that I'm not only gay but have been active in the gay political movement for a decade?"

Paul showed no surprise. "Yes, I know," he said with a smile. "I've had you thoroughly checked out."

"Okay. Just wanted to be sure. Frankly, I think you're going to catch hell."

"I know. The black [Communist] Party people are going to make a special stink. But I'll deal with it."

Subject closed. Yet I couldn't help but think that something of a puzzle remained. Paul said he was ready to turn his father over to history, to "give him up." But why so precipitously, to a man he'd met once? To a white, Jewish, gay activist? It didn't quite add up. There were any number of gifted, left-wing black historians around who, I felt sure, would likely have grabbed at an offer to do Paul Robeson's biography. Why me? And then there was the curious remark Paul had made during that first meeting, that both his parents had had "remarkably diverse" affective and sexual lives that until now had been totally concealed. He encouraged me to "tell all": "I feel my parents' responsiveness to a variety of impulses and people *adds* to their stature." The comment struck me as peculiar at the time; it wouldn't be until several years into the project that I'd link it to other comments Paul had made in the interim and would finally come up with a satisfying explanation for why he had thought me the ideal biographer for his father.

During the first long meeting in Frances's office, I picked up various clues about Paul's temperament and some of the likely pitfalls that awaited. I got the strong impression of an unused or stalled dynamo. I did like him—especially his articulate passion and vitality—though his penchant for long, repetitive monologues and his volatility (his "prickly and oversensitive" asides, as I put it in my diary) also came through loud and clear and foretold some potentially angry flare-ups. From the anecdotes he told (and retold) it was clear that he was given to concocting all sorts of conspiracies and plots emanating from a variety of quarters and based on thin evidence. I could easily see *myself* becoming the target of his suspicions. As I wrote in my diary, "I doubt if I exaggerate the potential hazards. Frances, not easily ruffled or annoyed, has already expressed exasperation to me over Paul's incessant monologuing and some fear that his bottled-up rage could at any point— probably some trivial, unpredictable point—erupt and engulf."

Yet at the time of our first meeting I mostly felt sympathy for his struggle. On the verge of giving up control over his father's story, he was facing a void in his life that I felt must be terrifying. At age fifty-four he typified the sufferer of the child-of-a-famous-figure syndrome. Though himself a man of considerable charisma and sharp intelligence, he'd never managed to find a satisfying career of his own; until recently he'd made his living as a translator of Russian, a job he said he'd loathed. Frances told me that he'd struggled painfully, "with much therapy and much help from his wife, Marilyn, to establish a separate identity," but was "so heavily invested in his father" that he'd spent most of his spare time and energy gathering and preserving the family's archives. I wrote that night in my diary, "Some difficulties, even serious clashes seem inevitable."

For now, puzzlement at being offered the assignment aside, I couldn't have been happier with the sudden turn of events. I had an extraordinary new subject to occupy my time and soak up my floating anxiety and felt "dumbfoundedly blessed at being handed the opportunity" to tell Robeson's story. Its immense possibilities—the scope of the canvas, the intrinsic drama and emblematic force of his life—was apparent to me, and I found the prospects exhilarating.

The publishing world, which had recently been slamming the door in my face, now clamored for my attention. As soon as the news surfaced that Paul Jr. had chosen me as his father's biographer, the phones started ringing in Frances's office: my situation had shifted overnight from trying to find a publisher to choosing among them. It was a feeling I had no trouble getting used to.

Frances consulted again with Alan Rinzler, who again advised her to "think big"—a $250,000 advance for hardcover—which in his assessment only five or six publishers in New York could afford. My own first choice of Roger Straus of Farrar, Straus, Rinzler added, wasn't one of them. Still, Frances agreed that we should sound Straus out. Known as an "old-fashioned" kind of publisher—super-loyal to his writers, super-tight on advances—Straus had a deserved reputation for being "difficult" but also for his legendary loyalty to his authors, who included Nadine Gordimer, Czesław Miłosz, Joseph Brodsky, and Flannery O'Connor.

During our visit to his office, Straus couldn't have been more cordial. He said he was delighted that we'd come to him first, that he thought the match of biographee and biographer "splendid," and was fully cognizant of the magnitude of the project and the sizable expenses it would entail. Despite all that, he said that Farrar, Straus had never offered an advance higher than $75,000—though he felt certain we'd have no trouble finding a publisher eager to come through with the $250,000—which he felt the project warranted.

After further consultation, and lunches with a host of eager editors, Frances decided to go with the strategy of an auction. She contacted those among the editors who'd expressed the keenest interest and who'd said that their houses could go "well above" Straus's offer of a $75,000 advance, and told them that on a given date they should phone in their best offer to her by noon. We would not, she added, automatically go with the highest bidder, but would weigh other factors as well—especially my sense of who among the editors I'd lunched with seemed the most compatible and astute. In my mind it had come down to three: Nan Talese at Houghton Mifflin, Hillel Black at Morrow, and Bob Gottlieb at Knopf.

When the day arrived, all but one of the contending editors dutifully phoned in their bids; they were very similar, hovering around the $150,000 mark. The one who hadn't called was Gottlieb. Frances waited an extra half-hour, then put in a call to him. As she later told the story, it was clear she'd outfoxed the fox himself.

"Why haven't I heard from you?" Frances asked sternly. "We thought you were extremely interested. What's the story?"

"What was the highest bid you got?" Bob coolly asked.

"I'm not going to tell you," Frances, a master negotiator, replied. "But I will tell you what we want."

"Namely?"

"Three hundred thousand dollars."

"Fine."

Brief pause while Frances recovered and calmed her nerves. "What does 'fine' mean?"

"Fine means—fine! I agree to your terms."

"Just hold on a minute—you haven't heard *all* my terms."

"Oh?"

"Marty's going to have to do a lot of traveling, including East Germany, maybe Moscow, to interview people. I want an additional $25,000 to cover those travel expenses."

"Consider it done."

And—stupefyingly—it was, though in exchange for the travel fund Gottlieb did extract the small quid pro quo of 20 percent of the English rights. Soon after I signed with Knopf, Gottlieb left to head up the *New Yorker* and my editor became Barbara Bristol, who turned out to be superb, the best editor I've ever had. But that story is down the road a bit.

Frances had just redefined *chutzpah* ($325,000 would today be the rough equivalent of five times that amount). Yet her astuteness deserted her when it came time to draw up a secondary agreement between Paul and me. What would prove a huge mistake might never have happened had she not been representing both of us simultaneously. What Frances suggested to me was that since Paul had given me total control over the contents of the book, I should magnanimously assign him the power to veto all subsidiary rights to the biography—including foreign, film, and TV. At the time Paul and I barely knew each other and had thus far gotten along well. I felt considerable gratitude to him for picking me out of the crowd (and out of my current malaise). I'd already volunteered to give him a portion of my advance from Knopf, and I agreed to Frances's suggestion without any hesitation (thus incurring some share of the blame). During these early days of the project, cordiality reigned, yet Frances had known Paul a long time and was aware, as I was not, that he had a reputation for being exceedingly difficult; that alone should have given pause—though to be sure, no one could have predicted quite the level of antagonism that would develop between Paul and me. Giving Paul the right of approval over secondary rights to the biography would become the cause of considerable grief.

WE WERE, in any case, launched. I happily put the rest of my projects on hold. Aside from a half-dozen entries and a few scratched notes, I stopped keeping any semblance of a journal for nearly two and a half years. I did hold on to one side project, "On Being Gay: A Modern Appraisal," which the higher-ups at New American Library had approved. I told Arnold Dolin, the NAL editor who'd pushed the project, that the Robeson biography obviously took priority and that I'd turn to "On Being Gay" only when and if I started feeling suffocated, overwhelmed, bored, or despairing over Robeson and needed a break. He said he completely understood. But the point never did come when I wanted to tear myself away from the biography, and finally, after five years of waiting, Arnold understandably got a bit grumpy. I solved the problem by converting the book into an anthology of new essays and brought in two coeditors, Martha Vicinus and George Chauncey Jr.; the retitled volume, *Hidden from History: Reclaiming the Gay and Lesbian Past*, would come out in 1989.

The contracts with Knopf were quickly signed, and with gratitude and zest I plunged into the research. Within the first few months of 1982 I'd already been to California (Paul accompanying me to make introductions) and to London for a substantial string of interviews. In L.A. the trip's highlight was meeting Lee and Revels Cayton. Revels was the grandson of Hiram Revels, the first African American to serve in the U.S. Senate (1870–71); himself a radical black labor leader, Revels had been Robeson's closest male friend. In London the highlight was a lengthy taped session with Peggy Ashcroft, Robeson's costar in the historic 1930 production of *Othello*. Both meetings had their startling aspects. Revels sent me several muted verbal signals—he was trying to warn me, he told me years later, to "be on my guard" with Paul, though the signals were so muted I didn't pick up on them at the time.

As for Peggy Ashcroft, we hit it off so well on a personal level that she ended up telling me—on tape—about her affair with Robeson during the run of *Othello*. She later thought better of the confession and asked me to return the tape—a request I managed to finesse with various unconscionable excuses until I was able instead to send her my completed chapter on the 1930 production. She responded with a brief, charming note saying in essence that I had "disobeyed her wishes" but that I'd done such a good job describing the production that she was willing to let the chapter stand "as is"—that is, would let me include the affair. I was thrilled to have gotten away with it and thrilled to have Ashcroft's blessing.

THANKS TO AN OCCASIONAL coke buy, along with an occasional trip to Rounds, I'd gotten close to being dead broke late in 1981—even falling into arrears on my maintenance payments. I was actually in danger for a time of having to sell my beloved new apartment. The advance from Knopf solved all that in a flash, though I realized that having extra cash on hand would be a standing temptation to return to indulgences immediately pleasurable but ultimately calamitous.

I did manage to avoid *one* indulgence: seeing Chris again. We'd now and then exchanged letters, and I had a standing invitation to visit him should I ever find myself in San Francisco. That distant prospect became a reality when I went to California in the spring of 1982 to conduct a series of Robeson-related interviews. Somewhat to my own surprise, I not only didn't contact Chris but wasn't much tempted to. After some rotten years I'd somehow landed on my feet, health restored and engaged full time in a deeply satisfying project; for once I managed to avoid plunging into a situation more than likely to sabotage my version of serenity.

But crafty Chris shifted back to the original board game: *himself* as pursuer, me as prey (to be eaten alive, of course, if ever caught). In the fall of 1982 he sent me a heartfelt tape followed by a phone call, full of awareness and remorse, his tone mellow and lucid—the result, he gratefully wrote, of all the insights I'd provided into his character. Uh-huh. I wrote him back a long, throbbingly sensitive letter, telling him that I felt "caught between conflicting emotions of renewed warmth *and* distrust." Mixed in with the warmth, I confessed, was considerable anger, leaving me ambivalent about seeing him again. "I do my best these days," I wrote, letting anger take the upper hand, "to avoid intimacy with people who—when pinch comes to shove—won't or can't care back, take but don't give." I assured him that I wasn't trying to cause him "needless pain," to "get back" at him—yeah, sure—but rather "to clear the air" in case we ever did decide on renewed contact.

Chris took my ambivalence well, praised my "clear and appropriate observations," acknowledged that he hadn't been able back then "to even see or understand" himself, and suggested yet again that we meet. I let the offer slide; I was in a good place in my life—a better place than I'd dreamed possible a few years back—and I wanted to safeguard an unfamiliar equilibrium I knew was fragile. I was startled, a full year later, to get yet another letter from Chris, this one telling me that I was often in his thoughts and that he "always appreciated" my "honesty and frankness." He was coming back East to visit his father, who'd been seriously ill, and wanted to see me. If I answered his letter, I didn't preserve a copy. I have found one letter dated as late as the spring of 1984 in which he refers to "our recent telephone call," again tells me he misses me and how "very important" I remain to him, and again suggests that we get together; this time, apparently, I didn't reply. Some years later I did run into him in a store in Manhattan. Flushed with confusion, I mumbled some response to his cheerful "Hello, Marty!" and rushed out of the store. His image haunted me for years. A passion that deep never entirely disappears. But after the store run-in, we dropped completely out of each other's lives.

AS THE HEART ATTACK—and Chris—receded further into the distance, I went back to my earlier gym routines and was feeling in robust health. (Maybe I *had* been a medical anomaly and was now anomalously well.) I dropped out of therapy, grown bored with the Self, its endless permutations and circular "understandings." With the biography taking up every inch of slack in my life, my intermittent mood swings evened out and acute emotional pain seemed a distant memory. Yet I've found one scrap of paper from this period on which I recorded a totally unexpected crying jag about my mother—it was now five years since her death—and another scrap in which I gave myself a stern lecture about "falling back into pre–heart attack mania," replete with an excess of coke and hustlers that could, I warned myself, end with the "willful sabotage of this extraordinarily fortunate turnabout, this second chance." A risky lifestyle, I further lectured myself, was *not* the key to creativity—"no, it was closer to self-destruction." I was well aware that beneath coke's glitzy surface effects, a deep, despairing fatigue lay in wait.

Later on I'd find it hard to heed my own warnings; with money in the bank, my long-dormant tendency to push the limits would be difficult to control. I'd then argue that the "sensible" lifestyle had never been a good match for my temperament, that I'd adopted it reluctantly, out of necessity. But for now I settled for an infrequent knocking over of the traces, and only when I could persuade myself that I'd been working in such an intense, concentrated way on the biography that it would be a service to the *biography* to blow off a little steam with a late-night raid on the Rounds cupboard.

My tours of Rounds, Haymarket, and Dallas (the newest stop on the hustling circuit) had been infrequent of late; when I did go, I usually came away feeling detached and lustless. "Just doing the scene," I wrote in my diary at one point back then, "any scene, produces a pleasant, low-grade euphoria: I cruise, therefore I am"; mechanics, in other words. Now, early in 1982, postdepression, post-Robeson contract, I had a notable uptake in energy—and in my visits to the bars. Dropping in at Dallas one evening I was startled to run into "Sean," someone I'd always found attractive but had never had sex with.

Just a few months before, he and I had spent all of one day and evening together, the electricity between us palpable. We'd talked on and on, Sean telling me far more about himself than he ever had—about his brutal police sergeant father, about his dream of becoming a sports writer, about his alternating involvements with gangsterdom, hustling, and, when in a "repentant" mood, driving a limo back and forth to the airports. He wanted a new start, wanted to stop draining off his natural gifts and energy into traditional channels of defiance. He needed help. We started to plot, with mounting enthusiasm, how he might get a leg up on the first rung of the sportswriting ladder.

Suddenly Sean blurted out that he'd long been physically attracted to me but was afraid of getting hurt—though he now felt "much, much more comfortable" about his feelings for me. That evening we tried some coke I'd recently bought but agreed it was mediocre; Sean volunteered to "get rid of it" at Rounds and to bring back some "first-rate stuff" in its place. When he asked if he could spend the night, I said, "Sure"—heart pumping, voice monotone—"I'll make up the bed in the living room for you" (don't push, don't push). Sean left at midnight, saying he'd make a quick deal and be right back. At 2:00 a.m. he called to say he was having trouble making a sale but should be back shortly. I waited up until 4:30, but Sean never reappeared nor called the next day.

Would he have bothered to rip me off for a small amount of mediocre coke, at the cost of alienating me? Had he again seized up with fear about getting "close"? Had he gotten in trouble—Sean had a reputation for a hair-trigger temper and for getting into fights—and could he be languishing in some jail, hospital, or morgue? Puzzles for Solomon. I never came up with any satisfying answer. I simply felt hurt and bewildered at how, yet again, some mysterious variable had intervened to destroy closeness all but coterminous with its onset. I tried hard for once *not* to assume that the fault was mine, that somehow I'd precipitated Sean's abrupt flight.

I had no way to reach him, and in the days and weeks that followed heard not a word; he seemed to have disappeared off the map. Then came a night at Dallas when I accidentally ran into him again. I never mentioned his earlier disappearance, and as before, we charged each other up on contact, talking for hours. This time Sean was accompanied by his younger brother, Ted, a nineteen-year-old marine, and the three of us commandeered a booth to drink and talk. Ted was a "tough," touching, grown-up boy, all open and bright-eyed, but with the same razor-sharp reflexes as his older brother, who clearly adored him. Sean kept egging on Ted and me to "do it," teasing Ted about never having "done it" with a man—the only area, I suspected, in which Ted was devoid of experience. I "shyly" deflected Sean's matchmaking, feeling sure that if Ted and I did go home together, that would permanently destroy my chances with Sean.

Both Sean and Ted stuck in my head for days afterward. I was surprised that the primary emotion they aroused in me wasn't lust— though that was certainly present—but poignancy. I wasn't sure why. I knew it had something to do with the contrast between them and the run-of-the-mill patrons of an ordinary middle-class gay bar. They were louder, quicker to take offense at any perceived slight, quicker still to erupt in anger—never deflecting their reactions with a campy quip or a haughty retreat. Sean and Ted were part of a breed of working-class young men, its royalty, of a perfectly crested physical intensity, fully in touch with their beauty and vitality and with the power it gave them over others, the attention it instantly commanded, the envy, the supplication, the profferings of devotion that automatically came their way.

Yet their easy physical confidence didn't translate into other areas—unlike the twenty-year-olds I grew up with, or the ones I taught in the Ivy League, whose class origins allowed them, quite realistically, to entertain a wide spectrum of career ambitions, of future prospects in general. Ted and Sean knew, in some deep, recessed way, that their speech patterns, the slight strut to their walk, the fullness of their energy and physicality betrayed their background, marked them out—and usually down. The working-class Teds and Seans have a hungry eagerness that cohabits nervously, sadly, with the knowledge in their nerve endings (knowledge derived from watching the fate of their relatives and friends) that their shrewd alertness to interpersonal nuance will carry them only so far. They sense the need to exercise caution, to rein in any urge to pursue what are in all likelihood unrealizable goals—and to distrust the motives of those who minimize the obstacles to advance and encourage them to "think big" about their future.

Consciously they have only a vague grasp of how the world that surrounds and encloses them works, which party is in power and what difference it might make, what contacts and alliances exist "out there," and for what purposes. But they do know in their bones, and shrug off the knowledge with feigned indifference, about the irredeemable inequities for which they bear no responsibility and against which, despite their everyday audacity, they're helplessly unarmed. Things are the way things are. Things they can't name, nor begin to assign merit or blame. They regard their own status, now and in the future, as the result of a preordained "system" not visible enough to understand—let alone combat.

That melancholic intuition helps to account for the cocky pugnacity we call "macho." It's all they're sure of, all they can fall back on, with an inner voice constantly reminding them—usually as they're asking you whether you think they might get into a college (or become a sportswriter)—that the odds are lousy, that they'll never be better off than at this moment, at the moment when their physical grace and vitality are intact. And when that inner voice whispers, they silence it with an extra bit of bravado, a rise in contentiousness, a brutal putdown of any lustful overture aimed in their direction.

So attuned are they on some semiconscious level to the likely limitations on their future that should you (also hearing that dark voice) try to reassure them about the open range of their options in a tone that suggests, even slightly, false encouragement (or calculated ingratiation), they'll retreat in sullen distrust, your unintended note of doubt having opened up a chasm of doubt in them—and a fierce resentment toward you, you who have what they want (an education, a career, a set of manners—or even mannerisms—a sense of comfortably belonging to the world of Success), you who at the same time are so casually disdainful of your prerogatives, especially when "humbling" yourself to win access to their bodies and their energy, all that they do have confidence in.

No wonder they withhold themselves, flaunt their physicality, use it. Anything—even to denying themselves the embraces they may crave—in order not to surrender (or, as it must feel to them, not to be *robbed* of) their one trump card, their one source of indisputable authority.

New York Native

As I launched full speed into the Robeson project, I had far less free time to fill and far less angst to medicate. Alternating research into the Robeson Archives with frequent trips to other archives and to interview his friends and associates, I found I disliked flying and sleeping in strange beds as much as ever. Yet I managed to cut out coke almost entirely, not wanting to risk a jagged "coming down" coinciding with a "meet and greet." When back in the city, I also sharply curtailed my late-night excursions; most archives opened at 10:00 a.m. and closed promptly at 5:00, and unless I matched my schedule to theirs and was rested enough to work at a rapid clip—a fearsome sight, I'm told—the biography could drag on for decades. (As it was, it took seven years.) Just before taking the veil, luckily, I'd met a hot, uninhibited Cuban hustler named Roberto, and being able to call him when I did get free and felt horny pretty much kept me off the late-night merry-go-round.

To clear the decks further, I withdrew from a few minor writing commitments I'd recently made and backed off from a few new friendships that hadn't really jelled. It was easy enough to stop writing for the *Quill*, the new national journalists' magazine, since I'd written only two columns for them (one, a piece on my hero Emma Goldman and her portrayal in the film *Reds*). Cutting ties with the *New York Native* was considerably more difficult. I'd grown very fond of its editor, Brett Averill, a thoroughly engaging and gifted young man, who would himself quit the turbulent *Native* in 1984, move to San Francisco, and become editor in chief of the weekly gay paper, *Bay Area Reporter*—before dying of AIDS in 1995 at thirty-seven. I felt great affection for Brett; I thought him wildly overworked and underpraised, surrounded by self-important, untrustworthy prima donnas.

Yet the *Native*—and even more, its sister publication, the literary monthly *Christopher Street* (founded in 1976)—were among the few outlets in the early eighties for explicitly gay writing. Before coming out in 1971 I'd often been invited to write on nongay subjects for such mainstream publications as the *New York Times*, the *Atlantic Monthly*, the *New Republic*, and the *Village Voice*; after I came out those invitations dried up rather abruptly, with the sole exception of the *Nation* (though even there my views were now solicited almost solely on events or books relating to sexual behavior).

One of the first gay magazines, OUT, lasted for exactly two issues in 1973, one of which inadvertently got me into a spat with Norman Mailer: a feature article, "Why Doesn't Norman Mailer Become the Woman He Is?," led him—on the assumption I was the guiding force behind OUT—to send me an angry letter denouncing me, the magazine, and the article. I knew Mailer slightly and managed to calm him down, though it took the exchange of several letters between us.

The other serious gay magazine, San Francisco's *Gay Sunshine*, was more radically outspoken, and I helped to support it with both literary and financial contributions; edited by Winston Leyland, a transplanted Englishman, it began as far back as 1971 and lasted until 1983. It was remarkably wide-ranging in its coverage and included interviews with such figures as William Burroughs, Jean Genet, Allen Ginsberg, and Tennessee Williams. As well, it branched out into book publishing, issuing a number of unique anthologies that featured gay-themed translations from Spanish, Japanese, and Russian literature. I sometimes thought Winston a bit touchy and overreactive (doubtless he had his own complaints about me), but as I wrote him at one point in 1982, "We *are* entitled to a misunderstanding [now and then]. After all, our record may have been a little too squeaky clean over the years to ring true; given the tensions of our lives (and our movement), *never* to have quarreled—over a decade!—smacks of unreality."

Mainstream publishing houses in these years were almost entirely closed to gay writers—unless, that is, you eschewed the label (as did Gore Vidal) or identified more centrally with being black (as did James Baldwin). There were only two editors known to be receptive. One was New American Library's Arnold Dolin, himself heterosexual, who'd signed up my "On Being Gay"; the other was the pioneering Michael Denneny, at the time the only openly gay man at a mainstream publishing house (St. Martin's). Lesbian writers had a somewhat larger number of outlets: a significant number of "out" lesbians were on the staffs of various women's presses, and there was also June Arnold and Parke Bowman's Daughters Inc., which published, among many others, my friend Bertha Harris's distinguished *Lover*. (When the novel was reissued by New York University Press in the 1990s, however, Bertha wrote a blistering introduction recounting her negative experience with Daughters.)

If gay cultural expression was on the upswing in 1981, the organized gay political movement was—on the cusp of the AIDS epidemic—barely limping along: the division between lesbian feminists and gay men remained pronounced; organizational ranks were thin; the agenda was "liberal" not radical (and centered primarily on the perceived needs of white men); and tactics were confined to the traditional tools of lobbying and the ballot box, the focus not on playing any transformational cultural role but on the mainstream goals of winning acceptance and civil rights. For gay men, being on the active sexual circuit marked you down as in the forefront of the "revolution." Being politically active won you condescension at best, mockery at worst. (Larry Kramer: "You just didn't want to get involved. It was not chic.")

Yet the late seventies and early eighties did mark something of a flowering of gay culture, and not solely in regard to the print media. (Think Keith Haring or Robert Mapplethorpe.) In terms of literature alone, the years 1976–82 had seen the publication of, among others, Rita Mae Brown's *Rubyfruit Jungle*, Ed White's *Nocturnes for the King of Naples*, Armistead Maupin's *Tales of the City*, Nancy Garden's *Annie on My Mind*, Paul Monette's *Taking Care of Mrs. Carroll*, Jane Rule's *Desert of the Heart*, and Andrew Holleran's *Dancer from the Dance*. Plus a large batch of younger writers was beginning to appear, including Dorothy Allison, Randall Kenan, Lee Lynch, Samuel Delany, David Leavitt, Brad Gooch, Jewelle Gomez, Cheryl Clarke, Essex Hemphill, and Christopher Bram. Both the *Native* and *Christopher Street* were primarily—no, nearly exclusively—gay white male publications. Lesbian writers had to look elsewhere in these years, to such periodicals as *Sinister Wisdom*, *Conditions*, *Azalea*, and *Feminary*. People of color, too, had to create their own outlets; they included *Blackheart* and *Black/Out*.

My own disaffection with the *Native* and *Christopher Street* came about gradually. From the very beginning I'd frequently had to protest the sloppy way the *Native* published my "About Time" history columns; along with grotesque typos, the material was often printed with arbitrary, unauthorized cuts and rearrangements that significantly distorted the historical evidence. I got neither apology nor explanation, and the ongoing carelessness finally led me to cancel the column. I held on somewhat longer with the more literary and polished *Christopher Street*, though often baffled by its behavior. When I offered to give a benefit for the magazine, they failed to return my calls, evading any attempt to fix a definite date for the party; mystified, I simply gave up.

Then, after I'd agreed to publish one of my one-act plays in *Christopher Street* and been told that "in a couple of weeks" they'd get back to me with a few suggested editorial changes, weeks turned into months without any word. At the six-month mark I asked to have the play returned, but Tom, the literary editor, expressed such profound regret, falling all over himself with apologies, that—I must have been in need at the time of a bite-size buttering-up—I reconsidered. A firm new date was set, *before* which, Tom swore, I'd *definitely* have his editorial comments. That date also came and went. I was on the verge of venting some high-horse anger when, during dinner with Brett one night, he handed me an envelope. "It's your play," he said, flushing with embarrassment. "Tom asked me to return it to you." Period. No letter in the envelope. No attempt at explanation. ("So much for you, fancy-pants.") I sent a duly outraged letter, saying I'd never again let them print anything of mine. No one bothered to reply.

The final straw for many of the *Native's* contributors, myself included, came in the spring of 1984, when the paper's publisher and chief honcho, Chuck Ortleb, first censored and then fired the columnist Doug Ireland. Doug was a widely admired political analyst of rich insight and wit—along with unimpeachable integrity. It turned out that Doug had dared to ridicule Gary Hart, who Ortleb had endorsed for the Democratic presidential nomination. The irate publisher announced that *he*, not Doug Ireland, nor anybody else, was "the political voice of the *Native*" and would no longer countenance opposing viewpoints from the paper's columnists.

I joined some twenty other writers, all of us present or former contributors to the *Native*—including such well-known figures as Dorothy Allison, Jewelle Gomez, Larry Gross, Amber Hollibaugh, Cindy Patton, and Vito Russo—in protesting Ortleb's treatment of Doug Ireland in particular and its staff in general. We cited, among other grievances, Ortleb's veto of a proposed women's section for the *Native* on the grounds that his male audience would react unfavorably to more coverage of lesbian-oriented news. We also deplored his repeated failure to pay his writers promptly: he was currently running three months in arrears. Ortleb's arbitrary mauling of the right to free speech, we wrote, was "repugnant and indefensible," and we would no longer be a party to it.

Ortleb's response was to print a half-page announcement in the *Native* proclaiming "YOU'RE NOT RUN BY COMMITTEE. NEITHER ARE WE"—a bald defense of autocracy. I learned from Brett that Ortleb had made a conscious decision to cater to the wealthier, more conservative segment of the gay male community, which meant curtailing material relevant to women, people of color, and progressives—a move that destroyed any pretense that the *Native* could be a representative community forum. The paper struggled on for a number of years but soon degenerated into a platform for Ortleb's latest crackpot conspiracy theory about the origins and treatment of AIDS. At different points the *Native* denied AIDS existed at all, labeled it a subset phenomenon connected to chronic fatigue syndrome, and insisted it was in fact the African swine fever virus. This lamentable decline was particularly poignant for a publication that had been the first to call attention to AIDS and to predict its looming magnitude.

I cut some other ties as well. When I went for a routine checkup before flying to London for a series of Robeson interviews, it was discovered—to my shock—that I had an enlarged liver. One doctor diagnosed a resurgence of hepatitis; another blamed the Procan medication I was still taking for the heart arrhythmia, pointing as proof to my occasional angina; my cardiologist dismissed both diagnoses as "nonsense" and blamed stress and parasitic infection. I blamed my doctors, and on a friend's recommendation switched cardiologists to Ted Tyberg, who proved both brilliant and humane. (I've been with him ever since and have never again had serious heart trouble.)

I bring all this up to illustrate what many people afflicted with serious illness seem to experience: there's nothing like it for separating the wheat from the chaff in regard to friendship. One friend's idea of being solicitous when hearing I was flat on my back was to invite me uptown to a party. Another—"acquaintance" would be more accurate—couldn't accept my recent silence as the result of illness and chewed me out for being unresponsive, for pushing "him away." Okay, I decided, how would it be if you don't hear from me *at all*?

I had to be careful, though. I had to acknowledge that I had never been particularly good at initiating social plans, even with people whose company I very much enjoyed; this had to do, somewhere below the fault line, with my deep hermit instincts. I also needed to keep in mind that most people are so burdened by their own issues that they have to tell themselves others don't have any—that others are trouble-free, have a serenely fulfilled life, and want nothing more than to be an empathic listener to their multiple woes. Should I reveal that I too house a hungry adolescent or lethargic depressive, they flee the news, even feel that in revealing my own limitations I've somehow betrayed them.

CUNY, Christopher Lasch, and Eugene Genovese

Back in 1972 I'd resigned from Princeton to accept a distinguished professorship at CUNY and had never for a minute regretted the decision. CUNY students were less polished and well-read than the Ivy Leaguers I'd been teaching, but also less self-satisfied and more available, generally, to opening themselves up to material that challenged their preconceptions. I'd of course found such students at Princeton too, though not as often, and some of the CUNY students, to be sure, were just as deadbeat as their Ivy League counterparts.

The liveliness of my CUNY classes was due in part to the subject matter: one seminar was on "the history of radical protest in the U.S.," the other on my newfound scholarly interest, "the history of sexual behavior," which—before the Robeson offer materialized and came to monopolize my energy—had dominated my scholarly research and writing throughout the seventies. I made a point in both seminars of coming out to my classes as a gay man. The reaction, predictably, ran the gamut, and at CUNY the hostile ones were more honorably vocal than what I'd experienced at Princeton.

In only one instance did my coming out lead to an overtly destructive situation—and that due not to homophobia but to remorseless infatuation. George, a graduate student at CUNY from France who'd enrolled in my sexuality course, sent me a letter declaring himself madly in love with me. I made the mistake, in my initial response, of trying to reason with him, making it clear that although I thought he had many fine qualities as a person, anything more than a potential friendship was out of the question. Hearing what he wanted to, George insisted that I felt the same ardor he did but was unwilling to admit it.

A flood of "love" letters followed: "I stole a book of yours. . . . I tore off the picture. . . . My shirt has a pocket on the heart side so your beautiful face is constantly in contact with my heart." When I didn't respond, his letters turned threatening: "I am a fighter!" he wrote in one. "I am approaching my physical limits. It is not a menace whatsoever." "It is hardly bearable," he wrote alarmingly in another. In a third the threat became more direct: "I honestly do not know where the horror caused by the absence of an answer [phone call or letter] would lead me."

After some six months of this I started to get frightened. Since my silence was apparently heightening his obsession, I decided to reverse course and tell him as directly as I could to leave me alone. "From our first meeting," I wrote him, "you leapt to a frenzy of demands and accusations—even to the point of insisting that I was in love with you but wouldn't acknowledge it! You've refused to hear and believe me, insisting instead on your version of reality."

That didn't work either. He now began to stalk me. One night he stood outside the Village brownstone I lived in, shouted up at my window, and rang the buzzer so relentlessly that he roused my neighbors, who finally got him to leave. Discouraged? Not George. Rejection only led him to intensify his campaign, now well into its second year. I finally reached the end of my patience when, after begging him yet again to leave me alone, he hid behind a sofa in my seminar room and when I entered, suddenly leaped out at me. That was it. The History Department itself became alarmed and posted a security guard outside the seminar room when I taught.

I myself turned for advice to two lawyer friends, Cary Boggan and Bill Thom, who'd formed their own firm. Bill sent George formal notification that would have frightened off any normal obsessive: "You have continued throughout the summer to telephone him and, in the past, have presented yourself at his home and his place of employment knowing that he did not wish to see you.... Future attempts by you to contact Professor Duberman against his wishes would violate Sections 240.25 and 240.30 of the Penal Law of the State of New York... and would subject you to civil liability as well."

Stern stuff, eh? Well, it turned out, not stern enough. After a month's pause George renewed his onslaught on my apartment, and his adamant refusal to back down began to seriously frighten me. Bill Thom decided on a second letter, this one uncompromisingly severe: "Contrary to my previous advice to him, Professor Duberman did not have you arrested and sent to jail on the spot. However, I have now received a firm and irrevocable commitment from him that any further unwelcome contact by you . . . will result in the immediate filing of criminal charges of harassment against you. Please guide yourself accordingly."

George's interpretation of that edict was to cease contacting me directly, but for an extended period of time he'd place himself within my line of vision whenever I gave a public speech or appeared at an event, glaring fixedly at me throughout. I learned to literally scan the room beforehand—and too often did discover his scowling face, which never failed to send a chill through me. George's "rational" justification for his irrationality centered on his birthright as a Frenchman to insist that passion must write its own rules, obey no strictures. I blessed the day when I heard that he'd finally returned to France.

Then suddenly—an unbelievable four years later—I picked up the phone one day and there was George on the other end, haranguing me as if he'd never left off: "I am *suffering*. You have the *obligation* to help me resolve my pain." I could hardly believe my ears. All this from a graduate student I had momentarily befriended, had never slept with, and had instantly—as soon as I recognized the psychosis—tried to disentangle from. And here he was again, mouthing the same words as years before. I was genuinely frightened, immediately got an answering machine, and took a solemn vow never to pick up the phone without knowing who was on the other end.

That was the last time I heard from him. Hopefully he got lost somewhere deep in the Ardennes forest. No one will ever have to explain to me the terror many women (and yes, some men) experience when being stalked by a claimant to their "love."

BY THE BEGINNING of the eighties I'd rounded a corner and, unaware that sharper ones lay ahead, became in general far less focused on my personal state and again more available for political controversy—its roots, in some instances, going back to the countercultural wars of the previous decade. In my rejoining the debate, personal angst took a (temporary) hike, giving way to an earlier form of comfort: polemical contention, the body politic. It was a welcome, needed respite, my ability to reengage itself a measure of marked recovery.

In 1980 Ed White published *States of Desire*, an account of his travels in gay America. The book's reception in the mainstream press positively glowed with antipathy. The *New York Times Book Review*, with its occasional genius for mismatching a book and its reviewer, assigned *States* to a straight man, Paul Cowan, a *Village Voice* staff writer. Cowan was a well-liked, left-leaning journalist who'd recently become immersed in Orthodox Judaism. He surprised no one by writing a savage attack on the book, the gay male subculture, and an author about whom he had no apparent knowledge or sympathy.

According to Cowan, Ed White, unforgivably, regarded "random sex"—which, according to Cowan, "most people find morally reprehensible"—as "an exalted activity," even "as proof that he's a radical." If so, Cowan continued, White is a man of "tragic self-delusion"; his journey through the gay baths and bars of America, replete with their "narcotized one-night stands," had, in Cowan's view, nothing in common, as White seemed to believe, with a brave new sexual revolution. The scene he describes was, to the contrary, "a modern-day inferno," a region "close to emotional darkness."

The *Nation* published a more moderate review of *States of Desire*, seeing some merit in White's argument that sex had "taken up the slack" left by the collapse of religious, patriotic, and familial values—had perhaps become "our sole mode of transcendence and our only touchstone of authenticity." The *Nation* reviewer likened White's position to the argument Christopher Lasch had made a year earlier in his widely admired book, *The Culture of Narcissism*, in which he deplored the current preoccupation with Self in American life. The linkage between White and Lasch, though, was only superficially plausible. Where White hailed the sexual revolution, Lasch denounced it as paradigmatic of a general collapse in values; he bundled women's liberation together with gay liberation as exemplifying the triumph of self-indulgence over the general good of the polity.

Lasch broadened his indictment of this lamentable "collapse" (when reviewing a biography of Carl Rogers, the founding father of humanistic psychology) to haughtily condemn the entire counterculture, sweepingly reproaching it for having rejected "binding commitments in the name of 'alternate life-styles.'" He denounced the entire New Left for its platitudinous "jargon of authenticity," along with its bromidic talk of "participatory democracy, human potential and other progressive slogans." And he held up feminism for particular scorn; in Lasch's view, it had led to a general deterioration in relationships between men and women, which in turn had seriously damaged the structural integrity of the family.

Lasch and I had been arguing these matters, publicly and privately, for more than a decade. Throughout our prolonged dispute we'd periodically pause to assure each other, like ceremonial samurai, of profound mutual admiration and to express puzzlement as to how two people who agreed on so much could simultaneously distort each other's positions so profoundly. Lasch and I did share many views: opposition to imperialist wars abroad and economic inequality at home, a belief in the *eventual* necessity for a new party *if* the Democratic one proved as hopeless in the future as it had been in the present, the conviction that decentralization wasn't a sufficient strategy for combating the *national* scope of our ills, and rejection of the view that the university was the incarnation of evil. Still, above and beyond all that, we had opposite attitudes toward the counterculture and the New Left in general. In this Lasch's hostility represented a good number of straight male lefties at the time—whereas if I spoke for anyone at all, it was for a mere handful of gay male radicals who the larger gay community generally regarded as kooky malcontents.

The argument between Lasch and me had begun way back in 1965 over a review I published of Eugene Genovese's first book, *The Political Economy of Slavery*. Genovese would become a hugely influential (and controversial) historian of the antebellum South, but in 1965 he'd already become notorious on different grounds entirely. During an anti–Vietnam War teach-in at Rutgers University, he'd told the crowd, "Those of you who know me know that I am a Marxist and a Socialist. Therefore, unlike most of my distinguished colleagues here this morning, I do not fear or regret the impending Viet Cong victory in Vietnam."

The statement had caused a national uproar, along with a demand that Genovese be fired from his Rutgers professorship ("Rid Rutgers of Reds"). His job was saved when New Jersey's Governor Richard Hughes, citing freedom of speech, stood firm against the clamor. I was among the many who signed a petition at the time defending Genovese's right to speak his mind; he and I had subsequently gotten to know each other, though our contact was only occasional and, by 1970, after he turned to the right, nonexistent. In my 1965 review of *The Political Economy of Slavery*, which appeared soon after the Rutgers controversy,

I praised the book highly, despite reservations, and along the way made some negative reference to an article Lasch had written which I'd read as a call for scholars to remain in the ivory tower and ignore the turmoil of public affairs.

In response to the reference, Lasch sent me an outraged letter denouncing my "gratuitous attack" and insisting that in my "uninformed and shoddy" review I'd "grotesquely" misrepresented him as a defender of the ivory tower. He also singled out my praise of Genovese for not letting his own commitment to Marxism distort his treatment of slavery as a "patronizing and backhanded compliment." Marxism, Lasch informed me, is a "theory of society . . . not a prejudice which needs to be 'curtailed.'" Genovese's book was "a good book," Lasch insisted, *because* it had looked at slavery from the perspective of "a coherent theory about society."

In response I was no less sharp. I wrote Lasch that Genovese had phoned me "to express his pleasure at my review—apparently unaware he had been patronized." I accepted Lasch's insistence that he was not a defender of the ivory tower but suggested that the ambiguity and abstraction of his prose style had allowed for the misrepresentation: "I am not responsible for what you *actually* think or what you *intended* to say; as a reader I can react only to what you *did* say." As for my remarks on Marxism, I pleaded guilty: "I do not view Marxism as an instrument of intellectual analysis on a par with the Darwinian hypothesis or the theory of psychoanalysis. I believe it has incidental insights to offer us, but in my view history written from a Marxist perspective *does* need apologizing for"—by which I meant an analysis based strictly on economic determinism.

And there it stood between us for several years. Then, early in 1968, I read a piece by Lasch in the *New York Review of Books* on Black Power— to which we were both sympathetic—and decided to send him a note saying that I thought it "very fine." I added, "Our tangle of two or three years ago has long bothered me. . . . Can we bury the hatchet?" Lasch responded cordially and said that he too regretted our quarrel. Soon after, we served on a panel together at the annual American Historical Association meeting, and having now met, it became "Kit" and "Marty."

Thinking to cement further our budding goodwill, I agreed to review his 1969 book, *The Agony of the American Left*, for the *New York Times*; I assumed that I'd like it as much as I had his Black Power piece (which was one of the five essays in the book). But, alas, alack, I didn't. I piled on the compliments in the review yet also registered my considerable objections. Among other things, I challenged Lasch's indictment of the Wobblies (the radical labor movement), arguing that he'd underplayed that movement's anti-authoritarianism and overplayed its hostility to politics. In regard to his call for a new party, I found his "description of its potential shape so vague as to leave me unconvinced that it holds any decisive advantage over working for a new coalition within an old party." Besides—and this constituted by far the area of sharpest disagreement between us (and with Genovese as well)—I wasn't convinced that electoral politics was going to prove the most significant catalyst for social change; in my view the counterculture had planted seeds that would have more far-reaching effect. From my perspective Lasch had paid insufficient attention to the radical young, settling for the simplistic accusation that they tended to turn public questions into tests of personal "authenticity." On that question he was immovable, writing me that he had "no faith at all in the new left's 'cultural revolution,'" that in his view it would lead to "political impotence and new despotism."

Genovese promptly got into the act. He let me know that he "hated" my review of Lasch's book. By then he and Kit had become close allies (though they would have a fierce and lasting rupture within a few years), and central to their alliance was contempt for (as Gene put it) "the nihilist and totalitarian elements of the New Left." In late 1969 they decided to write a book together on the subject, "Beyond the New Left," and sent me the manuscript for comment. I was surprised and flattered. In their covering letter they told me that they were also preparing to launch a new socialist journal and asked me to serve "on an editorial board of about 20 people." I reserved judgment on joining the board until after I'd read their manuscript, which I did with great care, well aware that their combined influence—and their shared bias against feminist and radical gay critiques of the traditional family—carried considerable weight in straight left-wing circles.

Their manuscript, "Beyond the New Left," made it unmistakably clear to me that our views were starkly incompatible, even irreconcilable. As I wrote Gene, the cultural revolution then gathering force was not—as he and Kit claimed—"a creation of Madison Avenue," nor was it mere "hedonism or nihilism." I suggested that if by "hedonism" they meant "pleasure in the body" and in "a variety of sexual experiences," they were, from my perspective, being far too puritanical and glib in their denunciation. "A new life style, whether or not we approve it," I wrote Gene, "*is* emerging, and may do more to create a new society than political action will. I don't say I'm convinced of that. I do say it's a real possibility, one that shouldn't be ignored or patronized."

Though the New Left, as exemplified by Students for a Democratic Society (SDS), was far more politically engaged than was the hippie version of the counterculture, Gene and Kit were no less sweeping in condemning it. To them, the "angry young men of the Left" (no mention of the angry young women) "denounce everything indiscriminately." The New Left, in their view, consisted of a "half-invisible leadership that systematically hides its premises and thereby manipulates it followers"; they "embraced poverty because they are bored or revolted by wealth." This all seemed to me disastrously wide of the mark.

"You're too smart," I wrote them, "not to make some finer discriminations here; you don't want to sound like J. Edgar Hoover (especially since he isn't right)." Their further suggestion that the New Left's "deep distrust of authority," which I regarded as the healthy sign of a questioning spirit, represented instead "a predisposition to paranoia" seemed to me bizarre. As for their furious attack on the countercultural suggestion that there were no functions that the "monogamous family unit" performs that can't be done better by "other possible institutions," I withheld judgment but urged them to have a look at the evidence Bruno Bettelheim provides in his *Children of the Dream* of communal child-rearing in Israel. (Both the man and his views subsequently came in for severe criticism.)

The cultural conservatism Gene and Kit expounded in their manuscript was expansive enough to include a bias against "avant-garde art" and what they called its "inability to communicate." The comment, I warned them, made them sound "philistine and reactionary." Of a piece was their further claim that the New Left's dissatisfaction with the standard model of university education (authoritarian teacher; passive, dutiful student) amounted to nothing more than the "denigration" of learning itself, voiced solely by students who were "inassimilable." The universities, they insisted, were "neutral, Platonic territory" and as the "guardians of humane learning" must be "de-politicized."

I thought that naïve, and said so; in my view the university has *always* been a political institution, one captive to the wishes and needs of those in power—as witnessed by the fact that several members of the Yale History Department (of which I'd recently been a member) were currently doubling as high-ranking agents in the CIA, preeminently Sherman Kent, who succeeded Harvard's William Langer (also a historian) as head of the CIA's Office of National Estimates. Those currently questioning the university's posture weren't "denigrating" learning itself, I argued, but rather its current misdirection and deceits.

Gene and Kit never responded to my comments on their manuscript; they made no effort either to counter my criticism or to further defend their own views. They no longer saw me as a potential ally, and the invitation to join the board of their new journal was never repeated—indeed the journal itself proved stillborn (and "Beyond the New Left" was never published; whether turned down or withdrawn, I have no knowledge). All communication from Kit came to an abrupt halt, though Gene and I hung in there for one more round of somewhat cordial disagreement. At some point during this two-year period, 1969–70, I remember making an unsuccessful attempt to get Gene a job offer from Princeton, where I then taught; he *was* a brilliant historian, however quirky I thought his political views. When, in 1970, Gene asked me to write a letter to the University of Rochester (where he was teaching) recommending Kit for an appointment there, I said I would; despite our disagreements I thought Kit too a skillful (if wrongheaded) cultural critic. "You could hardly do better," I wrote to Rochester, and Kit did get the job; soon after, his friendship with Gene permanently ruptured.

Some time later, when Kit wrote *The Culture of Narcissism*, his most famous work, he again denounced the "therapeutic sensibility" that had produced (he claimed) a "narcissistic personality structure" marked by a fear of committed, lasting relationships, as exemplified, in his view, by feminism and the "cool sex of promiscuity." In a subsequent book, *Haven in a Heartless World*, he would lump together "the growing tendency of profanity, sexual display, pornography, drugs, and homosexuality" as indicative of "a collapse of common decency." Gene, for his part, decamped for the antifeminist, antigay right and reembraced Catholicism.

I was taken aback several years later to get a letter from Gene in response to an essay review I'd done for the *Times* on the emerging literature on homosexuality. It began with the assertion—restating the view he shared with Kit—that "sexual regularity" was essential to maintaining the integrity of the family unit, which in turn was critical for society's "general functioning." But, Gene went on, "we know all about human frailty and know very well that many people will violate the established norm." Fortunately the law, Gene continued, "is a moral and educational force. It tells people what society thinks they ought to do and not do." Any society, in his view, had the right to make the judgment that homosexuality is "a deviation," and he became "alarmed" when told it does not. The basic difference between us, in Gene's estimate, was over the question of "just how much freedom a society can afford to dispense." Not enough, apparently, to sanction homosexuality and its "threat" to the family.

I responded in the same dispassionate tone Gene had adopted: "Of course the majority views 'sexual regularity,' including (at least officially) monogamy, as essential if society is to continue to function *as it is*—and it has the power to pass laws to that effect." As for his suggestion, though, that many people are "frail" and "will violate the norms," why "continue to honor the 'norm' as immutable if it seems to be at odds with human nature (or the nature of many humans)"? Why "must" we? "To preserve its 'health,' you seem to say. What health? I don't see much around me. I agree, though: society *will* continue to pass judgments. That, however, remains a function of power, not right. I'm old-fashioned (and utopian) enough to want to see those two kept separate."

In *The Culture of Narcissism* Lasch had spoken for many on the straight left when declaring that "the most prevalent form of escape from emotional complexity is promiscuity. . . . [It's] the protective withdrawal from strong emotion." Such a statement, of course, was an *opinion*, not a fact. Many gay men who indulged in frequent "anonymous" sex in the baths and backroom bars had a quite different opinion of their activity: they saw *monogamy*, not sexual adventuring, as the enemy of "strong emotion" and insisted that their activity *embraced* the "emotional complexity" that traditional marriage avoided. These sex radicals were at the heart of the pre-AIDS gay movement—though they never represented the majority of gay men. The gay male world at the dawn of the Reagan era was in fact no less diverse than the heterosexual one, and according to the Kinsey Institute, no more than 20 percent of gay men took part in the fast lane of recreational sex.

Still, on the eve of the AIDS epidemic, the equation of gay men with promiscuity had become well established in the popular mind, and that most assuredly included such self-declared socialists as Kit Lasch, who in regard to social issues was in fact more aptly labeled—as was most of the Old Left—"cultural conservatives." Why? The answer, I suspect, centers on their having been weaned on the doctrine that class status is determinative in human affairs and that the reordering of economic relations is of singular importance in creating a more equitable society; they saw all else as mere bourgeois diversionism—as self-indulgence.

Was the New Left any different in its attitudes? Yes—but only somewhat. The feminist movement was born out of the dissatisfaction many women activists in SDS and other radical groups felt with the traditional, patronizing attitudes of their male comrades. As for the latest kid on the block, the gay movement, the New Left had a mixed to negative record. Allen Young, the pioneering gay activist involved in a number of antinuke actions, recalls that the gay and lesbian contingent was treated by the other protestors as an "embarrassment"; their presence, it was said, ran the risk of tarnishing the demonstrations as "somehow kooky—and marginal." Oppositely, gay members like Dave McReynolds of the War Resisters League (despite the homophobia of the group's archangel, A. J. Muste) were made to feel comfortable and welcome—that is, so long as the antiwar cause, not gay liberation, remained at the center of their protest activity. And as early as 1969 the League's magazine, WIN, devoted an entire issue to gay liberation. Nothing remotely comparable happened within Old Left circles.

At any rate, most straight lefties, exemplified by Lasch and Genovese, shared with the general public a preexisting mind-set of hostility to gender and sexual deviations. And that was the mind-set in place when news arrived of a mysterious new virus.

The Onset of AIDS

Late in 1979, both in New York City and in San Francisco, various doctors began to see a slew of puzzling symptoms in some of their gay male patients: chronic fevers, swollen lymph nodes, thrush, strange purple bruises. The young men also shared similar sexual and medical histories: frequent sexual contact with a variety of partners, along with repeated infection with sexually transmitted diseases like gonorrhea, herpes, and anal warts. Mystification intensified when the bruises were diagnosed as Kaposi's sarcoma, a disease previously associated with elderly men of Eastern European origin, and when patients also began to come down with a deadly form of pneumonia: PCP, pneumocystis pneumonia. A few cases with similar symptoms were also reported among intravenous drug users, who, in common with the afflicted gay men, showed a decline in CD4 cells, a significant marker of immune suppression.

By early 1982 the syndrome had been given the label GRID (gay-related immune deficiency)—which was tantamount to declaring homosexual behavior the key factor in the spread of the disease. As more and more cases began to surface, right-wing conservatives could hardly conceal their glee or curtail their triumphant rhetoric about how the sexual revolution had begun to devour its children. Jerry Falwell announced that GRID was God's punishment for the "wicked practice" of homosexuality. "You can't fly into the laws of God," Falwell smilingly intoned, "without the price." For its part, the Reagan administration responded not with additional funds for research and treatment but with proposals for sharp *cuts* in the budgets of the Centers for Disease Control and the National Institutes of Health. During that same year the Tylenol scare, in which a grand total of seven people died after taking cyanide-laced pills, the federal government—within two weeks—allocated $10 million to investigate the contamination.

Further indicative of the federal government's apathetic reaction to "the gay disease" was the failure of both the CDC and the NIH to recommend that physicians give their GRID patients the inexpensive drug Bactrim, a *known* prophylactic against PCP. The failure was one of the more glaring signs of the government's brutal disregard for gay lives; in the years to come, thirty thousand patients would die from preventable pneumocystis pneumonia.

In New York City, Mayor Ed Koch, though widely rumored to be gay himself ("Nonsense!" the radical gay journalist Doug Ireland wrote. "Ed Koch isn't a closet homosexual; he's a closet human being."), let two years go by after the onset of the crisis before he'd agree to meet with representatives from the Gay Men's Health Crisis (GMHC) or any other organization set up to combat AIDS. By the end of 1983—two years into the epidemic—the Koch administration had allotted a grand total of $24,500, all of it to assist the Red Cross in providing home attendant care for AIDS patients. Further, under the guidance of his good friend (and ardent homophobe) Archbishop John O'Connor, Koch resisted all efforts to include AIDS education as part of the New York City school curriculum. Nor would he sanction the introduction of a needle exchange program to combat AIDS among intravenous drug users. This put Koch to the right of Margaret Thatcher, who early on embraced both AIDS education and a program of needle exchange in England.

In the dozen years since the Stonewall riots and the birth of the gay rights movement, the notion that "gay is good" had made considerable inroads against the once standard view that "gay is sick." The younger generation—especially many privileged middle- and upper-class white men—felt far less guilty about their sexuality than had previous generations. As early as 1981 a group of activists in San Francisco formed what later became known as the San Francisco AIDS Foundation, and soon after, New York City gave birth to GMHC, which rapidly became the largest organization in the country devoted to fighting AIDS. It inaugurated a host of initiatives to combat the disease and provide services to those affected, including a hotline, crisis counseling, support groups, a legal arm to assist patients in writing wills and fighting apartment evictions, and a volunteer buddy system to visit and assist those who'd fallen ill.

In the early days of the epidemic, many gay men, understandably, remained in denial; the leading national gay magazine, the *Advocate*, at the end of 1982 listed AIDS (as it had by then become known) as only ninth among the top ten stories affecting homosexuals that year. Among those who dismissed the early alarms were prominent pioneers of gay activism like Frank Kameny, Michael Lynch, and Jim Owles. Recreational sex, they insisted, was at the heart of the gay (male) movement—a more "natural" style of living than the monogamous model long imposed on mid-America.

The initial denial of AIDS as a passing and marginal phenomenon sprang from a variety of motives. With causes and treatments alike unknown, some were in denial out of sheer terror, others out of an unwillingness to believe that their favorite pastime, sex, might be implicated in a fearsome epidemic. The dance critic Charles Jurrist announced, "I will continue to be 'promiscuous.' I won't be scared out of seeking fulfillment. Nor will I consider my behavior in any way as self-destructive." A man like Jurrist—and in 1982 there were still many such men—was reacting to moralistic critics like Larry Kramer, who (sounding much like Christopher Lasch) in his 1978 novel *Faggots* had denounced those spearheading the sexual revolution as indulgent adolescents, contrasting them unfavorably with those who adhered to the traditional model of sex as a function of love, and the monogamous couple as the exemplification of maturity.

If some gay men were in denial, the national media was downright comatose in the shockingly slow pace it adopted in publicizing the rapid spread of the disease. During the entire year of 1982 a mere thirty articles appeared in the country's leading newspapers and magazines. Though New York City accounted for half the reported AIDS cases, the *San Francisco Chronicle* printed twice the number of stories as the *New York Times*, though it had only a third of New York's number of cases. It rapidly became obvious that in the face of the country's indifference, the afflicted themselves would have to band together to fight the scourge.

Michael Callen, who would go on to found the People with AIDS Coalition (and whose biography I would later write), was among the liberationists who loved having sex and did so as often as possible, cheerfully referring to himself as a "slut." Like other gay male sex radicals of the day, Callen was outspoken and unashamed about the frequency of his sexual contacts. But he wasn't an ostrich. He wanted to save the lives of gay men *and* save the sexual revolution. He appreciated all that GMHC was doing to alert the community, but he wanted a sex-positive approach to the epidemic and focused his activism on advocating for medically safe ways to have sex—emphasizing the use of condoms, jerk-off clubs, and closed circles of buddies. Callen insisted that the sexual revolution was and must remain at the heart of gay liberation, but he also insisted that, as he said in a speech early in 1983, "walking into the baths and backrooms with the delusion that you can check your responsibility at the door with your clothes is an act of personal and cultural suicide. . . . What is over isn't sex—just sex without responsibility."

As for me, back in the 1960s, when still in my thirties, I'd occasionally gone to the famed—and filthy—Everard Baths, but even back then had rarely indulged in multiple sexual partners; I was too inhibited, too body-shy. Nor, in the seventies, did I ever set foot in the flourishing S/M bars, the Eagle's Nest and the Spike, or in those backroom sex emporiums, most famously the Anvil and the Mineshaft, which specialized in orgies that outdid their predecessors in an encompassing tolerance for every known form of sexual expression (and a few that had merely been rumored).

I saw nothing wrong with such places morally; these were adults choosing their own forms of pleasure. I simply didn't fit in, psychologically and physically. Even in my twenties I would have been too guiltily self-conscious to have participated. And by the time I reached fifty (in 1980)—though told I looked younger and appeared "naturally masculine"—I would never have dared present myself as a worthy contestant in the hypermasculine "clone" (construction worker, cop, ditch digger, warrior) sweepstakes. Friends did once persuade me to go to The Saint, the huge gay dance and sex emporium in the old Fillmore East on Second Avenue, and I was duly awestruck at the hundreds of perfectly formed, drugged-out, glistening, half-naked bodies gyrating under a dome that opened up into a spectacular planetarium of shimmering stars. For me it was like stumbling as an amateur anthropologist upon a sacred site deep in the jungle and trying to make sense of the fertility rites taking place before my eyes in which katsina clowns were fucking female burros.

No, in comparison to the flamboyant sex clubs or, alternately, to the boring chatter of a gay dinner party (I was never one for chitchat, though campy gossip could be alluring), Rounds seemed a preferable, plausible alternative; there a fiftyish intellectual had far more currency (as it were) than on the frenzied dance floor or in the back of one of the trucks parked near the West Side Highway that specialized in anonymous nighttime orgies. As it turned out, I was exceedingly fortunate not to be a natural fit for the current sex scene; having a limited number of sexual partners put me in a position of *comparative* safety as the AIDS virus began to spread through the gay male world. Which isn't to say that the hustling scene where I primarily looked for sexual partners was germ-free—I'd had both amoebiasis and hepatitis twice—but I rarely got fucked (which, as would become known, was the chief conduit for the transmission of the HIV virus).

As the number of AIDS cases began its exponential rise, panic and denial swept the gay world, and rejection and harshness the straight. Hospital staffs were known to refuse AIDS patients admission or, if admitted, to ignore them; nurses, gowned and masked, would leave food trays on the floor at the doorway of bedridden patients' rooms, and orderlies would sometimes leave them to die on gurneys in the corridor. In the early years basic information about both etiology and treatment—Was AIDS bacterial or viral in origin? Was it transmitted primarily through blood or semen?—was sorely lacking. In their desperation, terrified patients and helpless doctors were willing to try almost anything; one San Francisco doctor started injecting his AIDS patients with huge (and useless) doses of vitamin C; another experimented unsuccessfully with applying DNCB, a photochemical used to treat warts, to Kaposi lesions.

Organizing against the disease—and against a hear-no-evil-see-no-evil federal administration—took on heroic proportions within the gay world itself. In its early phases the process was inevitably chaotic, and plenty of anguished tension got discharged against fellow sufferers. Despite the internecine squabbling, and though faced with terrifying unknowns, GMHC managed to put together a remarkable phalanx of volunteers and services, though Mike Callen and others rightly bemoaned the way it downplayed—in his view, falsified—descriptions of gay sexual "excess," failed to include organizational representation for people who themselves had AIDS, and, in the hope of liberating federal funds, deliberately overplayed the threat of the disease passing over into the heterosexual world. Although the gay community mobilized with remarkable speed, it wouldn't be until the advent of ACT-UP in 1987 that direct-action tactics against governmental and scientific indifference would replace traditional appeals for greater "understanding."

When Mike Callen and his coauthor Richard Berkowitz published their prescient article "We Know Who We Are" in the *New York Native* late in 1982, insisting that "the single greatest risk factor for contracting AIDS is a history of multiple sexual contacts with partners who are having multiple sexual contacts," it caused an uproar. The two were widely accused of "shouting guilt from the rooftops," and when they subsequently tried to explain that they themselves felt no guilt about having indulged their sexual appetites in the past and continued to believe in the centrality of a liberated sexuality to the gay movement, the accusations only became louder. All of which was predictable: in the absence of any sign of scientific urgency or governmental concern, and in the face of right-wing harangues about God's righteous punishment for "debauchery," simply maintaining sanity can be regarded as a major accomplishment.

The more the AIDS movement, with the onset of ACT-UP in 1987, turned toward the radical tactics of confrontational direct action, the more it sounded like the resurrected voice of the Gay Liberation Front that had formed in the aftermath of the 1969 Stonewall riots. But there was a difference. GLF had called for a broad alliance with other oppressed minorities and had reached out both to the Black Panthers and the Young Lords (who, riddled with homophobia, had disdained to reach back—with the single exception of Huey Newton). GLF, reflecting the mixed composition of protestors during the riots—street kids, people of color, transvestites and transsexuals (the term "transgender" came later)—continued throughout its life to have at least minimal representation for sexual and gender mavericks.

This was less true of ACT-UP. A significant number of those who joined had never been politically involved in the gay movement during the seventies, and in some cases had derided it as "unchic." Throughout its history ACT-UP would remain predominantly white and male, and when radical social analysis inclusive of issues relating to class, race, and gender did arise, it was primarily at the insistence of the group's lesbians—women like Sarah Schulman, Ann Northrop, and Maxine Wolfe—who had long histories of involvement with progressive causes.

Some of the middle- and upper-class white men in ACT-UP who'd previously been hostile or indifferent to the gay political movement did, through their activism, become more radicalized; coming up against the entrenched conservatism and bigotry of the medical establishment opened many an eye to the institutionalized injustices of the "system." But the prestigious and influential Treatment and Data Committee of ACT-UP remained primarily composed of entitled white men schooled from birth to believe that the world was their oyster; somewhere deep in the gut, they felt a kind of knee-jerk outrage that their presumptive destiny to lead comfortable, accomplished, untroubled lives had inexplicably run into a road block. Taught to overcome obstacles, they promptly devoted themselves to mastering the relevant science and, remarkably, became peers of the scientific experts. The Committee's focus would remain on medical issues—and who can criticize a determination to save one's own life?—refraining from involvement in "peripheral" issues of social justice. Eventually the Committee would break away entirely from ACT-UP and set up its own shop.

Ironically, just as a new generation of gay people was cutting its teeth on activism and relearning the earlier confrontational tactics of post-Stonewall radical groups like GLF and the Gay Activists Alliance (GAA), those groups had either disappeared entirely or transmogrified into mainstream political formations like the National Lesbian and Gay Task Force or the Human Rights Campaign Fund. It was as if two forks had appeared in the road. As the younger cohort of LGBTQ people associated with GMHC, the People with Aids Coalition, and ACT-UP grew more militant in protesting mainstream indifference to their plight, the older cohort was swelling its ranks under the banner of "We're Just Folks—Let Us In!," taking over non-AIDS organizations like the Task Force and steering them toward the less controversial shores of assimilationism.

For me personally the event that exemplified the division of forces—and foretold future conflict within the movement between pro- and anti-assimilation forces—was the Human Rights Campaign dinner held at the Waldorf-Astoria late in 1982 to honor Walter Mondale. One thousand strong and paying $150 a plate—the equivalent of about $500 today—the dinner-jacketed white males, along with a handful of women and almost no blacks, Asians, or Hispanics, cheered Mondale's brief, pedestrian speech. The event marked an apogee—for me, a nadir—in the mounting quest for mainstream respectability.

I attended the dinner and was appalled enough at the proceedings to write about it in the *Native*. It seemed to me that the appeal for acceptance on terms that conformed to majoritarian norms came at the cost of discarding our own subcultural values and perspectives, ones that had the potential to contribute to—perhaps to serve as the vanguard for—the creation of a political climate in which primary attention was redirected to the needs of the least fortunate. When the Waldorf crowd gave Mondale's lackluster speech a standing ovation— even though he never once mentioned the word "gay" and spoke in limp platitudes—it felt to me like chilling confirmation that mainstream gay politics had scrubbed itself clean of any trace of its radical roots. This was not the crowd likely to offer even a marginal critique of the country's growing concentration of power and privilege.

I doubt that most of the Waldorf attendees were actual Reaganites, but nor did they show any apparent interest in challenging mainstream mores. In their drive to establish our credentials as "everyday" Americans, they were implicitly *de*-emphasizing our "differentness"—which in turn was tantamount to denying our unique historical experience and falsifying the subculture it had generated. The pretense that we're "just folks" has the inevitable secondary effect of negating the potential contribution of our "off-center" perspectives to a much needed reexamination of traditional notions of "coupledom," "family," gender, and friendship.

Gay "differentness" is a reality, not a pipe dream. Diverse though our individual lifestyles are, collectively we challenge the rigid gender binary that assumes everyone is either male or female and that assigns certain "inherent" traits to one gender *or* the other—insisting, for example, that women are *intrinsically* emotional and men *intrinsically* aggressive. Taken as a group, it's also true—as multiple studies have shown—that LGBTQ people are more empathic and altruistic than heterosexuals and that lesbians are far more independent-minded, and less subservient to authority, than straight women. Most gay men, moreover, unlike straight ones, put a premium on emotional expressiveness and sexual experimentation.

When it comes to coupledom, both gay male and lesbian unions are characterized—much more so than straight couples—by mutuality and egalitarianism. Even the *New York Times* has validated the contrast. In a 2008 article summarizing scholarly studies to date, the *Times* concluded that "same-sex couples are far more egalitarian in sharing responsibility both for housework and finances" than their counterparts in heterosexual unions, where women still do most of the childrearing and domestic chores and men earn the higher salaries and pay more of the bills. The *Times* concluded that same-sex couples "have more relationship satisfaction" and—this is the nub of the matter—"have a great deal to teach everyone else."

As the Waldorf gathering made clear, the noisome, "impractical" visionaries of GLF had by 1982 (and probably by the mid-seventies) been pushed off center stage—no, out of the theater. The horde of prosperous white males who in the seventies had disdained association with gay politics had, on the eve of the AIDS epidemic, become the *official* movement—though without question the large majority of LGBTQ people held working-class jobs and salaries, were not affluent and not privileged. Yet no national LGBTQ organization was primarily devoting its resources to articulating their needs and agendas. The Waldorf crowd upgraded our image, made us more "acceptable"—but only by discarding in the process all claim to being a transformative social movement.

It was an old story, really. Political radicals who believe that *basic* institutional restructuring is needed, not just "liberal" tinkering around the edges, usually inaugurate movements for social justice in this country, but neither they nor the programs they advocate last very long. The radicals are quickly repudiated and replaced by those in a given movement who have a more accommodationist outlook. Thus the Garrisonian abolitionists ("Get rid of slavery *now*") gave way to the Free Soil Party ("No further *extension* of slavery into new territories"). Similarly the Knights of Labor—"One Big Union," skilled and unskilled workers combined—mutated over time into the AFL, catering only to skilled workers and denying admission to people of color. The same pattern is discernible in the first-wave feminist movement: the women who met at Seneca Falls in the mid-nineteenth century proposed a wide-ranging challenge to traditional gender roles that got watered down by the early twentieth into the single-issue demand for the right to vote.

I saw little reason to hope that the trajectory of the gay movement would follow a different path. The radical young were necessarily putting their talent and energy to work in combating the horrendous scourge of AIDS. Progressives of the older generation, long active in economic and labor struggles, were mostly staying put, and the small contingent who'd earlier been part of GLF and GAA had moved off to the sidelines. The large cohort of less-than-radical gay people were filling the gap, raising their centrist banners in organizations like the Human Rights Campaign Fund, and applying pressure not to changing institutionalized inequities but to opening the doors for *them* to its benefits and comforts.

Who was I to pass judgment? Beginning in late 1981 my own energy had become almost entirely absorbed in researching the story of a *past* radical, Paul Robeson. I could easily enough come up with reasons to justify my consuming engagement with the project: Robeson's history, never before told in any detail, was crucially important for understanding how the previous depth of black suffering (and accomplishment) centrally affects race relations today. Scholarship, I told myself, when done right, is itself a form of activism. Besides, wasn't I, a man in his mid-fifties who'd had a heart attack, exempt from lying in the street or assaulting the National Institutes of Health? Maybe, though when engaged in protests in the sixties against the war in Vietnam, I'd seen plenty of people older than that in the line of march.

The nagging feeling remained that I wasn't doing enough to help combat the AIDS crisis. I managed to feel somewhat better after I volunteered to answer the phones part-time at the People with AIDS Coalition, which I did for a number of years—yet only *somewhat* better. Later on, when people close to me got sick, it became obvious where to direct more of my energy. Yet something of an internal tug-of-war persisted. The demands of scholarship (and of my hermit instincts) have always compromised my counter impulse to engage more consistently in direct political activism.

Perhaps if I'd felt more at risk personally I would have reversed the ratio and invested more of myself in AIDS activism than in scholarship, but in fact I felt relatively safe, felt that my sexual history didn't closely align with the common profile of those who were coming down with HIV. No gay man with *any* sexual history, of course, could escape from the occasional sense of *certainty* that the unexplained bruise on his arm was Kaposi's sarcoma or that the congestion in his chest signaled the onset of PCP.

Completing *Robeson*

Throughout the eighties my research for *Paul Robeson*, published in 1989, alternated between manuscript archives and personal interviews. The main archive was the vast collection of Robeson family papers, previously closed to scholars, to which I had unrestricted access. It totaled some fifty thousand items, with a diary counting as a single item. In addition I consulted the archives of sixty or so of Robeson's friends and colleagues, most of them housed in research libraries scattered across several countries. Of the many people I interviewed, some three dozen entrusted me with correspondence and manuscripts in their own possession that added immeasurably to the storehouse of information. Leonard Boudin, who led the legal fight to win back Robeson's passport after it was revoked in 1950, opened his personal files to me; the radical journalist Cedric Belfrage shared his correspondence with London's left-wing county councilor Peggy Middleton, another staunch Robeson ally; the publisher Rupert Hart-Davis sent me a batch of letters revealing in detail Robeson's near-marriage to an Englishwoman named Yolande Jackson; Helen Rosen let me read Robeson's many letters to her during his psychological tailspin in the early 1960s; H. A. Murray offered letters and personal recollections about his involvement in the budding romance between Robeson and his future wife, Essie; Anita Sterner gave me the three dozen tapes she'd recorded for the BBC's program on Robeson in 1978. And so on. I was blessed by the willingness of so many of the people I interviewed to part with material essential to telling Robeson's story in full.

Many of Robeson's close friends and colleagues were still alive in the early eighties, and I had some memorable experiences talking with them. It was Paul Jr. who got me in to meet Indira Gandhi, then India's prime minister; she'd known Paul Sr. in the fifties through his association with her father, Jawaharlal Nehru. Motioning me to sit down next to her on the bed in a New York hotel room, she recalled the "wonder" she had felt at finding in Robeson "such gentleness in such a powerful frame."

Robeson's left-wing lawyer Leonard Boudin—whose daughter Kathy was then serving a twenty-year sentence for her role in the far left Brink's robbery that had taken the lives of two police officers and a security guard—recounted for me the long legal struggle to get the U.S. government to return Robeson's passport. Then there was my meeting—this one also arranged by Paul Jr.—with Eubie Blake, who cowrote (with Noble Sissle) the epochal black musical, *Shuffle Along*; it had opened in 1921 with a youthful Robeson in the cast, and Eubie (as he insisted I call him) reminisced warmly about how Robeson had been "the same all the time. . . . Success didn't change him. That's the great thing. . . . His head never got swollen. . . . He was a master gentleman." Within a year of our interview in 1982 Eubie Blake died, age ninety-six.

Ninety-year-old Oscar Brown Sr., who'd worked summers with Robeson at a hotel in Narragansett when both were teenagers, filled in a few more details about the young black staff's discussion of "current questions" relating to race. I also succeeded in locating a few surviving members of Robeson's undergraduate class (1915–18) at Rutgers. All of them white, some vehemently denied that there had ever been any racial antipathy toward him (he was one of only two blacks on campus), though others remembered clearly the "terrific beating" he took from his fellow football players during practice and the shouts of "Nigger" that would periodically emanate from the stands; they recalled too that he was routinely barred from traveling with the glee club (of which he was the star) and from participating in college dances.

One contact led to another, and I got particularly lucky when I found Robeson's first serious girlfriend, Geraldine Maimie Neale. The two had met when "Gerry" was a senior at a local high school and Paul a sophomore at Rutgers, and their affair was intense and prolonged. In her letters to me, which totaled some fifty pages, Gerry described how Paul's voice, even as an undergraduate, "got earnest, vigorous (not loud) when speaking about the subject of race discrimination." Paul pressed Gerry to marry him, but she resisted; as she explained to me, "I was not sure I loved him enough" to survive the difficulties of marriage to a man "I felt sure would be called upon around the world to be Everyman." Though she turned him down, he kept trying to get her to change her mind—even after he married Eslanda ("Essie") Goode.

Robeson was no fan of monogamy, domesticity, or parenting. Revels Cayton, the radical black labor leader and Robeson's closest male confident for many years, told me how, as young men, the two of them would go "catting" around Greenwich Village looking for sex. I eventually met nearly all of the women (most of them white) who at various points had had love affairs with Robeson. Two of them, the regal, feisty Helen Rosen (who laughingly described herself as having a "whim of steel") and the actress Uta Hagen, were among my most reliable truth-tellers, and Helen became a very dear friend. As I mentioned earlier, Peggy Ashcroft also told me about her love affair with Paul when they played opposite each other in the historic 1930 London production of *Othello*. That revelation came at the end of a long, cordial taping, and Peggy—unlike Helen and Uta—had an almost immediate change of heart about her frankness. Before I'd even left London she was phoning my hotel to ask that I return the tape to her. ("I've never before told anyone about my relationship with Paul, not even my husband.") I pleaded the necessity of temporarily retaining the tape so I could periodically refer to its richly detailed, unique revelations about the production's tribulations. (Though scholars tend to see themselves as noble truth-seekers, the successful ones have several less edifying personae: ruthless detective, devious scoundrel, charming con man.) I managed to keep Peggy at bay until I'd actually completed the chapter on the 1930 *Othello*, in which I *did* include a description of their affair. I sent the chapter off to her in advance of publication and awaited her reaction with trepidation. I've failed to locate the letter she sent me in response (it may be in my archives at the New York Public Library), but I remember its contents vividly, if not word for word. It was brief, firm—and enormously relieving. What she wrote in essence was that I'd disobeyed her wishes, but since I'd told the story of the 1930 production so well, she would not ask for any changes. That's one of the higher compliments I've ever gotten.

When Robeson performed his second *Othello* in 1943, on Broadway, he and his new Desdemona, Uta Hagen, also became sexually and romantically entangled. In Ashcroft's opinion, the affair was "possibly inevitable . . . a lesson in the power of drama to encourage a portrayed emotion to become a fantasy of one's own." (Othello: "She loved me for the dangers I had passed, and I loved her that she did pity them.")

Uta's explanation was less poetic. I spent two days alone with her in her house in Montauk, New York, and we got along famously. I liked her immensely, found her warm, real—and remarkably frank. Our sole outing during two days of taping was a dinner party at the home of Dore Ashton, the art critic. Our fellow guests were the painter Hedda Sterne and, to my amazement, Alger Hiss. I was at the time convinced of his innocence, and even now feel confused and unsettled about the evidence that he was a Soviet spy. Though I liked both Dore and Hedda, I had eyes only for Alger. Amid the usual disconnected chatter of a Manhattanesque dinner party, I found him (as I wrote in my diary) the only one who "stayed in focus," sustained "a line of conversation beyond the launching pad," gently adding an underblown opinion here and there, "soothing and connected."

As for Uta, she was full of feisty bravado that night, revealing a boisterous, hilarious side that deliciously complemented her generous, warm nature. Back at her place in Montauk, we talked far into the night, a kind of raucous candor taking over after our umpteenth drink. With ribald directness, she pantomimed the night during the Broadway run of Othello when she and Paul were standing in the wings awaiting their entrance: Paul "took his enormous hand—costume and all—and put it between my legs. I thought, 'What happened to me?!' I was being assaulted in the most phenomenal way, and I thought, 'What the hell,' and I got unbelievably excited. I was flying!"

She loved him not "for the dangers he had passed" but for the frankness and confidence of his sexuality. From that night on they became lovers, though Uta had only recently married José Ferrer, who (unbelievably) was playing Iago in the same production! José was having an affair of his own and seemed indifferent to Uta's liaison with Paul, which continued uninterrupted for two years. Uta and José formally separated, yet friendliness reigned on all sides—until, that is, the shocking evening when José abruptly appeared with a lawyer and a detective in the house where Uta and Paul were staying. To this day, Uta told me, she remained puzzled over José's motives. Her best guess was that he had decided on the raid to avoid having to pay alimony.

Uta also told me that she found Paul's reaction to the raid "most peculiar." He "paced up and down in a sweat . . . talking himself into more and more fear. He panicked. He called all his friends," several of whom arrived, some carrying guns, henchmen apparently of the notorious Ellsworth "Bumpy" Johnson, head of the black mafia, a longtime friend and protector of Robeson's. Though Uta felt Paul was overestimating the potential danger, she did see merit in my view that it was realistic, not paranoid—especially in those years—for a black man caught with a white woman to fear for his life (a famous black man who'd recently berated President Truman to his face for refusing to back antilynching legislation and who the FBI was currently tracking and possibly attempting to set up on a rape charge).

READING THE LEFT-WING magazine *WIN* (long since defunct, but back then influential) one day, I was startled to come across a book review that concluded with the flat-out statement—as if well-known and incontrovertible—that Paul Robeson had been bisexual. I immediately called Frances Goldin, my agent, who was just as astonished at the "news" and highly skeptical of its truth. She called Paul Jr., then got back to me with his reaction. This is what I jotted down after her call: "He was bland and undefensive about it, saying something to the effect that, yes, his father did have an occasional fling with a man (including Sergei Eisenstein) but in fact Essie, his *mother*, was in her fifties the more 'bisexual' of the two, turning increasingly lesbian in her later years."

I suddenly flashed back to that very first meeting with Paul in Frances's office. After we'd talked for hours and agreed that it was a match, Paul had said something along the lines of "I want you to show all sides of my father. I don't want a plaster-cast saint whom nobody can identify with. My father was very human. To give you just one example, both he and my mother were free of prejudice about anyone who was homosexual. My father even had an affair himself—with Sergei Eisenstein." Stunned at such wholly unexpected and potentially volatile news, Frances and I hadn't dared even to look at each other or to press Paul for further details.

But as soon as the ink was dry on the contracts, I set out to check the accuracy of Paul's remarks. I managed to locate a gay man who'd lived in Moscow during the 1930s and had known Robeson (who visited Russia often during that decade), as well as Eisenstein's sister-in-law, Zina Voynow, then living in New York City. When I ran the news by them, both broke out in laughter. Voynow said, "Sergei *was* homosexual, but Paul was possibly the most rigorously heterosexual man I've ever known." I also tracked down the author of the WIN article and asked him what his sources had been. "Hearsay," was all he could come up with.

When I told Paul that I'd been unsuccessful in finding even a scintilla of evidence to confirm his father's affair with Eisenstein, he turned on me angrily. "What the hell are you talking about?!" he shouted and proceeded vehemently to deny that he'd ever said such a thing. By then I'd had a taste of Paul's uncorked rage and didn't want another go-round. "Well," I said, as neutrally as I knew how, "it's easy enough to check out—Frances was in the room at the time." Paul simply stalked away. But I did call Frances, and she confirmed Paul's words; I hadn't hallucinated them. Some considerable time later, Frances called one day to say, "Marty, sit down—and *don't* make any effort to check out what I'm about to tell you. Paul was just here, and after we got through our business and were chatting, he said, 'Did I ever tell you my father had an affair with Marc Blitzstein [the composer]?'"

Frances was right: the remark was more of the same and not worth checking (though I did, since Blitzstein was gay). But I stored away Paul's bizarre false leads, and eventually the fog would slowly lift around the long-standing puzzle of why he'd come to *me* to write his father's biography. It would take a while longer before I felt confident that all the pieces did truly fit together. In the interim, whenever the question of Robeson's purported bisexuality came up, in public or private—and the rumors had spread some distance—I firmly denied them. Ironically, as antagonism between Paul and me deepened over the years, he would periodically appear in Frances's office—she would always call to tell me—to "rage" (her word) at length about how "Duberman is trying to claim my father for gay liberation!" I learned not to respond.

OF THE DOZENS of people I interviewed for the Robeson biography, few were as forthright and as trusting as Uta Hagen had been. Yet almost all of them contributed at least some information to help me flesh out a particular incident or relationship or to better understand the inner workings of, say, the Council on African Affairs or of Robeson's shrouded and contested relationship with the Communist Party USA.

The degree of Robeson's commitment to the Party—and to the Soviet Union—was probably the most difficult question I faced in writing the biography and the issue around which I did the most interviewing.

Some of the leading black figures in the CPUSA—among them Pettis Perry and Benjamin Davis Jr. (one of Robeson's closest friends)—were already dead when I began the research process. Their widows agreed to talk with me but kept the conversations pleasant and mostly superficial. ("Rose Perry," I jotted on a scrap of paper, is "soft, gentle, not wanting to say a bad word against anyone.") The affable Howard ("Stretch") Johnson, one level down in the Party structure, was more forthcoming, but such information as he had, or was willing to share, merely confirmed Robeson's personal appeal ("he exuded magnetism and charm and charisma") and had little to say about the nature of his CPUSA connection.

A few leading black figures in the Party—in particular, Marvel Cooke and Esther and James Jackson—refused outright to see me. They based their refusal, I later learned, on the assumption that if Paul Jr., who they regarded as a political renegade, had chosen me as his father's biographer, than I must be his unsound surrogate. A British filmmaker who did succeed in gaining access to the Jacksons and to several other black CP figures who'd turned me down confirmed that they were uniform in their distrust of Paul Jr. He quoted Marvel Cooke to the effect that for years she had her husband answer the phone to avoid having to talk to him.

One of the few other people who refused my request for an interview was Harry Belafonte. When we were introduced at a Woza Africa benefit at Lincoln Center, I told him that I was writing Robeson's biography and hoped he would talk to me about their relationship. He interrupted, his tone snappish: "Under whose auspices are you doing the book?" "Paul Robson Jr. has opened up the family archives to me," I foolishly responded. Without a word, Belafonte turned on his heels and walked away. I'd obviously given the wrong answer, and that door remained permanently shut.

I had better luck in Chicago with Ishmael Flory, head of the Communist Party in Illinois, who'd run for governor of the state in 1972 and 1976. In advance of our meeting Flory had sounded like a bear on the phone and I'd felt the odds were high that if he agreed to see me at all, he'd skim across the surface and evade the hard questions. I couldn't have been more wrong. Flory greeted me with a warm smile and an amiable pat on the shoulder. He was a hugely likeable man, and he knew everyone. He took me all over Chicago and introduced me to, among others, Rev. Louis Rawls, founder of the Tabernacle Missionary Baptist Church, and Julia Lochard, widow of the *Chicago Defender* editor Metz Lochard. He also took me to lunch with friends who owned the Soul Queen restaurant, and we ended up on the first evening of our two days together in the locker room of a black male gym on the South Side chatting away with some of the younger political radicals, like Chapman Wailes, about the National Labor Conference for Black Rights, as well as a range of race-related issues. Along with much else, Wailes told me about Robeson's passionate speech at the mammoth Chicago Peace Congress in June 1951, in which he denounced the recent jailing under the Smith Act of various communist leaders. Wailes also related the incident he witnessed in the lobby of the Persian Hotel when the jazz great Charlie Parker spotted Robeson, who at that point had had his passport lifted and was under constant FBI surveillance, went up to him, and said, "I just wanted to shake your hand. You're a great man."

By then, at Flory's insistence, it had become "Ish" and "Martin," and I was able to check out with him at length the tentative conclusions I'd reached about Robeson's relationship both to the CPUSA and to the Soviet Union. I'd found no evidence, I told him, that Robeson had ever become an actual Party member, though the FBI believed otherwise and though he had close personal ties to several of its leaders, including Ben Davis Jr., Earl Browder, and Eugene Dennis. As Dennis's widow, Peggy Dennis, had put it to me, "The Party was just a small part of Paul's life." (On yet another scrap of paper I jotted, "Peggy Dennis: likeable, warm, guarded, remarkably unembittered.") When I interviewed the admirably candid, down-to-earth Dorothy Healey, the former communist leader in California, she confirmed Peggy Dennis's view: "Ninety percent of the inner-CP stuff," Dorothy said (with her it was immediately first-name friendly), "was either unknown to Paul or, if known, considered unimportant."

Yet John Gates, a leading figure in the Party and editor of the *Daily Worker*, revealed to me that he was present at a secret meeting of four of the Party leaders indicted by the U.S. government under the Smith Act when Robeson offered to join the Party as a public gesture of solidarity just before they were jailed. According to Gates, none of the four encouraged the idea; they felt it would be "a personal disservice" to Robeson, reducing his influence in the black community—and thereby reducing his usefulness to the Party. That "usefulness," as I was ultimately to write in the biography, was "directly proportionate to the fact that his stature did not derive from it."

In the 1930s, at a time when racism and colonialism were rampant in the United States, Robeson—and many other progressives—saw the Soviet Union as a bulwark against imperialism, fascism, and racism (though Robeson never wavered from his firm insistence that blacks themselves, not the Party, should serve as the vanguard in the black struggle). Robeson's sanguine view of Soviet intentions may have been shaken (there's no concrete evidence either way) by the Nazi-Soviet Pact of 1939, but if so, his optimism was reaffirmed after Russia joined the Allies to defeat Germany in World War II.

Subsequently, however, the cold war between Russia and the United States set in, followed in 1956 by Khrushchev's shocking revelations about the murderous extent of Stalin's crimes, which led most progressives still sympathetic to the Soviet Union to turn their backs. If Robeson shared their disillusion he never spoke about it openly, apparently unwilling to provide ammunition (as he saw it) to right-wing fascists. He remained tight-lipped, refusing all comment, even, Paul Jr. told me, within the confines of the family.

Flory (and others) thought plausible my view that Robeson's silence is probably best understood as a function of his stubborn conviction that the socialist experiment in which he continued to believe had been only temporarily derailed by Stalin's malignant leadership. Robeson's political identification had all along been primarily, as I would write in the biography, "with the Soviet Union in its original revolutionary purity." In the thirties, when he initially championed the Soviet Union, "it was playing the most visible role in the liberation of American and colonial peoples of color." He "aligned himself with the principles of black liberation and socialism, not with national or organizational ambitions."

Robeson apparently remained convinced, I wrote, that the unhappy detours of the Nazi-Soviet Pact and Stalin's pernicious leadership "would prove temporary and that socialism, still humanity's best hope, would triumph." In the meantime he chose silence, refusing to join the anti-Soviet chorus, not wanting his own fame enlisted in the campaign to condemn a country and an experiment that had once held out such promise—and that might again. His refusal to denounce the Soviets— or to hail American "democracy"—led the U.S. government, as the cold war heated up, to brand him a "traitor," to lift his passport, to destroy his career, to destabilize his health, and to drive him in his final years to living anonymously in a room in his sister's Philadelphia home.

The *Salmagundi* Controversy

I had a phone call one day in 1982 from Robert Boyers, editor of the well-regarded literary quarterly *Salmagundi*. He invited me to contribute an essay to a planned issue of the journal devoted wholly to the topic of homosexuality. Boyers told me that George Steiner would serve as guest editor of the issue—news apparently designed to impress me but that in fact made me wary. Steiner, a portentous polymath with a flair for obscurantism, was a High Culture guru, a sort of male Susan Sontag. At some party back in the sixties he and I had gotten into an angry argument over his defense of the U.S. role in Vietnam.

Various gay worthies, Boyers added, including Michel Foucault and Stephen Spender, had already said yes to his invitation. (In the end Spender did not appear in the volume.) Boyers said further that some nongay intellectuals would also be invited to contribute—not to oppose the "liberationist" point of view but to add specialist perspectives derived from various fields of professional inquiry (anthropology, sociology, etc.). The overall aim of the volume, he assured me, was (as I quoted him in a letter) "to help consolidate and clarify the recent onslaught of information—help us all better to understand where the state of the inquiry now stood."

All of which sounded reasonable enough, but I told Boyers that I needed time to talk the matter over with a few "politically sophisticated" gay friends and would get back to him. Those friends shared my view that to date liberal academics had demonstrated (at best) an acceptance of homosexuality premised on the view that we were "just folks," sharing their values, measuring up to their behavioral standards. Despite the insufficiency of that premise, my friends and I were flattered by an invitation that seemed to take our lives and issues seriously. We managed to convince ourselves that the promise of reaching a prestigious academic audience with information and arguments that went beyond the "just folks" assumption outweighed the risks. For myself, I needed a break from the intense pace I'd set on the Robeson biography—a chance to turn away for a brief spell from my absorption in "objective" research and to do something entirely personal.

The "liberal" take on homosexuality had recently been exemplified by the Kinsey Institute's Alan Bell and Martin Weinberg in their book *Homosexualities*. In reviewing the book for the *New York Times*, I'd called it "the most ambitious study" to date of male homosexuality, and to a degree had praised it. But I'd also challenged its conclusion that homosexuals didn't differ in any essential way from heterosexuals. Radical-minded gay people, I pointed out, would view that conclusion not as praise but as patronization. I proceeded to explain why in some detail—far more detail, the *Times* editor decided, than was warranted. When the review appeared that section had been cut.

In the excised portion I'd argued that although most gay people *did* share the prescribed values and aspirations of mainstream culture, a radical minority, lesbian feminists in particular, did not; that minority firmly rejected the liberal view that our national institutions were basically sound and that a little tinkering here and there around the edges would make them better still—rejected, in other words, a state of affairs in which entrenched privilege and power remained in the hands of a few, mostly white and, presumably, straight men.

At the conclusion of the *Times* review I offered what I called "certain general principles" that gay *radicals* shared: that you cannot adopt the dominant values of a culture and at the same time hope to reorder those values, and that the token adjustments which the power brokers grant from time to time are insufficient to dilute (and in the long run may strengthen) "our society's instinctive distaste for substantive change, its zeal for homogenization and its entrenched suspicion of the very human diversity it rhetorically defends." The liberal Kinsey Institute, I argued, champions out of one side of its mouth the vigorous scrutiny of traditional assumptions about sex and gender but then blindly accepts a set of assumptions about human nature most in need of scrutiny— like the belief that a "maternal instinct" is innate, that recreational sex denotes immaturity or, conversely, that monogamy signifies adulthood.

For my own contribution to the *Salmagundi* issue I decided to print excerpts from a diary I'd briefly kept as a graduate student at Harvard in the mid-fifties, along with my current (1982) comments on those excerpts. I wanted to demonstrate how oppressive the social climate had been during the fifties and the frightening extent to which many of us had internalized its self-denigrating message. It was a risky, perhaps foolish choice: I not only dropped the protective armor of academic discourse; I dropped my underpants too.

A few sample excerpts will convey what George Steiner in his preface would describe as "confessions born of vehement privacies. Their mere publication points to a radical shift in the limits of socially-admissible sentiment and speech."

What is far more shaming to me today in reprinting those fifties excerpts is the extent to which they reveal what a dutiful creature of the culture I then was, the extent to which I'd viscerally absorbed middle-class—and psychiatric—values of the day. I'd all but wholly bought into the then standard definition of the "homosexual condition" as "sick" and "second-rate," as well as the culture's overarching sex-negativism.

Here are a few of the sample diary entries, along with my 1982 comments on them (as included in the *Salmagundi* article):

Boston. September 21, 1956:
Big scene with Dick [Buckley, at that point my lover of some three years]. I told him the plain truth—I don't want to lose him but can't be completely faithful. What a Goddamn mess I am. Simply not capable of love. Can anything be worse than a life of promiscuity, of objects not people? This is what I'm faced with and have to accept.

1982: Part of the trouble, probably most of it, was the going social definition of what constituted being a "mess." Homosexuality was sign enough, as the current consensus saw it, but to want to sleep with more than one man during a lifetime was considered the equivalent of being unable to "love."

New Haven. November 26:
Pick-up bars don't allow for any other form of contact. Sex is the basis of meeting, and sex is the first, rather than the final expression of the relationship. I tell myself how meaningless this anonymous cycle of body and body is, but I continue to repeat it; partly, no doubt, because of the necessity to keep proving myself, but also because the means of forming a healthier, more complete relationship are slight.

1982: *I was mouthing the standard social values and thera-*
peutic vocabulary of the day: sexual pleasure can only be justified
within the context of a "meaningful" (i.e. "caring," "permanent")
relationship; disconnected lust leads to emptiness and disgust. The
self-recriminations that followed my failing to measure up to stereotypic
norms were more than a strategy of atonement, they were expiation for
having experienced pleasure not officially sanctioned.

November 5, 1957:
To New York. Ended up going to Everard's two nights in a row.

    1982: *Everard's was a gay bathhouse. . . . My usual pattern at the*
baths was to meet one man and go to a room with him. I avoided
orgiastic scenes, especially the steam room. If I was going to be gay, I
was going to be gay in a way that was "seemly," in a way that ap-
proximated how straight people—sensible, adult, healthy, straight
people—behaved. You find one person and stick with him (her).

New Haven. December 1:
Disappointing holiday in Boston. Dick and I got along only
sporadically. My feelings towards him, as always, fluctuated
between deep affection and sudden antagonism. . . . But I still
feel so tied to him—in some deeply neurotic way—that I can't
seriously envision cutting off all contact.

    1982: *Why "neurotic"? Because of the fluctuations in feelings? But*
that's true of all deep attachments. Maybe our arc swung wider and
more often than most, but I automatically ascribed that to personal
deficiencies, never to the self-distrust engendered in us by a culture
insistent that it was wrong ("sinful," "neurotic"—depending on
whether the choice of rhetoric was religious or psychiatric) for two men
to be physical lovers, to care "too much" about each other.

New Haven. December 20:
I present an exterior of manliness, and in much of my actual sex
life, play the dominant role, but there is a parallel and conflicting
desire in me—sometimes very strong—to be passive sexually.
In some complicated way I think all my homosexual activity is
an attempt (among other things) to identify with a masculinity I
never was sure I had.

1982: A "real" man penetrated, dominated, fucked. This kind of sexual stereotyping—still so prevalent—was an integral aspect of the medical model of sexuality with which I identified. It managed all at once to be homophobic and patriarchal: a "real man" was heterosexual and unyieldingly dominant. All sexual acts intrinsically denoted "active" or "passive" attributes. There seemed to be no understanding that the muscular contractions of the anus, say, or the vagina, could by several definitions, be considered "active" agents in producing any cohabitation worthy of the name.

You get the idea.

The official title of the *Salmagundi* issue for Fall 1982–Winter 1983 was "Homosexuality: Sacrilege, Vision, Politics." A title of such obvious pretension was at the same time linguistically puzzling. Who was committing "sacrilege"? Or was the term possibly meant to be taken sardonically? Not likely. As for "vision," surely the plural form would have more accurately described the varied points of view expressed in the volume. (Or might that have been too suggestive of "hallucinations"?) In regard to "politics," of the eight contributors to that section, only one was known to be gay, and her article was devoted to the Beat generation. None of the other seven paid much attention to what was actually going on in the gay political movement in 1982; there wasn't a word in either the journal's title or its contents about the movement's strategies and goals, past or present, nor about the AIDS plague that was inexorably advancing.

The presumptively heterosexual essayists—more than half the total number of contributors—relied on arguments that can best be characterized as sophisticated homophobia (though they would deny the charge). The issue's three major pieces were by Herbert Blau, a theater director and critic; Jean Bethke Elshtain, the political theorist; and Elizabeth Moberly, author of *Psychogenesis: The Early Development of Gender Identity* and *Homosexuality: A New Christian Ethic.* Blau's long essay, "Disseminating Sodom," was so drenched in postmodern posturing as to be nearly impenetrable. When "confronted with the homosexual discourse," he patronizingly announced at the top, he had to conclude, "I understand homosexuals far better than they understand me." One example of his "understanding" will suffice: "Anyone who approaches not only male buggery but the even more lurid aspects of the new experimental sex may as well, without false tolerance, stake out his aversions and limits." And Blau proceeded to do so at inordinate, unctuous length, all but figuratively holding his nose. "What is most disturbing about the increasingly licensed excesses of homosexual behavior," he announced with unearned authority, "is that it is being consciously enunciated as an ideological critique. . . . Sodomy has become a paradigm of sexual innovation . . . demanding more and more territory for their imperative desires." Translation: "Possibly this far—but absolutely no further."

In contrast to Blau's haughty opacity, Elizabeth Moberly adopted a tone of sweet reasonableness. Her underlying assumption is still popular today: "we must do justice to the traditional evidence of pathology" in homosexuality. But her argument had an unusual twist: the aim of homosexual behavior, in her view, was to repair the traumatic lack of attachment to the parent of the same gender during childhood. Male homosexuality represented a *legitimate* attempt "to fulfill needs that properly belong to the pre-adult developmental process." Homosexuality, in other words, was not an abnormal sexual drive but a normal developmental one—"the persistence into adult years of certain pre-adult developmental needs" that haven't been met. It followed, in her cosmology, that heterosexuality retained its primacy as *the* goal of the developmental process.

From that underlying assumption, a host of questions arose that Moberly carefully avoided: How many times must homosexuals have same-gender sex before successfully repairing their damaged childhood and earning their credentials as functioning heterosexuals? Does it matter whether or not we *enjoy* same-gender sex—does pleasure accelerate or impede the process of winning our heterosexual stripes? Couldn't that goal be less messily achieved through same-gender *friendship*, or perhaps worked out psychotherapeutically, thereby avoiding the distasteful experience of homosexuality altogether? In Moberly's moral universe, what accounts for bisexuality? Is it a case of having achieved "some" but not "enough" attachment to the same-gender parent?

Though Moberly fails to address such quandaries, on one matter she is concrete and confident: "It is mistaken to assume that the divine purpose for homosexuals is that they should remain as they are." Ah! There's the clincher! *God* is against homosexuality. We are in the realm—the vacuum—of faith, against which rationality is a weak instrument. Moberly's bottom line is that we can justify same-gender sexuality *up to a* certain *reparative point* (never defined), but if it continues beyond that, we are disobeying the divine plan for the universe. At which point, presumably, Satan takes over and scoops up the lot of us for a nasty descent.

Salmagundi's other "major contribution" to "consolidating and clarifying" the recent debate about homosexuality—Boyers's original claim to me for the volume—was Jean Bethke Elshtain's article "Homosexual Politics: The Paradox of Gay Liberation." Elshtain was the best-known of the heterosexual contributors; author of some twenty books and the recipient of nine honorary degrees, she was a George W. Bush appointee to the Council of the National Endowment for the Humanities.

The central premise of Elshtain's article is that homosexuality represents an assault on heterosexual marriage and the family; as such it poses a dangerous threat to "civil political morality." ("Would that it was so!" was my initial reaction. The main thrust of the gay movement in the years since her article appeared has been in exactly the opposite direction from the one she predicted: it has adopted, not challenged, the mainstream institutions of marriage and the family. The barbarian horde has turned into pliable in-laws.)

Elshtain explicitly defends those homosexuals who merely seek protection from harassment and discrimination—who operate, that is, within the framework of a traditional civil rights agenda. But for the "other kind," for those radical homosexuals who make claims that go beyond the civil rights agenda, who challenge the traditional verities of marriage and monogamy, Elshtain has nothing but contempt. She labels such gay radicals "maximal liberationists" and angrily rejects their attack on heteronormativity in the name of "celebrating a kind of abstract, rarified Eros."

It is a celebration, Elshtain insists, that ignores the necessity of erotic "constraints" and "prohibitions"—though she never tells us where she'd draw the line. Does she want to "prohibit" oral sex? Anal sex? s/m? Is devoted adherence to monogamy a necessary plank in her platform? In her central concern for the family, would she sternly disavow premarital sex, or divorce, or remarriage? She calls for "a politics of limits which creates and respects a zone of privacy, where what goes on between people is nobody's business but their own or that of those who love them." Does that make wife-beating *in private* okay? And kissing in public *not* okay? Oh, and at what age does an individual's zone of privacy need to be respected? Do teenagers qualify—and if so, can those two doting heterosexually paired parents so central to Elshtain's moral order be successfully barred from questioning them?

Elshtain tries to dismiss gay "maximalists" with the argument that the "heterosexist 'dictatorship'" (of marriage and monogamy) they deplore must in fact be "a terribly inept system if it creates so many who are implacably set against it." But it *hasn't* created "so many." Even in 1982, at the time she was writing, the gay movement's initial, short-lived radical challenge to "things as they are" had already been shunted aside by gay "moderates" hell-bent on embracing centrist values and winning acceptance from the traditional American mainstream. Prosperous white males in the early seventies eschewed the countercultural gay movement that had erupted in the immediate aftermath of the Stonewall riots as utterly alien to their personal style and goals. Then, starting gradually in the early seventies, those same gay assimilationists began to take over the movement's national organizations and remake them in their own "moderate" image.

Bland in deportment, narrow in social vision, the movement on the eve of the AIDS crisis was busily pledging allegiance to The American Way. It downgraded all talk of our "differentness," discarded any concern for the plight of the underprivileged (straight and gay), and energetically lobbied for the right to participate fully in a system that increasingly concentrated power and wealth in the hands of a few. Now and then, under extreme provocation—the Anita Bryant "Save Our Children" campaign or the California Briggs amendment to bar openly gay teachers—large numbers of angry protestors would take to the streets. (Yet even those were, at base, protestations of our ordinariness.) Those of us who—naïvely, perhaps—had believed the gay movement had the potential to become an instrument of transformational social change were shocked at the swiftness and ease with which it underwent a major face-lift and became a mere supplicant for equal "citizenship."

The AIDS crisis *would* reintroduce confrontational tactics, as well as demands for substantive change in standard health care procedures and the structure of medical research, but in the end ACT-UP's imaginative lobbying only peripherally challenged existing social arrangements. The axis of privilege did not shift; the economic order did not reconstitute. Following the advent of protease inhibitors in 1996 and the shift in the focus of AIDS activism to a global dimension, the national gay movement featured, to the exclusion of almost all else, the assimilationist agenda of gay marriage and gays serving openly in the military. The gay "maximalists" Elshtain had so feared either retreated to privatism or got politically involved in marginal new organizations like New York City's Queers for Economic Justice, which devoted its limited resources to organizing gay people forced to live in homeless shelters—and which had to close its doors in 2014 because it could no longer raise even the tiny sums that constituted its pathetically small budget.

WHAT MORAL DO I draw, all these years later, from this recounting of *Salmagundi*'s attempted, and pathetic, intervention in the debate on homosexuality? As a major outlet for sophisticated liberal commentary, *Salmagundi* in the early eighties was, along with a few other prestigious journals like *Partisan Review* and the *Yale Review*, serving—though they would furiously deny the characterization—essentially as cultural police. This was certainly true in regard to homosexuality—and to the radical gay fringe in particular. "Well-meaning" liberals either didn't get it or got it and hated it—as they still do. They can't be trusted as allies in any effort to understand, let alone encourage, a transformational agenda regarding matters relating to gender and sexuality—and yes, race and class. Liberals often see themselves as our allies and tend to adore their own sense of magnanimity. But their key allegiance is—as with Elshtain—to mainstream American values and institutions. The moral? Should your typical heterosexual liberal extend his or her hand, keep one eye on the hand—and the other on the holster.

Let Robert Boyers himself draw the moral. Though he claimed in 1982 that he'd decided to devote a whole issue of *Salmagundi* "to help us all better to understand where the state of the inquiry [on homosexuality] now stood," he'd in fact made up his mind two years earlier. In a 1980 piece for the *Times Literary Supplement* he'd written that gay men who frequented the steam baths "are likely to be disturbed, yes, disturbed and crippled people enacting fantasies of release or liberation that can at best relieve momentarily the fear or impotence they experience when they confront real people capable of making complex emotional demands." Need anything more be said?

Paul Robeson Jr.

Throughout the first three years of my work on Robeson's biography, I stayed in pretty close contact with Paul Jr. He played a central role in setting up and even participating in some of the interviews I did; as well, I sometimes turned to him to decipher and fill in the background for arcane references in the family archives or incomplete hints of the sectarian intrigues, say, of the CPUSA. The more I got to know Paul, the better I appreciated his steel-trap mind, his ability to retain information and to recall in minute detail the most convoluted exchanges and events.

Yet a certain amount of friction and misunderstanding between us was there from the beginning, and surely inevitable: sons and scholars do not share the same agenda. As sons go, Paul was far more deeply invested than most, and it became increasingly difficult to deal with his unwavering insistence that *his* version of events was the only plausible one. Especially since he would frequently contradict on Tuesday his own prior interpretation on Monday—with equal vehemence on both occasions—making it difficult, sometimes impossible, for me to ascertain the "truth" of his testimony (for example, the exact nature of his own relationship to the Communist Party USA and the Soviet Union).

There were other problems. His repetitive monologues were often interminable, his moods unpredictable, and his periodic outbursts of abusive belligerence cumulatively intolerable. I couldn't help but wonder if he suffered from the same bipolar affliction his father had; denying the diagnosis for his father, Paul was unlikely to confirm it for himself. One occasion of his abusiveness stands out: in the car on the way back from visiting Doxey Wilkerson, a leading black figure in the CPUSA, Paul furiously berated me for "playing Uriah Heep" and for not having done sufficient homework on the intricacies of the Party's internal politics. On both counts he had a point. Though temperamentally I'm more forceful and proactive than laid back, my interview style can be, by design, bland and tactful, sometimes veering unappealingly off into parodic humility.

As someone who's always been a compulsively hard worker, however, Paul's accusation of a lack of homework, should have been tempered, I felt, by some understanding that in the early stages of my research I couldn't possibly master all at once the many worlds in which his father moved. It would have been impossible for anyone to become an instant expert on everything from the history of football to the sorrow songs and to 1930s filmography, and in the first few years especially I did sometimes miss, for lack of sufficient information, an opportunity to probe an interview subject more deeply. It was, I believe, an inevitable, and transient, shortcoming.

Real as my initial inadequacies were, I felt confident they didn't warrant Paul's outburst on our drive back from the Wilkerson interview. Working himself into a fine frenzy and shaking with anger, Paul actually threatened me, telling me in effect that if I didn't watch my step he had a cousin who from a hundred yards (or something like that) could put a bullet through a man's head. Stunned at the ill-disguised threat and the ferocity with which he delivered it, I demanded that he pull over to the side of the road and stop the car. Taking a deep breath, I said something like, "That's it, Paul. This time you've gone *way* over the line. As far as I'm concerned, you can have your goddamned biography back! I quit!" That wasn't, it became apparent, what Paul in fact wanted, and he quickly shifted to a more conciliatory tone. Once back in the city we talked for hours that night and managed, as it were, to stanch the bleeding.

But the incident did make it crystal clear to me that if I was ever going to finish the biography, I had to steer clear of Paul's accusations and tantrums. From then on I held him at arm's length and gave my agent the burden of letting him periodically rage around her office, his indignation at full tilt as he denounced me for this or that infraction, until she could succeed in reassuring him about my intentions and quiet him down. In one of her calming letters to him—she always sent me copies—she pointed out that the content of the book was, by contract, "the author's province," that although I had appreciated his help in the early stages of my work, he now (in Frances's words) had to "stop trying to steer Marty in directions compatible with your conception of your father and events which transpired in his life."

I give Paul credit for *trying* to back off, but his floating anxiety was at such an intense, consistently high level that I was more than a little unnerved when a typed, unsigned postcard appeared in the mail in the spring of 1985 warning me, "P now says that he intends to 'liquidate' you. As a dear friend of Eslanda [Robeson's wife], I hope and pray that in his madness he does not do anything terrible and disgrace the memory of his parents." I took a deep breath and told myself that the anonymous writer was indulging some wild private fantasy and that Paul's fits of anger would never lead him to do something *that* extreme.

When Paul wasn't threatening or belittling me, I was able to feel considerable sympathy for the difficult hand life had dealt him. He'd suffered profoundly, I felt, from being the only child of two people ill-suited to the job of parenting. His father had never been cut out for domesticity—and had never pretended otherwise—nor had he wanted children. Essie's focus was on being Paul Sr.'s wife, not on being Paul Jr.'s mother. The emotional absence of both parents couldn't help but have a damaging effect on him. His "inconvenient" childhood led to his being sent to live for two years in the Soviet Union, chaperoned by his strict, unloving grandmother; it was "for his own good," he was told, "to spare you from being permanently damaged by pernicious American racism." A good reason, certainly, yet inseparable from his parents' wish to skirt any impediment to their roaming the world unburdened.

Failing to get the attention he craved, and which should be every child's birthright, Paul became a deeply unhappy, raging storm of a man, unable, apparently, to face and express his justifiable resentment at having been "cast off." He psychologically coped with his resentment of his father by converting anger into adoration, making himself into a kind of amanuensis, a tormented, unfulfilled keeper of the flame (and dumping the anger on his mother, who he tried to convince me at various points put speed in his father's heart medication and was a double agent for the CIA and the KGB). Paul may never have acknowledged any of this consciously, but as I saw it, the lifelong effect on him of loveless neglect was profound and irremediable. Naturally gifted, sensitive and smart, he never found a satisfying outlet for his own considerable gifts. His thwarted ambition, his anguished yearning to *matter*, made for a seething, bristly, deeply scarred man.

As I ultimately came to understand it, Paul's actual—as opposed to his professed—feelings about his father ranged far more widely than the unalloyed adoration he demonstrated publicly. His father's closest friends, including Helen Rosen, Freda Diamond, and Revels Cayton, all agreed with my view that Paul harbored an intolerable, unexamined truth: his father had been essentially indifferent to him as a child, and as an adult hadn't much use for him. Paul compensated by clamorously claiming—over and over—that he, and only he, had his father's full confidence, knew his innermost secrets, served as his most trusted lieutenant. I never directly challenged any of that in the published biography; it would have been needlessly hurtful, inhumane—though the simple fact that he isn't present during many of the critical turning points in his father's life indirectly makes the point. He isn't, in the book, at the center of his father's life nor portrayed as his most trusted confidant—which is how Paul had long presented himself publicly. Not surprisingly he hated and denounced the book, and it would be then—in the late eighties—that he and I would have our most bruising struggles.

Depression

As the number of AIDS cases doubled, and then doubled again, cause and cure alike elusive, terror continued to mount among gay men; for a time controversy over closing the orgiastic gay bathhouses became *the* lightning-rod issue. In San Francisco there was a rash of public demonstrations against bathhouse closures; one protester carried a sign that read "TODAY THE TUBS, TOMORROW YOUR BEDROOM." In New York, Mike Callen, who'd done so much to alert the community to the need for practicing "safe sex," took it upon himself to do a one-man tour of the bathhouse scene. Callen loved sex, had it often, and initially opposed bathhouse closings. But he'd done so on the assumption that their owners were cooperating in putting up safe-sex posters advising condom use and the avoidance of any exchange of body fluids, thus helping to make the baths a safer site for recreational sex than, say, the Central Park Ramble or the West Side piers.

Callen considered lots and lots of sex—healthy abandon—a necessary antidote to the strictures of a puritanical society; to him, sexual pleasure was at the heart of the gay revolution and an essential corrective to mainstream prudery. But what Callen found on his tour of the bathhouses deeply troubled him. Their bulletin boards posted notices of every kind *except* for the safe-sex posters that GMHC and other groups had donated free of charge. Callen felt torn. He was sensitive to the civil liberties issues at stake—to the danger of allowing city and state officials to dictate what was or wasn't permissible erotic behavior and the "acceptable" places for indulging it. He also recognized, without overstating, the democratizing aspects of the gay bathhouse scene, where wealthy white businessmen gratefully serviced Puerto Rican delivery boys.

Yet his tour of the bathhouses convinced him that their patrons were ill-informed about safe-sex practices and the owners unwilling to spread information they feared might frighten off potential customers. As a prudential—and he hoped strictly temporary—measure, Callen reluctantly shifted sides in the bathhouse debate and joined the ranks of those advocating closure; he did so fully aware that closing down the bathhouses was unlikely to have much effect on the escalating crisis, since alternative sites for unregulated casual sex remained available. In any case Mayor Koch announced in 1985, "You can't sell death in this city and get away with it," and he issued an order to close the gay bathhouses (though not straight sex clubs like Plato's Retreat). At the end of 1985 only four out of fifteen were still hanging on.

By then twenty thousand cases of AIDS had been reported in the United States, and the scientific community had coalesced around the view that the HIV virus was the culprit. President Reagan had still not uttered a single word about the epidemic, let alone sanctioned a vigorous campaign against it—though he had no trouble appropriating vast sums to support brutal dictatorships in El Salvador and Nicaragua. On the other hand, there was no absence of voices raised to denounce homosexual degenerates who'd brought down God's wrath on themselves. Congressman William Dannemeyer introduced a resolution on the floor of the House to set up a series of concentration camps similar to those inflicted on Japanese Americans during World War II. Others, like the well-known psychologist Helen Singer Kaplan, insisted that gay men had the *obligation* to submit to the new ELISA blood test, the implication being that those who tested positive would be held in quarantine to protect the rest of the population (that is, the people who *mattered*) from possible contamination. According to one reliable poll, 57 percent of the general population thought gay and lesbian relations should be declared illegal.

For liberationists like Callen, the safe-sex "condom code" was far preferable to either monogamy or celibacy. I myself wasn't so sure, even though, as someone who rarely got fucked or swallowed cum, I was in a comparatively low risk group. Since I wasn't in a committed relationship at the time, monogamy was a nonissue. But for a considerable period—out of a mixture of dread and total immersion in the Robeson book—I chose celibacy. Though I hadn't kept a diary for some two years, I now went back to occasional entries, writing at one point, "Being celibate isn't proving a problem. The only surprise—& that mild—is how little I miss it. Plus how foreign sex feels when it briefly hovers into view.

It suggests that during baby-making years the need for sex feels urgent. Subsequently it becomes more a knack than a drive, a socially acquired set of habits; and like all learning, can be forgotten if not persistently repeated."

I soon grew less blasé about celibacy, and angrier at the heterosexual world's smug admonition to accept uncomplainingly the "modified" forms of sex still available to us; I wondered how well straight men would do with the rigorous self-policing necessary for strict adherence to the "condom code." "I accept the current wisdom that sexual contact is inherently risky," I wrote in my diary,

> but I won't accept the conventional solution. Better no sex at all than a stricken, truncated version. . . . "Modified" sex is like telling a wine fancier how to appreciate—nay, to love—the beneficence of a single sip. I'd prefer none at all. . . . Is this petulant extremism, that old familiar "all or nothing"? I think not. It feels closer to an ability to tolerate deprivation (much like the way I choose these days not to play with cocaine *at all* rather than falling for the illusion that a safe middle way exists). Hell, it's only sex.

Today that reads like pouty defiance. But in fact it was denial. I currently lacked any pressing *interest* in sex, which was itself the product of renewed physical symptoms that of late I'd been busily ignoring—no, not symptoms we'd all learned to recognize as harbingers of AIDS but rather the blahs that signify depression. My energy level had gone way down. I was constantly tired, yet at night often unable to sleep, even with medication. My appetite fell off, and I began to lose weight. I even had occasional chest pain, uneasily aware that it might be angina but strangely unwilling to call my cardiologist—though ordinarily I wasn't one to tough it out. Setting up an appointment felt like *immense* trouble; I was too listless to exert that much energy in chasing what I told myself were phantom symptoms.

I had no ready explanation for the pronounced shift in mood. The body's mysterious chemistry? The loneliness of not having a partner? Who knew? I finally decided that what I needed, simply, was a change of scene. I'd been working too hard on the Robeson book, I told myself, without a break. I should get away—away from the intensity of doing interviews and from the long, lonely hours locked in some archive doing research. Ordinarily I shunned taking time out or going on vacation.

I had never understood why friends thought it necessary for me to give up my engrossing routines in order to stare at a stand of interchangeable pine trees or sleep on a too-soft mattress in some drably interchangeable hotel room. Even as far back as the sixties, when I stayed with Leo on Fire Island or, later, when I rented a house with Dick in Quoque—when, in other words, I had dear friends close at hand for comfort—I'd had to flee back to Manhattan periodically to maintain sanity. Greece or Italy, yes, but I'd been there, done that. Besides, I'd always hated flying. (Who's in control? Who's in control?) I'd rather work than play, since I (usually) considered them one and the same. Relaxation was all but guaranteed to make me more, not less anxious, counting the days when I could "legitimately" return to my overbooked, overwrought life in New York. Idling just wasn't my thing.

Yet hoping to abort a deepening depression, I put aside my hard-earned wisdom about *not* needing vacations and called up my friend Penny, who'd settled in Maine with her son and boyfriend, and asked her to look for a cottage I could rent for a few weeks, nothing fancy, and invited her to take some time off and join me. Penny was enthusiastic and within days called back to say she'd rented a comfortable cabin in the woods, located on a stream. (A *stream*? The *woods*? I thought sure I'd said "near the ocean." Oh well, it would be good to spend time with Penny again; we'd been very close when she lived in New York and it had been a while since I'd seen her for more than a few hours.) My fantasies leaped expectantly ahead to idyllic days canoeing near some mythic waterfall, aglow with the wonder of nature's splendor—and conveniently forgot that when plopped into nature in the past I'd felt at best bored, at worst mysteriously threatened.

Since it was the height of the summer season Penny had to rent the cottage for a full month. I knew I'd never last that long—especially after I actually saw the wretched little cabin. When I'd suggested "not fancy" I had New York standards in mind; by *Maine's* standards, the place was a dump. "Now, Marty," I lectured myself. "Don't start! You don't have to sit it out for thirty days. You can go back and forth to New York." This was my version of optimism.

The first few days went better than I'd feared. I'd been to Maine many times, and in a rented car Penny and I happily barreled down the familiar, long-fingered peninsulas, the roads that ran on and on, surrounded by dense clumps of impenetrable trees—until suddenly the road opened up into a gorgeous still life, a harbor filled with fishing boats and yachts, the houses snugly fit, radiating warmth (my runaway favorite: Northeast Harbor in Acadia).

I came down to earth with a considerable thud when Penny told me after the first weekend that she couldn't stay away any longer from her home and her nursing job in Canaan but would "soon" return for occasional day trips. My understanding had been that we'd *both* return to our respective homes after a week and would thereafter rendezvous for a few days here and there back at the cabin. Later, when I tried to iron out our disparate expectations, and my resentment at what I felt was her abrupt change in plans, she told me she'd been so "shocked" at first seeing me in "such bad shape" that she "had to get away," my "debilitated state" frightened her, filled her with apprehension. Uh-oh, I thought, here we go again, the Dick Poirier syndrome: "If I can't fix it, I can't hang around." I hadn't bought the excuse when Dick employed it after my heart attack, and I couldn't get myself to buy it from Penny. (Doesn't "adulthood" mean that the occasion *sometimes* calls for putting someone other than yourself first? "Get it together: your 'dear friend' is in far more pain than you are and needs you.") Not that I said anything at the time. I did want her to come back.

So there I was, alone in a cabin in Kehail Point, Maine. The "alone" part is for me almost always fine—that is, in *New York*, surrounded by familiar comforts and routines of work, but not in a cabin in the woods. I was the provincial urbanite personified, and one who, in the bargain, happened to be teetering on depression. Out came the diary. I scratched away in it like never before:

> *July 4, 1984:* I've watched my third tide come in, washed my
> underwear, clicked a roll of film from the rocks and killed a yellow
> jacket. Now what? . . . I listen to the sound of water against
> the rocks, awaiting the soothing regularity anciently described.
> Nature (as all else here) sounds unpredictably *ir*regular. Doesn't
> soothe, disquiets: The unadvertised randomness unnerving.
> *4:00 p.m.* Squeezed a pimple, marveled at wind through
> pines, jerked off (Ray staring at my crotch on Charles Street roof,
> groans, "I can't do without it much longer"), read *People* magazine,
> registered awe at sudden shifts of light on water, considered
> growing a beard, listened to live radio from Augusta ("Breakdancing!

TONIGHT!!"), scooped daringly away at Breyers' burnt almond, caressed mosquito bites, resolved on a morning hike to the Point, yawned at ennobling life close to nature, danced a knee-locked Las Vegas solo in the kitchen to the sounds of ABSENT Penny's ear-splat Dolby system, stayed appropriately (a.k.a. the firs) motionless at sunset (though the rocks, disconcertingly, begin to *palpitate!*). . . . My non-resting place, as is more obvious with each passing second, is destined to be forever Nueva York. . . . Audre Lorde, *The Cancer Journals*: "I must be content to see how really little I can do and still do it with an open heart. . . . I want the old me, bad as before."

July 5. 5:00 p.m. Spirits sinking. Sitting alone in the cottage, locked in by fog so thick I can barely see the water below, the damp so heavy the soles of my bare feet stick to the linoleum as I lumber across the kitchen floor. . . . Radio broadcast: "Come enjoy the York Musical Theater of Maine's production of *Cabaret*, located in the Dexter Shoe building next to the Dairy Queen." . . . "Newscasts," so called, have yet to make reference, within my (fairly frequent) earshot, of wars in Iran & Lebanon, the election in Israel, the coal strike in England. . . . The news centers instead on arts & crafts fairs, the tides, ads for pickup trucks, night crawlers and Smuckers' wondrous grape jelly, mounting drama in the Maine baseball league battle, button-popping reports about museum openings devoted to the story of logging and steamboat operations in the Moosehead region. A different reality. Not better or worse (I'm supposed to add) than Manhattan's. But not mine, so for me worse. Beyond that, can't something more be ventured about, say, the dangers of insularity, of regional pride translating into smugness? . . . My hateful (dehumanizing) intolerance of the ordinary.

Penny returned for two days. I buried my grievances and a trip to the beach at Popham, plus dining on the deck of a good restaurant in Frenchman's Bay—a perfect sunset, complete with red-sailed schooner in the foreground, the crew swabbing down the deck right under our noses (Lao Tzu: "Gravity is the root of grace")—all gave my spirits a boost. What kept them afloat for a few more days after Penny left was a brief visit from my friend Michael Kimmel; he and I were in a men's group together in the city, and we got some transient pleasure out of dishing a third member, Roger Enlow, the starchy, ill-tempered director of the Office of Gay and Lesbian Health Concerns.

After Michael left, I raced back to the comfort of diary-keeping:

> *July 10–11:* Beyond irony today. Impacted stool causing too much discomfort to head up the coast towards Belfast and Bar Harbor, as planned. Bag packed, sun shining, but moored here alone. Too chilly even to read on the deck. . . . The fight's gone out of me. . . . Heading back for Manhattan. . . . Sum of insights gained:
>
> > I do enjoy some people around some of the time.
> > Nature isn't serene.
> > Manhattan remains home.
> > My political rage can't be reduced to personal ills: the country *is* nearing terminal atrophy. It's grumpy (at "pests": gays, blacks, feminists—at "Anti-Americans"), uninformed, co-equally scared and smug. Manhattan, too, but much less so than Maine. Manhattan has more of what I value: people-mix, differentness, surprise, energy; elements worthy of retreating from.
> > Such surprises as surfaced were not so much discoveries as re-discoveries: the fun of driving a car (for an hour); the turbulent peacefulness of a proper beach (Popham)—give me water over trees; the real pacifying force of TV. . . .
> > Simplification *is* the right direction, less of everything. I've reaffirmed that I can pretty much do anything (excepting again pushing the coke/sex boundaries), but there isn't much I want to do.
> > Greeted in Manhattan by the *chutzpah* line of the year: Bruce Jenner has announced that he "has a lot of respect for life." One solar system acknowledges another.

EVEN AFTER I'D returned to the safety of Manhattan, the renewed diary habit stayed with me. Had it not, I would never have remembered, some thirty years later, that I broke my twin resolutions regarding celibacy and coke much sooner than I cared to remember. My return from Maine coincided almost to the day with the arrival of David, my California coke contact, in Manhattan for a three-week stay.

I had a ready-made excuse at hand for giving his latest batch of "absolutely superb stuff" a try: the looming deadline of September 31 (1984) for a collection (it would appear the following year with the title *About Time: Exploring the Gay Past*) that I'd agreed to put together combining the documentary material I'd been publishing in the *Native* with a selection of essays and reviews I'd written between 1972 and 1984.

I've always liked working on two or three projects at the same time; when one felt stale or at an impasse, I could always turn to the other—heaven forbid I should ever not be working on *some* project. In fact I hadn't at any point grown bored with the Robeson biography nor felt the need to put it aside. Rather it was a case of wanting to focus all my energy on finishing the research for it by clearing the decks—gathering up my recent shorter pieces into a book, and thereby putting a period to writing incidental articles until after I'd completed the biography.

Readying the material for publication felt more like a chore than a pleasure. And as a chore it naturally followed—nay, mandated and justified—an assist. And what better than an inert powder rather than a living editorial assistant. I'd twice experimented with assistants but with poor results; one of the two chose to see himself as an already anointed (though unpublished) genius above mere grunt work, and the other—a Southerner, naturally—had been utterly disdainful of the "uncivilized" pace I set him, and quit.

My spirits had taken an upswing once I got back to Manhattan, but I hadn't recaptured any real vitality. Hauling my laundry to the corner felt like a major chore. A shiatsu massage yielded a diagnosis of "extreme fatigue." Sheer tenacity was driving the engine, with the motor threatening to stall at any time. Or so I told myself. I knew perfectly well that when it came to coke I became remarkably inventive in producing claims of necessity. I even admitted as much in my diary: "I'm working up a super rationale for another 'experiment' (what's left to learn?) with coke. Yes, I was able to write a significant number of books before discovering the white powder's seductive powers, but I was young, healthy, energetic. Besides, I didn't write very well. Answers: (1) nor do you on coke, except briefly (2) you're still young *enough* to proceed (3) you'll die unless (1) and (2) convince." I can't pretend, in other words, that I wasn't fully aware that my so-called justifications for turning again to coke weren't utter hogwash. But I went right ahead anyway. It's called an "addictive personality."

During the first two weeks of David's stay in New York, I managed to resist his twin blandishments of coke and the hustler bar Rounds. I simply felt too debilitated—even as I continued to puzzle over the cause. Had the trip to Maine been *that* traumatic? I didn't think so. Was I having a return bout of hepatitis? I doubted it—my eyes weren't yellow and my stools were still brown. (Staring at them, I came up with a new definition of self-absorption: "being unable to decide whether the color of one's stools is most accurately described as tan or beige.") Was the process of readying my collected short pieces for publication carrying me back to an earlier time, when I was full of zest and confidence— and was the inevitable comparison with my current state underscoring my incapacity and loneliness? Yes, maybe. But trying to figure out a logical explanation and sequence for my current fragility was like trying to lasso water—a fool's game (not that I gave it up, trained as I was in the power of reason).

In mid-August the day came when I felt somewhat better and—as if the tooth fairy was in charge of my destiny—I instantly capitulated to David's persistent offers. Down to my apartment came Marc, a stellar recruit from David's nightly plundering missions to Rounds. David hadn't exaggerated: Marc was both handsome and pleasant. Too pleasant: it got in the way of my ability to conjure up a stereotypic— workable—fantasy from the old file cabinet (e.g., card #63: one-sided servicing of macho-indifferent-stud). Marc proved too real to fit that or any other preprogrammed mind-set; fatally, I *liked* him. And he was smart: he described David as "a terrorist who enjoys swallowing piss." Who could get a hard-on after *that*?

The downward slide had begun. The next night I said yes when David suggested he drop by with a sample from his latest shipment. The initial rush *was* euphoric, yet not (as in the past) urgently seductive. I didn't push greedily on, didn't—as so often before—plunge headlong into a frenzy of passion or work. So perhaps—I wrote hopefully in my diary—"the last five months of tedium and discouragement will turn out to mark some genuine turning point."

No. Within days—and *not* under the influence of coke—I was feeling far gloomier. I decided, despite all my negative experiences with psychotherapy and skepticism about its transformational power, to look for help from Bill Trevor, my most recent therapist. Maybe, I thought, he can find some sort of explanation for my spiraling decline.

That would take time, he told me. In the interim he suggested some concrete steps to keep my head above water. They seemed wondrously simplistic:

1. Darvon for pain (from ongoing impaction of stools)
2. Exercise to release endorphins
3. Writing a play for a change of pace

Yes, "simplistic." Two days on Darvon made me spacey and nauseous but did nothing for the pain. Exercise required more effort than I was able to sustain. And the notion of writing a play seemed as remote as hopping aboard a space flight to Mars. Yet after seeing Bill I did, for a brief time anyway, feel a little better, if no less lethargic. Maybe it was just seeing him again—seeing someone who I felt did care about me, did truly want to help me get my depression and anxiety under control (though I continued to doubt that therapy had the power to do so).

One sure sign of improved spirits was that the political world came somewhat back into focus. I'd long ago learned, when rethinking the antislavery movement back in the early sixties, that disabling neurosis—of which the abolitionists, along with most radical reformers in our history, have long been accused—makes one a most *unlikely* candidate for political involvement. The guy (me) who at 3:30 one morning scrawled "Nausea, sweats, felt dizzy and sick when I got out of bed" isn't likely to stay out of bed long enough to read the daily *Times* and angrily phone his congressman. A certain degree of contentment about who one is, a sense of feeling safe, seems to me an essential prerequisite for any sustained involvement with the plight of others. Most of my life I've felt secure enough to be aware that lots of other people were in pain and had enough energy to try to do something about it. But not during this lousy five-year stretch from 1979 to 1984, during which, for much of the time, I was too consumed with my own anguish—what I've rightly learned to call "first world problems"—to care much about anybody else's.

But for a few weeks in the fall of 1984 my head stayed above water, and when a Californian, prominent in the gay movement there, asked if he could come by to discuss current alternatives on the "gay agenda," I eagerly agreed. As it turned out, I didn't take to him personally, nor did he and I get very far in discussing political prospects. Yet he did evoke in me some retrospective disgust at how I'd moved myself to the sidelines as middle-of-the-road white men had taken over the national gay movement; disgust too at my inability to follow through with the GMHC training I'd started to become a "buddy" to someone afflicted with AIDS. I had to remind myself that I *had* been politically active for the better part of the seventies and it wasn't my fault that currently my private demons had become disabling. I also needed to remember that (as I wrote in my diary) "hell is never individually induced nor uniquely experienced. It is Martin frightened; it is Martin, gay man in America." But self-flagellation was part of my DNA, and to that diary entry I added this: "How boring ultimately, how stupidly self-absorbed, with so much work in the world to be done, with such endemic horror."

Maybe, I thought, maybe, maybe the horrors of the summer were at last receding and a new, more positive cycle emerging that would allow me (as I put it in the diary) "to shift from selfish ego-centrism back to active re-engagement with political issues." My long-standing conviction was that *the* marker of restored vitality was a renewed desire and capacity for sex. Did I pass that test? Did I have the goods? I thought so. Where should I go, or who should I call, to find out? The answer was predestined. I automatically ruled out the gay bar circuit, where youthful gym-buffed clones eagerly cruised each other. No, the most convenient and promising venue was surely my old stomping ground, Rounds, where a man in his mid-fifties with discretionary income was considered—by half the bar—the ideal patron.

And thus it was that I found myself—it really did feel like I lacked volition—back in the forever-renounced Rounds, where in quick succession I downed *five* drinks (two was my usual maximum), chatted up a few old numbers, and eventually went off (as I later wrote in my diary) "with an unlusted-after trick, and snorted the despised cocaine until 7:00 a.m." I awoke from a dream (my diary tells me) "of furious verbal onslaught against me and all homosexuals, in a military court; recess—and looming threat of physical violence in the corridors. I feel vulnerable and scared, but determined to resist. . . . Preparing by night for pending disaster. . . . Feeling like carrion on a cliff."

Somewhat to my surprise, perhaps disappointment even, my tentative recovery survived, the reanimated carrion flew off—briefly, at least. A few nights later I was actually at the theater seeing David Rabe's *Hurlyburly* and sensate enough to play the critic ("promising first act, then descent into self-indulgence"). The downside of such wondrous resilience was the lurking conviction that I could *always* skirt destructive behavior without any lasting consequences. A toxic conviction, ultimately.

And so it went for the next few weeks, a seesaw of sex/drug binges alternating, bizarrely, with several perfectly normal social lunches, interviews with Alice Childress and Indira Gandhi, and consultations with my lawyer that concluded with a decision to bring a lawsuit against the FBI for refusing to release, under my Freedom of Information Act request, their voluminous files on Robeson. (Thus does sanity, the moralist concludes, live side by side with imbecilic folly.) I made only two entries in my diary from mid-October to early November. One was determinedly political, expressing "horror" at the Reagan administration's pro-Contra carnage in Nicaragua.

The other began as a paean of praise to Randy, my "hot new coke contact," in whose apartment—locks running from top to bottom of his iron-plated door—I ingested snort after snort while enduring, in real terror, his dusk-to-dawn addle-pated tirade against phantasmal foes. That diary entry ends with a grim assessment of my attempts to have sex: "Sweats, impotence, utter lack of desire—as in all my 5–6 forays of late. . . . Nothing works anymore."

There was one more set of scribbles, too jumbled to qualify as a diary entry: "Fearful of going under. . . . Terrified. *Unsafe.* . . . Getting by on bluff. . . . Careful calculations of energy expenditure. . . . Mere survival hinges on super-delicate calibrations of fear and strength. . . . Shopping for food too charged an obstacle course, a trip to the corner presaging imminent collapse. . . . Reaganism and AIDS, the social parameters of terror, grandiose reference points for my own state."

Then, for three weeks, the diary goes blank. I can recall almost nothing during those weeks except closing the shades, getting into bed, and telling myself it was time to "check out." I was in and out of consciousness.

ON NOVEMBER 9, 1984, I finally made a new entry in my diary:

> The first day I feel I'm coming back. . . . Being cared for by Doreen Poule (arranged by Aunt Tedda and Barbara), an angelic Guyanese in the U.S. two years. . . . Starting to eat & get out of bed. . . . A

nightmare few weeks, still mangled in confused chronology with no discernible center in a physical/emotional crack-up involving factual bits of black-outs and sedative overdose, as vivid as they're peripheral, along with the muddied clues of enraged, unfair, furiously bitter accusations I hurled at Barbara (especially), Michael [Kimmel], Penny, & Terry [Collins, another longtime friend], and equally uncharacteristic (for the rational Marty) days of bottom-line despondency & wanting to "check out" that I knew (but can't "know" meaningfully now) contain the meaning of this bizarre freak-out. I can see the major outlines, though, and won't try for more now: a determined test to prove myself unloved, to force out all possible candidates; and unworthy of being loved, having never gotten over my grief for having been (I'd somehow decided) "a bastard" to Ma; proving nothing & no-one (certainly not myself) was worth hanging around for. None of that's quite "it." I'm close but still too crumbled to describe inner scenario that's taken place well enough yet. And probably shouldn't have even made this much effort one day into the clearing. Leave it alone for a while. Enough to say for now I had to throw both legs over the cliff to prove love existed & only the luck of a hand grabbing onto a branch has kept me here.

Much, much later I tried to extract more details from the friends who'd come to my rescue, but each one had only a piece of the puzzle, and the pieces never fit together into a coherent whole. Barbara remembers that when she was unable to reach me by phone, she came by to check on me—I'd long since given her a key to my apartment—but when I heard her put the key in the lock, I screamed obscenities at her, demanding that she put the key outside the door and "leave me the fuck in peace."

She did, but she called Terry and Michael, and all three returned to the apartment. Michael says they found me in the darkened bedroom, that I looked emaciated—and "smelled bad." He carried me into the shower and cleaned me off—yes, I had shit in the bed. They guessed that I'd been there "for some time," maybe a week; nobody could be sure. Barbara called my therapist, Bill Trevor, who, she later told me, expressed reluctance to come over but eventually agreed. They huddled about what to do. I remember I got out of bed long enough to say *something* to Bill—but can't remember a word of it. They decided that for the time being—even though Terry recalls some doubt about whether or not I "would make it"—to try keeping me at home, apparently feeling that I "couldn't handle" being hospitalized.

The second night after regaining some kind of coherence was, as I scratched on a piece of paper, "terrible . . . no sleep, & panic over it . . . crying again." (I can see in retrospect that making myself write, *wanting* to write, was a sign that the worst was over, that I wanted to come back.) I don't know where Barbara and Aunt Tedda found Doreen, but she was, I scribbled, "so extraordinary, caring—really so—to a stranger." I didn't feel that "I *deserve* such loving responsiveness—*from anyone.*"

By the third day I was able to talk on the phone with Bill and apparently went on and on about what "a shit" I was, what an ingrate, what a shabby excuse for a human being. Bill finally interrupted the flood of self-denunciation with a zinger: "Your chest-beating is a strategy for not changing, for defusing guilt without really examining it, without finding out whether and to what extent it's justified." I wasn't at all sure what he meant, but I dutifully wrote it down. "You've hit rock-bottom emotional pain," he added, "and continuing to sedate yourself in order to sleep is a strategy for not facing that pain." I understood that much fully, but didn't think this was any time to be facing anything. I told Bill that given the poor physical shape I was in, I couldn't risk total sleeplessness, risk my defensive walls caving in.

"I'm too cowardly for that," I told my friend Michael. Maybe I need to reclaim my political rage, I said—a grandiose notion—maybe that's the way out and back for me, focusing my anger on the "gallivanting indifference" (as I put it, in a weirdly bloated way) "to primal human misery." Michael humored me: "Well, yes, maybe that is the ticket." Having wrenched polite agreement out of him, I promptly reversed fields and told him that I was (as I also wrote on a piece of paper) "washed up, no purpose to go on, no possible political outlets still open to me, no prospects of any kind."

The next day I had back-to-back panic attacks, and terrified of not sleeping, I kept trying to reach Bill. When I did get hold of him he provided no reassurance: "We don't really understand the cause of panic attacks." Great, wonderful, just what I *didn't* need to hear. Despairing, I begged him to let me double the dose of my nighttime sedative Placidyl (a "hypnotic" taken off the market in 1999). He at first refused, said he couldn't continue to sanction my "self-indulgence." I could care less at this point about something as trivial as "self-indulgence"—gimme a break! When I persisted, Bill finally gave in: "Okay, take the second Placidyl." I instantly calmed down. "Am I being a coward—*again*?" I asked Bill. "No, no," he said reassuringly, "it's okay. Don't worry about it." The last thing I remember was scrawling on a piece of paper, "I've done the best I can for tonight."

The Placidyl knocked me out for a few hours, but I awoke with chest pains and a return of my old arrhythmia problem of irregular, skipped beats. I became convinced that the accumulated stress had made another heart attack imminent. Doreen tried to coax me to take some food, just a piece of toast for starters, but I refused. (I later learned that I'd dropped thirty pounds and weighed only 125). Somebody—I have no recall who—insisted on calling my cardiologist, Ted Tyberg. He told them to take me immediately to the emergency room at New York Hospital.

The next few days are a blank. All I know is that I was put in the medical unit of the hospital and for three days underwent a variety of heart and liver tests. After my first EKG, a maverick intern let me know that there'd been a "finding" and they were going to repeat the test. My anxiety level shot back up, but I was soon told they'd decided the finding "wasn't significant" and had canceled the second EKG. Were they *sure*? Was I *really* physically in the clear? "Well, your pulse is 160 over 100, but that's to be expected, given your anxiety."

Finally persuaded that the news *was* good, and with the fog in my head beginning to clear, I expected to be released the next day. My doctors— there was now a posse of them—had other plans. They decided I needed to undergo a slow—three to four weeks—supervised detoxification and were shifting me to the Payne Whitney Psychiatric Clinic. "What?! Isn't that the looney bin?" Back came the calm reply: "The patient population is mixed. You'll find a few seriously ill people in the ward, but most, like you, are suffering from various degrees of depression and anxiety." I wondered what the difference was but decided not to ask. Was it the difference between hopelessness and fear? Don't I have both?

And so it began. A nearly month-long stay in Payne Whitney that was a decided step up from the black despair of the previous few weeks, but in its own right dispiriting enough.

Hospitalization

We were *not* a jolly crew. I was put in a room with two other men who wanted above all to stay in bed and be left alone—windows and shades pulled down, door shut tight, air quality putrid.

Compared to them I was a carnival busker, a gregarious extrovert. I had, in fact, helped talk the second man, who arrived soon after I did, into staying. He was a young Orthodox Jew so terrified that he'd become entirely mute. He kept trying to back out of the room, but the friend who'd brought him held him firmly in his grip. I called out something from my bed—the exact words escape me, but that I spoke at all now seems to me unimaginable; I assured him that he'd be fine here and would soon feel better. The friend gave me a grateful nod, wished the incapacitated patient "Good *shabbas*," and fled the room with a parting "L'chiam" (To the good life)—about as appropriate, I thought, as telling someone boarding the *Titanic* that he was in for the trip of a lifetime. An attendant got the young man into bed, where he stayed for days, barely moving, never speaking—until the stench got so bad that the attendant picked him up one day and carried him bodily into the shower. Thereafter he was somewhat—but only somewhat—more alert.

Payne Whitney had in the past been known for its celebrity "guests": Marilyn Monroe in 1961, Robert Lowell and Mary McCarthy among those who followed, and James Schuyler, who, subsequent to his stay in 1972, published an eleven-part sequence *The Payne Whitney Poems*. In recent years the stars had migrated elsewhere, and the hospital's loss of status was reflected in the decay of its physical structure. (It would be completely demolished in the early nineties.) In 1984 the building contained a series of self-contained wards—locked wards—with a dozen patients in each, its own kitchen (complete with a large population of cockroaches, some of whom made their way to my night table and bed, making their own contribution to my anxiety level), and a mostly benign staff. The exception was Tom, a very large, threatening-looking nighttime guard, who came around every twenty minutes and shined a light in everybody's face to make sure they hadn't killed themselves or had somehow managed to flee.

My underlying resilience held me in good stead. When, on my second day, a female psychiatrist and her gaggle of students came to the ward looking for a patient they could interview, I proudly volunteered. It didn't go well. The bright-eyed students, apparently still immune to life's misfortunes, fired one insensitive question after the other at me ("How come you never injected cocaine?" "Why is sleep so important to you?"), until I finally called a halt. I wasn't *that* resilient. The female professor was also appalled and later sent back the least compassionate of the bunch to apologize to me (which he mechanically did, making me angrier still).

Once I started to feel better, I realized I had to notify the CUNY History Department that I'd "taken ill" and wouldn't be able to teach in the new term soon to begin. Though I was an august Distinguished Professor, I knew perfectly well that the sole ground on which I could be fired was "moral turpitude" and that cocaine use would certainly qualify as such in the minds of most of my colleagues (especially if, as I'd long suspected, several of them were distinctly homophobic and would be delighted to be handed an excuse for getting rid of me).

And so I concocted an elaborate story about how a bout of the flu had led to an elevation in my liver tests, followed by a dangerous arrhythmia that had sent me to the emergency room; I was being kept in the hospital for a prolonged period of rest and for an elaborate series of tests, including looking for the possibility that my heart medications were themselves responsible for the arrhythmia and needed recalibrating. I also made sure that the department chairman was notified that with the exception of a few family members, I wasn't permitted any visitors. In fact I myself limited my visitors' list to exactly three people: Barbara, Michael, and Aunt Tedda—all of whom could be relied on not to say a word about what was actually going on with me.

By the time detoxification began on my third day, I was in much better shape physically, eager to begin the process, and full of inflated optimism about the wondrous changes that were about to take place in my life. So wondrous that I would record every momentous step in my diary, certain that at the very least I would come away with the secondary gain of a new play. Since I hadn't done cocaine in several weeks, the detox was mostly about permanently kicking my long-standing addiction to sleep medication, the brand and dose having shifted many times over the years.

The underlying theory was that the pills had been masking anxiety and depression that had to be allowed to surface if they were ever to be understood, faced—and vanquished; besides, I was sternly informed, taking sleeping pills was eventually bound to have a deleterious effect on my liver. The theory, in retrospect, strikes me as highly suspect. I wanted to yell (but didn't), "*You* try growing up in the fifties as a gay man bombarded with denunciation as an 'abomination' and see what it does for *your* self-esteem." *Not* to develop anxiety and depression over being a benighted, despised creature was the equivalent of being devoid of feeling—or immune to socialization.

The wonder is why I didn't simply put on my clothes and go home. I suspect the answer comes in several parts: my collapse had been truly awful and I didn't want to risk a repeat; as a creature of the fifties, I was still prepared to believe that something was radically wrong with me and needed drastic correction; and, critically, my mother's unconditional love had imbued me with a certain irreducible amount of self-regard that continued to make me available for rituals of self-improvement. I remained game, even confident, that despite what I'd been through, I'd be able to dispense with psychopharmacological remedies for pain and lay bare—and live with—my raw nerve endings.

Yet I may also, contradictorily, have been looking for further punishment for the original sin of being queer. If so, the detoxification provided it in full measure. I have the notes to prove it. They begin with an optimistic "Strategy for Sleep." I worked out, step by step, how in the future I would cope with a medication-free life: "Get in bed *expecting* not to sleep *at all*. Stay in bed midnight to seven a.m. *Assume* you'll be lying there for seven hours. If you happen to doze now and then, fine. But don't *expect* even that much. And if at some point during the seven hours, you find yourself anxious, simply repeat and remember: I'VE ALWAYS SURVIVED THE NEXT DAY WITH NO SLEEP IN ME AT ALL!" Having mapped my plans, I hastened to caution myself against trying to be " 'the perfect patient.' Be easy on yourself. You're not here to win first prize; *that*, you must finally learn, is self-defeating." On your mark, get set—GO!

Just before take-off, I read "Rules of the Unit" and learned that I wasn't eligible for "self-transport" to the eighth-floor recreational area until after detox had been completed. That meant long hours confined to the unit, and with both Barbara and Michael too busy to visit other than every three or four days (my aunt came daily), and with my attention span too limited for reading, that meant, as I slowly began to feel better, the looming problem of boredom.

I started to get to know a few of my fellow patients. I was drawn particularly to Margaret and Gail. At the moment they seemed at opposite poles on the manic-depressive scale: Margaret couldn't stop talking and *had* to be always at the center of attention; Gail wanted to sleep all the time and had trouble getting out of bed even for meals. I was leery of Margaret as a competitor for attention and jealous of Gail as possessing the one attribute I most coveted: sleep. Though the doctors had scheduled a slow detoxification, within two days I was sleeping only one to two hours a night. Since nobody believed me, I made a point of waving at Tom whenever he came around with his flashlight at twenty-minute intervals. Tom had to acknowledge that I missed few inspections.

When the first weekend of my confinement came around, I learned that only a skeleton staff would remain on duty and few doctors would check in. Lack of staff produced considerable anxiety among the "clientele." Margaret, for one, declared the situation "dangerous." What would we do, she loudly asked, "abandoned" as we were on a locked-in floor, in case of fire? The question was enough to send Gail straight to bed. I decided to cheer everybody up by organizing a penny ante seven-card stud poker game. Only four of the twelve patients in our ward showed up, two of whom quit after the first few hands. If salvation *did* "lie with other people," as I'd euphorically written on a piece of paper, we seemed some distance from paradise.

There was a ratty little "lounge" at the end of our single corridor with a functional TV set. Watching a newscast one day, I was shocked when Kitty, one of the nurses, sat down in the chair next to mine and allowed herself to laugh at something on the screen. She'd dropped the authoritarian mask the rest of the staff kept rigidly in place, reacted in a recognizably human way. In blurring the division between staff and patients, she made me realize that we were being treated—and had come to regard ourselves—not as "clients" but as "prisoners," locked away in a total institution, turned over to our guards and keepers to be kept out of sight.

The awareness did wonders for reviving my rebellious spirit, buried under layers of exhaustion and fear. I promptly told my two roommates that it was fine with me if they needed to stay in bed all day with the shades drawn and the door closed—I was well enough by now to stay outside the room most of the day—but the air became so foul at night that I hoped we could at least leave the door partway open. Jeff, the young Orthodox Jew who'd been mute up to now, immediately agreed, softly mumbling that we needed to compromise on all our needs. I was even more surprised when he added his thanks for "the words of comfort" I'd spoken to him when he first arrived. The acknowledgment lifted my spirits still further—I considered it "thrilling confirmation" (as I manically wrote in the little notebook I was now carrying around) that "even at a time when one or both of the people are barely functional, a connection does register somewhere in the depths and ignites some prospect of hope, however dim, to hold on, come back."

Over the next few days my optimism held, even grew. I started to plan ahead, to list priorities after my release: I'd repaint the apartment and I'd throw out the accumulated clutter; then maybe I'd go back to Maine to visit Penny and rest up; then, on return, I'd avoid all distractions and single-mindedly focus on writing the first draft of the Robeson biography. Convinced that I'd bottomed out, that the worst was behind me, I confidently told myself that "the broken bone, once mended, is stronger than before." Alas for my optimism. Every time I thereafter opened a window or the door to our room even a crack, as soon as I left Jeff would get out of bed and shut them again.

By the end of my third week at Payne Whitney, my optimism had drained away still further, in tandem with the last of the sleeping medication leaving my system. Having previously been fairly amazed at the speed with which I was bouncing back from a pretty low bottom, I now rapidly returned to feeling lousy. "Shaky," I jotted down. "Zero drugs, zero sleep. The hard part begins. Nothingness, mortality." I'd been assuming that the Payne Whitney doctors were right, had bought into the medical theory that the sleeping pills had in fact *long since* stopped working for me and in recent years had reversed their effect and themselves become responsible in part for my sleeplessness. Well, maybe the theory was true for some, but not for me. I remembered with a rush what they'd told me years before, at the close of my bioenergetics intensive: "Now we understand why you have trouble getting off sedatives. There's an unexploded volcano lying in wait. If you ever do go clean, *be careful.*"

Rage alternated with tears. I drew up a formal list of complaints and presented them to one of the staff, a Dr. Maroz, whose French-accented irritability did nothing for my own. I told him I wanted "self-transport"—free access to the eighth-floor recreational area—*now*; I wanted to start attending the Cocaine Anonymous, Drugs Anonymous, or Alcoholics Anonymous meetings the hospital itself ran; and above all, I *had* to have more help with sleep, had to be given some relief from my miserable discomfort. The response wasn't entirely negative: Yes, I could go to the eighth floor. Yes, I could go to one or two meetings— the exact number was "under review." No, I would not be given any new medication to cushion the withdrawal. They were "working on" finding me a substance abuse doctor. "Your emergent anger," Dr. Maroz testily informed me, "is better seen as 'displacement'; it is *centrally* related not to hospital conditions or the difficulty of withdrawal but to deeper issues—it's a vignette about your *life.*" A *vignette*? He made my despondency sound like a French farce.

My first DA meeting produced an ambivalent reaction that would remain a constant throughout the subsequent years of attending meetings. As I scratched in my notebook, "People heal people (not 'GOD'); reliance on mutual support (not 'spirituality' or 'GOD') promotes the confidence to change." I summed it up this way: "Talk of 'putting ourselves in the hands of a higher being' is for me nearly as likely as Placidyl to produce a blackout." After my first AA meeting I managed to isolate what I took to be some of its inherent contradictions: they insist that alcoholism is a disease, a biologically caused condition; if so, how can it be cured by an act of will (i.e., "Day by day I'll *decide* to stay sober"). How is it possible all at once to "surrender to a higher power" and through *my own* volition decide to "chill out" or "take a moral inventory"?

Besides, I'd read somewhere that the relapse rate from cocaine addiction was highest among those from the lowest socioeconomic groups. That seemed to me conclusive proof that addiction is at base a social, not a biological phenomenon—despite all the fancy new theories pushing the latter view, including the rhetoric about "enzyme deficiency" that I heard at the meetings. If you give people hope of jobs and of human connection (which is what the meetings do), they are more willing to reengage life than to numb themselves against its pain.

AA, I decided, was a philosophical mishmash: we were all at once to throw ourselves on the mercy of the deity and at the same time pull ourselves up by our own bootstraps—Calvinist resignation impossibly yoked to ahistorical optimism. What could be more American? Never mind, another voice counseled—forget the ideological confusion and concentrate on the warmth of the fellowship; focus on the ritual of "sharing" and avoid the familiar self-sabotage of logic. All you need to know is this: the emphasis in society is on competition and confrontation; the emphasis in AA is on cooperation and commonality. As Americans we're encouraged to find the other person's weakness—and use it. In AA we're taught to look for the other person's strength—and support it. AA is a nurturing oasis in a desert landscape.

As hot flashes and muscle spasms joined my collection of withdrawal symptoms, I appealed once more for some pharmacological help. Down came word from the staff meeting: "It's time you developed 'good habits.'" In other words, NO. The Victorian principle would continue to reign supreme: "Suffer and be still." Dr. Maroz assured me that I "couldn't be in better hands or in a safer environment; should anything go wrong: we have all the necessary equipment." Meaning: Should you fall off the bridge, rowboats, we promise, shall dot the waters below. Translation: SUBMIT. We know what's best for you. Maybe they do, I thought. Maybe it's only the furious infant in me that feels violated, protests in outrage. But was it really babyish to want some comfort during a time of intense stress? "Babies," I scribbled down, "being natural, bawl." Only certain kinds of adults—stoics and puritans—unnaturally bottle up their feelings, giving babies a bad name. Was anxiety at the level I was experiencing it really a necessary prelude to constructing a life of "good habits"? Had the medical staff really weighed the risks involved in going cold turkey—in prolonged sleeplessness—for a cardiac patient? Their answer was loud and clear: "You've developed the wrong strategies over the years for coping with anxiety. Our scientific model for 'distress management' will provide you with more 'appropriate' ones." The bottom-line message was patently clear: If you want to get out of here, behave.

So I more or less did—while seething inside. "In addition to sleeping pills," I wrote irately in my notebook, "what further past indulgences,

SINFUL ACCOUTREMENTS, must be acknowledged and foresworn? Sheets on the bed? Honey in my milk? Scented soap for showering? If I tell them I've been constipated for a day, will they promptly insist on an exploratory colonoscopy?"

NEARLY FOUR WEEKS after I entered the hospital, the magical day of release finally arrived. On December 6, 1984, I found myself standing alone on the sidewalk in front of Payne Whitney, staring dizzily at the sun, ecstatically breathing the cold, fresh air into my lungs. None of my holy trinity had been available to pick me up at the assigned time for release, and I hadn't been willing to wait a minute longer than necessary. I walked to the corner, hailed a cab, and twenty minutes later was standing in the middle of my apartment, still blinking at the miracle of being home.

That night (as I wrote in my diary) "jerked off on heavenly home mattress with (besides erections) long-forgotten porn and poppers. Instantaneous pop, then instantaneous guilt—Oh God, the bloody popper! Isn't it, too, a drug?! Should it not, too, be forever foresworn, as kit to the kaboodle?" Oh give it a rest, Marty! Worry about it tomorrow. Or better yet, not at all.

Getting Clean: AA and CA

I'd drawn up a clear-cut battle plan in my head. For the next three weeks, I would do nothing but catch up on undone chores (get my cavities filled, replace the broken toilet seat); go to two to four Alcoholics Anonymous (AA) or Cocaine Anonymous (CA) meetings a day; put the finishing touches on "About Time," my collection of documents and essays (it appeared in 1986); and reestablish something like a normal social life—whatever that was. Then, starting the first of the year, I'd devote myself wholly to writing the first draft of the Robeson biography—which would mean, necessarily, putting "Being Gay" (the book I'd contracted for with New American Library) not merely on the back burner but entirely on hold, along with a contract I'd signed with the WPA Theater for a play about Paul Goodman. If either NAL or the WPA pressed me, I would buy out the contracts and cancel the projects.

As for the fleeting notion I'd had in the hospital of returning to Maine for a rest, where did I come up with that idiotic idea? For one thing, Penny had never shown up at the hospital and had given the usual excuse: "I couldn't bear to see you suffer." (Yeah, sure. Don't forget to call if you're ever in Oshkosh.) Had I already forgotten that Maine had been the jumping-off point for my roller-coaster ride to Payne Whitney? *Really*, Marty, what new tricks is that weird psyche of yours plotting behind your own back? Yet more drama and humiliation? No, no, NO! I was "sane" again. I had a bright new agenda laid out. If I knew anything, it was that I left Manhattan—or maybe I meant my apartment—at my peril. STAY PUT. New York City is in *every* sense home.

"Life's back in focus!!" I wrote excitedly in my diary. Two weeks later I added, "Best I've felt in years." My high spirits had nothing to do with sleeping better (which I wasn't) nor with returning to Placidyl (which I hadn't). No, above all it had to do with the meetings, which I attended faithfully and frequently. I was no less annoyed and cynical than before in regard to AA's philosophical underpinnings, but that came to matter less and less. I defined the "disease" of alcoholism in my own way: I called it the disease of *loneliness*. And the cure was to interact on a consistent basis with others. That, to me, was the entire essence of AA, the whole reason for its success. Connectedness: steady association with people much like myself—that is, suckers for theatrical amplitude, emphatically competitive, insistent perfectionists who put a premium on honesty, carry around a shit-load of concealed pain (or is that everybody?), have difficulty curtailing expectations, and are wide open to limited relationships. (Or, as someone put it at a meeting, "I don't want a lover, I want someone to hold me while I isolate.")

AA, I decided, represented—and facilitated—a restoration of faith in people. That was its curative power. It fulfills (I wrote in my diary) "our dream of utopian harmony and cooperation—or at a minimum approximates it. The premium at the meetings is on sharing, giving, acceptance, gratitude." We're encouraged to channel our energy in the direction of availability—and away from attitude. There was a starry-eyed streak among my fellow CA addicts that I found endearing: intolerance for what *is*, insistence on the prospects for change, on different, more, and better.

For the first few weeks after coming home I still wasn't getting much sleep and I sorely missed my nightly dose of Placidyl. The drug "*did* work," I wrote in my new diary, "*did* take care of the pain." Three weeks in, though I still saw the clock strike nearly every hour, I thought I'd begun to catnap more. Unlike sleep, my sexual appetite came storming back; my frequent erections made me feel like a teenager. This go-round, instead of turning to Placidyl for sleep and Rounds for sex, I made an appointment with the Sleep Disorder Clinic at New York Hospital and also started seeing a substance abuse therapist, who I'll call Dr. Kleiman.

At my initial interview at the Sleep Disorder Clinic, a Dr. Dunkell suggested that I "listen to music on the radio" while trying to fall asleep. "Talk about up-to-date methodology!" I wrote cynically in my diary. My first appointment with Dr. Kleiman went no better. His top-of-the-line advice was "Take control of the excessive, obsessive ruminations which interfere with your falling asleep." Oh—okay; now exactly how do I go about achieving that major miracle? Well, Kleiman responded, begin by "reducing muscle tension in your calves"—yes, my *calves*. ("Dear God," I silently muttered, "*this* is supposed to replace Placidyl?! *This* is state-of-the-art substance abuse therapy?")

It would have been easy to throw in the towel then and there, though I'd been clean for six weeks. Instead I wrote in my diary that I was firmly "on guard against allowing my warranted cynicism to ease over to an unwarranted justification for picking up a sedative." Well said, Old Man, I thought proudly—but what I wrote in my diary was a good deal more plaintive: "The condition of sleeplessness—oi vey!—begins to feel permanent." Yet I held firm, and the next day's entry was again euphoric: "Life feels rich—words I never again expected to write." I went to the famous "Living Now" AA meeting in Greenwich Village and heard the legendary Liz Bailey—"Thirty-three years sober!"—wow the crowd with her down-home honesty and wit.

In some moods I veered toward outright silliness, which for me felt good after so many dour months. Within weeks of getting out of the hospital, I'd put on twenty pounds, which inspired this giggle: "In order to have an ass, you have to have a paunch. This is the sum of my accrued wisdom from ages 45 to 55." Or this variation: "All these years I've been told that sedatives suppress feelings. No, they suppress *fat*. My new love affair with Snickers bars has produced a midsection spread—and provided a new focus for obsession."

As the number of days "clean and sober" continued to mount, I dutifully went both to the Sleep Disorder Clinic and to Dr. Kleiman. With each visit to the Clinic, my confidence in its efficacy diminished. Dr. Dunkell had a pronounced penchant for pontificating about the obvious. During one entire session he labored over the fatuous—and two-decades old—"revelation" that continuously repeating the word "one" gradually induces sleep. It didn't in me. Was he next going to recommend a glass of warm milk?

Nor was I taken with Dunkell's lyrical description of how, having himself finally experienced a trace of insomnia, he'd come to realize that "a certain euphoric lightness of body accompanies the process of falling asleep." "Yeah," I growled, "I seem to remember." That was the same day Dunkell revealed to me that he disagreed with Payne Whitney's diagnosis that I suffered from "a mild, generalized anxiety." (The word "mild" alone made me bristle. I'd like to see how long Dunkell lasted without *his* props.) "No, Mr. Duberman," he went on, "you're not *sufficiently* restless, fearful and sweaty" to warrant such a diagnosis. What I had was a "protracted abstinence syndrome." Translation: I suffered from drug-withdrawal symptoms. Yes, quite. But why, I asked the good doctor, did I resort to cocaine and sedatives in the first place if not out of an attempt to self-medicate for anxiety? Bug-eyed stare from Dunkell, as if I'd mumbled some obscenity. I stared back—and made the instant decision that this would be my last visit to the Clinic.

Things were going quite a bit better with Dr. Kleiman. I found him absurdly quiet and nonreactive—a near-parody of the outmoded analytic model of blank-slate neutrality. Still, when the Buddha did speak, he made some telling comments. "He thinks," I wrote in my diary,

> that I describe varied events and feelings in a similar tone, as if investing them with comparable emotional weight. I complained about the trivial malady of a cold but expressed no deeper concern over more serious ailments—the heart attack, insomnia, addiction. Or as Kleiman put it, "You present all in an equally minimizing tone." The result, he suggests, is that it can be difficult for others to know when I'm in serious trouble and need help— especially since I almost never ask for it directly. I think he's right; Dick or Penny, among others, have their own issues regarding friends in need but I make it easier for them to turn away from difficult situations.

Kleiman also seemed on target when pointing to my suspicious tendency to overextend myself at the *beginning* of a relationship. For example, when hiring a young assistant, Gary, to do last-minute fact-checking on "About Time," I started off by saying, "I leave it to you to set whatever hourly price tag you consider fair." And when Gary grandly announced that his fee was $25 an hour—then more than double the rate for a qualified graduate student (which he wasn't), I felt unable to protest, to go back on my original casualness. As a result I was left feeling "taken advantage of" and resentful. Applying Kleiman's insight to my failed relationship with Chris, *he* may have done the immoderate pursuing at first, but once I'd fallen for him I overpromised to love him faithfully forever. When he then drew back, I felt betrayed. Chris was responsible for the deceitful, abrupt way he withdrew, but I'm the one who hastened us too quickly to the altar.

IN JANUARY 1985 I did begin, as planned, to write the first draft of the Robeson biography. I had a ton of research under my belt and was full of excitement at the prospect of making sense of it. Yet initially it didn't go well; I felt rusty. At the meetings friends told me I was "rushing it" and quoted assorted program slogans at me: "Easy does it"; "One day at a time"; "Don't be too hard on yourself." After all, they said, I hadn't even reached the magical marker of "Ninety Days Clean and Dry." Kleiman too urged caution: "Don't rush to bury under a blizzard of 'productivity' the horrors of November before you've fully come to grips with them." He added his "strong impression" that the process of writing was for me closely interconnected with "physicality": "You can't work well unless you feel good, feel physically comfortable. It ties in somehow with your lifelong alienation from your body, which, paradoxically, exists in tandem with your deeply sensuous nature." Now *that* felt premature. How was I to digest so grand a pronouncement (especially coming from the Silent One) short of devoting a lifetime to it? No, I needed to get busy *now*. I wasn't any good at long-term reflection, at dawdling. I grabbed the reins and cracked the whip. And this time I was right about impatiently plowing ahead: the more I wrote, the easier it became.

My dreams, though, continued to send me warning signals: time and again I'd awake from a dream miserably convinced that I'd had a coke slip. At the meetings they reassured me that such dreams were commonplace—and positive: better to have my slips unconsciously than when awake. Yet consciously—which was puzzling—I had only a minuscule amount of longing for coke; the curtain on that show had definitely come down, and I felt reasonably certain that cocaine was behind me. I'd fully come to realize that a heart patient playing around with cocaine was a bizarre, even suicidal variant on Russian roulette, and—as medical opinion now confirmed—it was a miracle I'd survived it. Not, however, a miracle I ascribed to divine intervention. I would inevitably squirm when hearing someone at a meeting describe a narrow escape from this or that temptation and attribute it to "my Higher Power watching over me." Wasn't He or She just a trifle too busy these days to worry about whether John Doe did or did not pick up a drink? (That is, if you believed in Him or Her in the first place.)

What I yearned for wasn't alcohol (which had never appealed to me) or coke—but rather sedatives. I'd flushed my supply of Placidyl down the toilet the day I was released from Payne Whitney, but there was never a night, as I tossed around between brief periods of sleep, when I didn't yearn for a sedative, and yet—puzzlingly again—I never once dreamed that I'd had a sleeping pill slip. The ongoing temptation of Placidyl, or any variant thereof, kept me faithfully going to two to four meetings a day. That summer I was flabbergasted to read in the *Times* that William Rehnquist took Placidyl for ten years—a huge dosage, no less, of 1,500 milligrams a day. I end up in Payne Whitney; he ends up as chief justice of the Supreme Court! Some day, I vowed in my diary, "I'll stare into the national TV cameras and say, 'Yes, I once got into trouble with drugs—just like Chief Justice Rehnquist, I overdosed on Placidyl.'"

AA groups, I soon discovered, had distinctive personalities. A well-meaning friend took me one day to the Lenox Hill meeting, and I was astonished at how closely it reflected its Park Avenue address. It was strictly white and upper class: members of the reception committee wore name tags, costumes were by Brooks Brothers and Rosemary Hall (circa 1950), exclamations of "Gross!" and "Horrid!" were frequent, the coffee cake (this I assigned to the New England Brahmin contingent) was appropriately stale and offered in stringently small slices. It should have come as no surprise to find that class distinctions were as marked within AA as without. What I didn't expect was that I'd feel far more comfortable in meetings representing the downscale side of the class line, in particular the Living Now meeting in the Village; maybe my father's immigrant roots were resurfacing.

My "home" group, though, became Ninth Avenue, a gay meeting right around the corner from where I lived. I migrated to it out of convenience, not compatibility. Most of the gay men I met there, and sometimes went out for coffee with, were annoyingly conservative—smug, house-proud Chelsea-ites, wholly unconcerned with any issue that didn't relate directly to their own well-being.

In my diary I described one particularly disturbing dinner with some of my fellow gay alcoholics from Ninth Avenue. The talk somehow turned to the ongoing plight of black Americans; with the exception of one other person at the table (his proclaimed hero was Dorothy Day), the rest "went in full cry after the 'malingerers,' the outcasts and poor who remain so because 'they won't do anything about their lives.' I angrily took issue and got nowhere—other than angrier."

I felt there was something "peculiarly repellent" about their refusal to acknowledge that the opportunities that had characterized their own lives as middle-class white men didn't apply to most blacks. As far as my tablemates were concerned, obstacles to advancement were easily overturned if only blacks would learn better habits and made the needed effort to "pull themselves up by their own bootstraps." I found it disheartening to hear such claptrap from gay men, themselves often branded as "good-for-nothing degenerates." Knowing how ludicrously false that description was of their own lives, why couldn't they see that the "lazy malingerers" stereotype was equally wide of the mark as a description of blacks? Instead, like peacocks in heat, they pridefully strutted about congratulating themselves on having "come through"— stayed sober—and refused to allow other (less advantaged) sufferers into the club.

AA itself thoroughly encouraged an apolitical attitude; it was filled with people who insisted that sobriety was a full-time job; getting involved in other issues and concerns was viewed as a dangerous distraction. I didn't buy it. To me, part of coming alive again was to reengage with the world—to become politically aware and active. I frequently heard people in the meetings quote a favorite AA slogan: "Accusing the times is but excusing ourselves." That always set my teeth on edge; I wanted to yell out "*Can be*, not *is but*"—the difference between exaggerating the influence of social reality and acknowledging it. Maybe in the early stages of sobriety AA should be regarded as a kind of cloister, protecting one from the outside world. But surely after a point it was vital to exchange the nun's habit for ordinary street wear.

Fortunately I went to a variety of other meetings besides Ninth Avenue, and usually preferred the CA meetings to the AA ones. The difference between the cokers and the alkies, I decided, was that the cokers wanted more of everything, the alkies less; the former sought heightened amplitude, the latter diminished feeling. Put differently, the contrast was between people intent on unlimited sensation and getting their way and people who'd given up on daydreams and aimed at dulling their pain. I clearly belonged in the former group, enjoyed the

CA meetings more, and even made a few friends—"charming impossibilists all," as I described them in my diary. For them, like me, the best meetings combined what I called "the flavor of a frat house, a secret society, and a utopian commune." I often jotted down some of the wit and wisdom I continued to hear in the rooms, like when a black woman gave her version of a white woman's low point: " 'When my husband fell off the deck of our cabin cruiser, I was so drunk I had trouble calling the Coast Guard.' That was her bottom. Hell, I never even been to the Boat Show."

There were other gems:

> "For years I've been addicted primarily to feeling miserable."
> "I can't understand how some people start a job and stick. Some people even retire."
> "The Mafia gave me money to open a flower shop on Fire Island."
> "Once my head got clearer, I knew I was insane."
> "I may have had another drink in me, but I didn't have another recovery."
> "We all come into AA as stars and gradually work our way into the chorus."

I was impressed over and over again at how casually accepting most CA- and AAers were about my being gay—though in the country at large a considerable homophobic backlash was well under way. The gay men and lesbians I heard speak at meetings invariably made their sexual orientation known, but did so in passing, without any notable emphasis, any indication it might be an unusually weighted topic—indeed a "topic" at all. (A male qualifier: "And then I fell in love for the first time. He and I . . .") And the news was invariably received by others at the meeting with nonchalance. Maybe, I thought, it's a case of those who'd hit bottom in their own lives learning to feel compassion for other outcasts; maybe, on recovering, they develop a different set of priorities, a keener sense of what really matters—and a person's sexual orientation *didn't*. Then, too, in my first flush of enthusiasm, I may have exaggerated the tolerance for differentness—either that or I'd exaggerated the amount of racism among the conservative gay men at the Ninth Avenue meeting.

In regard to the AIDS crisis, certainly, I wasn't overstating the sympathy I found at meetings. I vividly recall the day when several people at a meeting talked about the pain and grief they felt over the death of friends from AIDS, or as one of them put it, "the disappearance of laughter from my life." Remembering my own losses, I burst into tears—to my amazement—and when I did people rushed up to hug and comfort me. It brought back the recent nightmare I'd had that I'd been diagnosed with AIDS, and how I'd awakened into a panic attack, bathed in sweat and fear.

Then there was the meeting when a young man spoke up about having had "yet another" slip. He told us that he was going to give the program another chance, then added, "Though since I have AIDS I wonder why I bother, given how little time I have." It was heart-stopping. We surrounded him with embraces and tears. As far as I recall, he never did return to another meeting.

A similar episode happened as we approached Christmas. The meeting room was decorated with a tree, and a platter full of holiday cookies was on the table. One young man hesitantly put up his hand and, when recognized, told the group he had AIDS, no money, and the previous night had dialed the suicide watch. He asked us to pray for him. Four or five people gathered around him after the meeting, gave him effusive hugs, and offered their phone numbers. He drifted quietly out of the room, holiday spirits closed over the empty space, and cheerful chatter quickly obliterated his absence. "Another one," I wrote in my diary, "has dropped noiselessly off, momentarily mourned, instantly trod under. The ants don't do it more efficiently."

AS MY ONE-YEAR anniversary "clean and dry" approached, my starry-eyed gratitude to AA and its sister meetings had given way around the edges to more grouchy discontent—maybe because no miracle had been wrought in regard to my sleep, which remained erratic and insufficient. I also continued to have a problem with AA's religiosity and kept trying to come up with an equivalent personal version of "spirituality" that I could live with. The best I could manage, as I formulated it in my diary, combined "the qualities of seriousness, struggle, and a search to connect with the importance of claims beyond the self." I thought such qualities might legitimately be called "spiritual"—an admitted stretch—and in any case I found those qualities "in abundant supply in the rooms—and in short supply outside them, where triviality reigns instead."

If one of AA's capsule bits of "wisdom" bothered me more than any other it was "God only gives you what you can handle." Every time I heard it, I'd flush with anger; I viewed it as on a par with "Every day in every way I get better and better"—in other words, as moronic claptrap. One day I let loose about it at a meeting: "Do the young men dying of AIDS get 'only what they can handle'? Are they too getting better every day in every way?" On I vented, raging against the simplistic generalities, the hollow pontifications and backslappings, whose chief effect, I said, was to minimize the reality of human suffering. No one came up to me after the meeting to congratulate me on my "honesty"—a habitual response at meetings—or on "getting in touch with and sharing" my anger.

Despite my complaints, I continued to go to meetings, though less frequently than before. More often than not it was simply the *contact* that would leave me feeling lighter and more centered than when I'd arrived. I was still learning that with AA, as with everything else, there are highs and lows and that unless those states become extreme and incapacitating—at which point they require medical attention—people are a more reliable antidote than any sloganeering ideology. Yet I was reaching the point—a healthy point, I think—where I was growing bored with exploring my own "inner process," both in AA and in therapy.

Writing remained *the* mainstay, the most reliable guard against exaggerated mood swings, and the most functional—productive of outside validation and not notably threatening to the body. At the turn of the year (1986) Arnold Dolin, my editor at New American Library, began to make noises about my overdue manuscript "Being Gay," and I decided I had more writing assignments than I could sensibly handle. I suggested to Arnold that we convert what had originally been designed as a personal narrative into an anthology of original essays by various scholars summarizing what we knew to date about the history of same-sex relations, thereby helping to map the emerging field of LGBTQ studies. Arnold immediately liked the new formula, and as a sideline diversion from my center-ring focus on Robeson, we started to put together what became *Hidden from History: Reclaiming the Gay and Lesbian Past*, which would appear in 1989.

East Germany and After

I had been able to attend multiple meetings a day because I'd been on leave on a Rockefeller Foundation Humanities Fellowship. At the beginning of the new term in February 1985, I returned to teaching my two seminars, Radical Protest Movements in the U.S. and The History of Sexuality. It was good to be back, good to feel so fully present and to recover the pleasure I took in engaging with others about controversial material. I was also socializing again—I even gave a fund-raiser for an openly gay candidate for New York's City Council. (He lost.) Though my hermit instincts were alive and well, I was now going out more regularly—with friends to dinner, the ballet, or a movie—much more than when I was hunkered down in intense isolation, snorting my lines, lost in unswerving admiration for my prose. (I never understood how people used cocaine for casual partying.)

I was also still doing some mopping up on the Robeson biography, traveling here and there to research an archive or interview someone. As always, it's only when I begin to write that I'm able to see the gaps in evidence that need filling. I spent a delightful day right here in New York talking with John Hammond, the legendary music producer. He was funny and frank, if a bit effusive, and he filled in any number of missing details for me. He seemed to have known everyone and to have perky anecdotes about each (a few of them sounding suspiciously time-tested). He described Claude McKay as "snotty," Countee Cullen as "charming," and the civil rights activist Walter White as an "opportunist; Robeson's closest friend when the two men were in their early twenties, the underappreciated physician and novelist Rudolph Fisher (*The Walls of Jericho*), who died of cancer at age thirty-seven, was "as nice as he was talented."

To get a better sense of Robeson's youth—for which evidence was thin—I flew up to Boston to interview H. A. Murray, the renowned psychologist; at ninety-three, bedridden after three strokes, he remained agile, witty, and urbane—and he solved the puzzle for me about how Robeson and his wife, Eslanda, first met. I then succeeded in locating the charming eighty-five-year-old Sadie Davenport Shelton in nearby Montclair, New Jersey, who'd married the only other black student at Rutgers. She confirmed my hunch that even as an undergraduate Robeson had initiated serious discussions among their friends about racial issues—though he maintained a bland, polite exterior when among whites. She also confirmed that Robeson "always liked light-skinned women" and that he'd fallen deeply in love with Gerry Bledsoe—who I'd also managed to locate and who had proved a wellspring of information about the youthful Robeson and her love affair with him.

Sadie Davenport Shelton's testimony further underscored what was already clear to me: that throughout his life Robeson's major romantic and sexual affairs were with white women and, to a far lesser extent, with light-skinned women of color. When I later said as much in the book, Paul Jr. furiously denounced me and claimed in public that he'd given me a list of his father's black lovers but that I had ignored it. Not true. If such a list ever existed, he never passed it on to me (though he may have meant to and thought he had). In all of my many lengthy conversations with Paul, the only black women he ever mentioned as having been intimately involved with his father were light-skinned: besides Gerry Bledsoe, casually with the actresses Fredi Washington and Nina Mae McKinney and, improbably—she was lesbian—Ethel Waters.

It wasn't until I was five years into the research that I caught wind of a "Paul Robeson Archiv" in East Berlin (when it *was* East Berlin), though nobody seemed to have a clear picture of what was in it. *A lot* was my hunch, and I decided to make the trip, hoping that I'd also get a chance to interview some of the expatriate Americans who'd been friendly with Robeson and were still living in the German Democratic Republic (GDR). Above all, I wanted to talk with Alfred Katzenstein, the doctor in charge of Robeson's treatment for bipolar disorder when he'd been a patient in East Germany's Buch Clinic in the early sixties.

The paperwork involved in getting a visa almost did me in at the start. The League for German-American Friendship "somehow" kept failing to send the East German Consulate in D.C. the necessary confirmation that I was an official guest, with the result that I got on the plane without a visa, armed only with the unconvincing assurance of both the League and the Consulate that I would have "no trouble at all" in crossing the border from West to East Berlin. "Will I be able to take my tape-recording equipment?" "Ja—maybe. If there's trouble, tell the border guards to call the League." Ja, sure. I could see the guards jumping to attention to accommodate me.

The GDR Consulate instructed me to disembark in Frankfurt and proceed to Checkpoint Charlie in Berlin, where, they assured me, I'd be issued a day visa. From there I was to proceed directly to the Palast Hotel in East Berlin, which was reserved—that is, cordoned off—for foreign guests. Nobody, predictably, behaved according to plan. The border guards kept me sitting for endless hours at Checkpoint Charlie, periodically glaring at me menacingly through the car window but saying not a word. When I finally arrived, exhausted, at the Palast Hotel, the hostile clerk deigned to let me register but informed me that I'd be shown to a room only *after* Dr. Katzenstein had seen me. A car, I was told, was waiting to take me to his home.

A pleasant, nondescript man, Katzenstein led me through a mine-field of questions obviously designed to establish my political sympathies; perhaps because I was too groggy to argue about anything, I passed muster (not as a communist but as at least acceptably left wing). We then talked for most of the day, including an invaluable five hours of taping, with Katzenstein cordial and forthcoming throughout. He described Robeson's depression as "very low," though he disagreed with the "excessive" number of ECT (electroconvulsive therapy) treatments he'd received at the Priory, London's psychiatric hospital, before transferring to the Buch Clinic.

That had been Paul Jr.'s position as well. Prior to my Berlin trip he'd harangued me over and over with denunciations of the CIA's "deliberate attempt," in conjunction with its British counterpart, MI-5, to "neutralize" his father with a needless and destructive course of ECT treatments. I took Paul's accusation seriously, knowing our government's long and malignant record of working to disable left-wing antagonists and regimes; it was in these very years of the early sixties that the United States helped to sabotage Salvador Allende's government in Chile and was implicated in the assassination of Congo's Patrice Lumumba.

I wouldn't have been surprised—or displeased—to discover the CIA's complicity in Robeson's decline, and I tried hard to find the evidence that would document it. With the help of the left-wing Boston lawyer Ed Greer and citing the Freedom of Information Act, I initiated a lawsuit against the FBI for the release of its voluminous Robeson files. The suit dragged on for three years, but when Judge Vincent Broderick (former police commissioner of New York City) ruled in chambers that my suit involved "issues of fact" and could therefore proceed to trial, it looked as if, against all odds, we might succeed.

By then, unfortunately, I'd spent $20,000, had run out of money, and was nearing completion of the book. Ed Greer urged me to agree to an out-of-court settlement; as he put it, "The FBI has a battery of lawyers on retainer and can litigate forever." When the Bureau offered a compromise—it would let me choose some dozen items from a prepared list of the "most important material," with each item briefly described—Ed advised me to take it and, reluctantly, I did. The brief descriptions proved bogus and the material of only limited value. My heart sank further when Ed repeated a remark from a wisecracking FBI agent: "Funny—the 103 volumes of Robeson records we had in the New York and Philadelphia offices are now fifty-six volumes. The others seem to have unaccountably disappeared." Oh swell, I thought: the end result of my lawsuit has been the destruction of nearly fifty volumes of material likely to have been the most incriminating of the FBI. It was a lesson in powerlessness.

In further trying to verify Paul's contention that his father had been "fine" and had never suffered from severe depression—that is, until the CIA decided to "neutralize" him through ECT—I immersed myself in the literature on electric shock therapy and also consulted with various specialists, including Dr. Max Fink of SUNY, Stony Brook, then the leading expert. The overwhelming consensus was that in a case like Robeson's, where the patient is in dire straits and unresponsive to other forms of treatment (the arsenal of psychotropic drugs was then limited), ECT was rightly seen as the only appropriate recourse. That Robeson *was* in dire straits was further confirmed by a number of his intimates. Helen Rosen was in London at the time, having been summoned by a distraught Essie to help deal with the crisis. Helen found Robeson curled up in bed in a fetal position, delusional, shaking in terror. There was no question in her mind, nor in Essie's, that his suffering was acute.

When I tried to discuss the current literature on ECT with Katzenstein, it quickly became apparent that he wasn't in command of it. Nor had he, though a clinical psychologist, ever attempted with Robeson any sort of traditional psychotherapeutic approach—not because psychosis doesn't yield to such treatment but because, as he himself put it, "I didn't go too much into personal questions." Though Katzenstein denounced the "excessive" use of ECT in Robeson's case, he also freely acknowledged, "Here in the GDR we generally consider British psychiatry to be superior to ours." If Katzenstein's amiability and openness surprised me, I was still more taken aback at his substandard medical knowledge. I came away from our long afternoon of talk forced to conclude, sadly, that although he was a gracious, empathic human being, he was not a top-flight practitioner.

I had better luck with the Robeson Archiv at the Akademie der Künste. My hunch paid off: it proved a rich collection of manuscript letters and first-person reminiscences of Robeson. While in East Berlin I also got to interview several American expatriates who'd been Robeson friends or associates; the standout for me was the witty and shrewd cartoonist Ollie Harrington, who regaled me with Robeson stories.

During my ten days in East Berlin, I had little free time, but I did get to walk through the melancholy and deeply moving Jewish Cemetery and also managed a rushed visit to the Pergamon Museum, where the astonishing Ishtar Gate floored me. I even got a peek into gay life in East Berlin. Earlier, in New York, I'd met Irene, a visiting East Berliner—I forget how or why—who'd promised to show me around should I decide to make the trip. Irene had many gay friends, and during my stay she threw a party for me and also arranged for a group of us to tour the gay hot spots. I was surprised there *were* any—and even more surprised when we arrived at a gay disco (which served as a high school during the day!) to find the music, dress, and attitudes so familiar I could easily have been back in clone city (Manhattan). Irene tried to persuade me that East Germany was far more tolerant and hip than the West, but Klaus, one of the gay men she introduced me to, solemnly recounted how he'd been thrown out of the Party two years earlier for presenting "a formal series of demands" on behalf of gay people.

Klaus also told me that the neuroendocrinologist Günter Dörner of the GDR's Humboldt University was gaining support for his conclusion that the "mistake" of same-gender sexual orientation occurred between the third and fourth month of pregnancy and could be "corrected" through hormonal intervention. Dörner claimed complete success in his experiments with rats and was only awaiting official sanction to move the experiment to humans. Meanwhile in Prague, Klaus reported, a still worse situation existed. His friends there had told him about a "brain operation" being performed with some regularity to "destroy" any lustful same-gender inclinations; since the operation induced epilepsy, Klaus and I "joked," that *would* tend to distract the mind from sex. The same operation, he added, was also being performed in Hamburg. The GDR, in other words, represented the best of a bad set of conditions in Eastern Europe, and that best—despite East Berlin's gay disco, and despite all of our setbacks back home—was no match for the vigor and assertiveness of gay life in the States.

By the time I returned home from the GDR, the hostile climate for gay people had deepened. Yes, New York City had finally passed a gay civil rights bill, but simultaneously the U.S. Supreme Court had issued its notorious *Bowers v. Hardwick* decision, upholding a Georgia statute that in essence declared it illegal to engage in homosexual activities even in the privacy of one's own home. Chief Justice Warren Burger, writing for the majority, gave voice to the raging homophobia then rising in tandem with the sharp increase in the number of AIDS cases. "The infamous *crime against nature*," Burger wrote, is "an offense of 'deeper malignity' than rape, a heinous act 'the very mention of which is a disgrace to human nature.' . . . To hold that the act of homosexual sodomy is somehow protected as a fundamental right would be to cast aside millennia of moral teaching."

For gay people *Bowers* was brutally demoralizing. My friend Tom Stoddard, then executive director of the Lambda Legal Defense Fund, called it "our *Dred Scott* decision," and another friend, Joe Chaikin, founder of the Open Theatre, phoned to say that he felt we should issue a public statement declaring our refusal to abide by any law which in essence denied our right to sexual expression. I told Joe I'd sign it but wasn't convinced of its tactical value, since I doubted if we'd get many signatories. What about, I suggested, a mass rally instead? It would at least provide an outlet for our anger. Or maybe we should revive the tax refusal tactic some of us had employed against the war in Vietnam, as if to say "We won't support a government that withholds our basic rights." Neither seemed plausible. All that was clear was that *some* response was necessary, both to rally our own troops and to underscore the fact that we weren't struggling against a phantom oppression nor overstating the obstacles in the path of equality.

Many others were having the same reaction and feeling determined to express it publicly. The *Bowers* decision, in combination with rage over the federal government's gross indifference to the mounting scourge of AIDS, eventuated in the massive—some half a million people—1987 March on Washington, which I was proud to join.

BY EARLY SPRING 1985 my five-month run of sustained good spirits began to shift to a more realistic pattern of ups-and-downs. Run-of-the-mill physical symptoms—an atypical headache, a simple cold—would bring to the surface the lurking fear of most gay men that pneumocystis pneumonia was about to descend. When I could assign a glum day to a particular cause—say, the FBI continuing to stonewall my effort to get Robeson's files released or the failure of Gary, my fact-checker, to keep up the pace we'd agreed on—I always revived more quickly than when the blahs descended unannounced and unassignable to any obvious explanation. In mid-April, seemingly out of nowhere, I fell into a depression worse than any I'd experienced since leaving the hospital. A sense of acute loneliness surfaced that the lockstep pace of my renewed routines had previously managed to block. "Without a companion or a religion," I wrote in my diary, "I lack the two standard insulations against terror."

A period of undefined melancholy ensued. One particularly nightmarish morning I awoke in terror at what I described in my diary as

> the stark awareness of someday not being. This really is all
> going to end. Couldn't shake the dreaded knowledge. . . . I need
> a metaphysician, not a therapist—a specialist in annihilation,
> not perfectionism. In AA they would view this state as a positive
> development: "I'm giving up controls, surrendering." . . . I'm more
> comfortable with the familiar vocabulary of existential dread. . . .
> Now I know why I sedated myself for years. . . . Yet the routines do
> go on—in the face of all counter-indications of futility. . . . I tried
> to share some of my angst in a meeting today. A few well-meaning
> slaps on the back, but basically ignored. Even shunned: a morbid
> spoilsport. The focus in the rooms is on our "miraculous" escape
> from premature death—which tends to get equated with escape
> from death itself.

The angst gradually eased into a low-grade depression. Initially I did try to "figure it out"—and of course managed to come up with any number of "reasons," equally plausible, equally impossible to corroborate. Yes, my close friend Barbara had gone into what became a prolonged retreat from me, apparently fearful—though she never said as much—that her husband had become angrily insecure over the intensity of our relationship.

And yes, Paul Jr. had flown into an abusive rage when he learned that *About Time*, my collection of gay-themed documents and essays, would soon be published. "Your sole priority," he stormed, "is *my father's legacy*—that, and only that, should occupy your time!" I reminded him that I'd had a life before the biography and hoped to have one again after it was published, but beyond that I held my peace. I did decide on the spot, however, that if I was ever going to finish the book, I had to put more distance—a lot of distance—between Paul and me. I'd come to realize that responding to his assorted accusations only briefly appeased him—and were in a real sense beside the point. He periodically *needed* to vent accumulated anger—not least at his own history, at his father's unbearable disinterest in him—and to compensate for it by adopting the role of having been his father's closest confidant and staunchest defender, the fiercest of all defenders of the faith. It was pitiable, and I wouldn't dare attempt to unmask the charade; doing so would redouble Paul's wrath and accomplish nothing. But I did need to remove myself from his constant, furious interruptions.

I would never lose the habit of trying to come up with logical explanations for what were not wholly logical situations; nor, as an academician trained in rational analysis, would it take much to get that near-automatic gear system cranking up again. But I now understood better the essential disorder of experience, the underlying chaos of a lived life, and the difficulty of re-creating and understanding it; childhood experiences, for one, are the least retrievable part of our memory and yet the most formative part of our experience. And that applies to the undecipherable element in our mood swings as well. The arc wasn't nearly as wide for me postsobriety as during my drugging days. (Ironically I'd originally started in on sedatives and cocaine in part to deal with depressive moods.) Part of being alive, I belatedly realized, was to be hit now and then with the doldrums—and for no obvious reason. Brought up as a Prince of the Realm, I was supposed to have a life free of pain and full of accomplishment. Fortunately I began to develop a marked *dis*interest in trying to solve the conundrum of mood swings—in the truly hopeless pursuit of "puzzling it all out."

Luckily for my character, I'd never in fact had a life free from considerable emotional pain (though many people, I realized, saw me that way), as well as serious physical bouts with polio, hepatitis, back surgeries, a heart attack, fibromyalgia, and prostate cancer. Growing up gay in the 1950s had been psychic pain enough, and its effects enduring. I'd spent years in therapy trying to erase this "condition" and had been almost as abused by incompetent therapists as by the homophobia of the culture at large. Yet being part of a despised minority was also a form of salvation: it contradicted and leavened my mother's presumption that I was one of the "elect," entitled to exemption from distress of any kind. The distress was at times severe enough to help account for my turning to drugs—and to work—in order to suppress any interruption in my onward march to Success (to proof of worth). Yet the generalized unease that always accompanied that march also helps to account for my pronounced antagonism to authority, to established "truth"—and for my consistent siding with the underdog.

Drugs and work had all along been interconnected, the one fueling the other. Dr. Kleiman pointed out to me one day that, so long as my life continued to be eventful, it seemed hardly to matter to me whether the onrush of activity produced good news ("The *Voice* will run your article) or bad ("We can't produce your new play after all"); either way, it kept the whirlwind of activity spinning—and kept depression at bay. In staying busy I was staying taut and animated, distant from the perils of relaxation.

Emerging from the haze, I'd come to feel that problems and mood swings are in fact *gifts* of survival; if I'd continued down the drug-addled path I'd been on, I wouldn't be worrying about and trying to figure out why Barbara was in retreat or Paul off on another tear. Only in the past few months had such luxurious problems become available to me. Now and then I continued to need more amplitude, a renewed sense of danger. So I'd have two chocolate bars instead of one or eat my forbidden Pepperidge Farm cookies out of a brown paper bag.

The Theater Again

Six months into sobriety I was still celibate. The thought of having sex began to feel like an invasion of privacy. I didn't miss it; my libido wasn't groaning in the night. Fear of AIDS contributed to my abstinence, but more important, I suspect, was my uneasiness about having sex stone-cold sober: I felt sure I'd be inhibited, probably impotent, and certainly unsatisfied—and that, in turn, might tempt me to try a joint or some other drug I hadn't yet abused. I kept telling myself that I had enough going on in my life—teaching, writing, meetings, exercise—to take up the slack. "It's a trade-off," I wrote in my diary, "boredom for sanity. I'm not sure I can maintain it, should one ingredient in the mix—like the Robeson book—run into a snag, or conclude. I'd rush for a replacement—but in which direction?"

Often I was too tired after working on the Robeson book all day to go out at night. Still, I managed it fairly often, though I picked my occasions pretty carefully: I wanted contact, not arousal; pleasantry, not turmoil. "No drama" became the byword. Dinner with Tom Stoddard was what I had in mind—a lively companion, but hardly a prospective mate. Or dinner with Helen Rosen, Robeson's long-term lover, with whom I'd become very close over the years; though in her seventies, Helen remained zestfully engaged with life and was appalled at my extended celibacy.

Another guaranteed low-wattage event was the annual American Historical Association convention. Though the "gay history" panel proved tedious, it was pleasant to reconnect with various queer colleagues in the audience who I hadn't seen in a while. I reconnected with still others at excursions to hear the Gay Men's Chorus (too many show tunes for my taste), to attend a benefit at the Lesbian and Gay Community Center (where the diversity, from Eastern Orthodox Christians to Hikin' Dykes, was dazzling), and to attend the premiere of the film

Before Stonewall (in which I was one of the talking heads), where I was delighted to run into Barbara Gittings again ("rounder but as exuberantly positive as ever") and also the Australian gay rights activist Dennis Altman. The invitation I was quickest to turn down was to a gay AA dance; in my mind the two worlds didn't mix: the discomfort of a cruising environment, however decorous, would do nothing, I decided, for my "serenity."

I was still diligently attending board meetings of the New York Civil Liberties Union (though I was soon to resign) and still naïvely startled when that presumed bastion of human rights breezily vetoed—by a vote of 22 to 6, no less—a proposal to end the organization's connection with Israel's Bank Leumi, due to Israel's remaining South Africa's second biggest customer. As always, NYCLU's sophisticated liberals used rhetoric—in this case, in defense of Israel—that carefully avoided gross, transparent forms of bigotry, assuming instead a guise subtle enough to allow them to disguise from *themselves* the extent of their prejudices.

To further prevent any threat of free time in my schedule, I joined a health club and started to swim three times a week, gleefully warning myself in my diary "to be careful not to overdo *health*, since I'm likely to overdo *whatever* is at hand." I also dutifully went to the theater now and then, though I'd learned to limit my outings—and expectations. I found no surprises: Christopher Durang's *The Marriage of Bette and Boo* had, as I wrote in my diary, "some hilarious Thurberesque bits, but cartoons can't sustain a play." As for Larry Kramer's *The Normal Heart*, I thought "the most shocking thing about the play was Larry's unembarrassed self-aggrandizement." Still, I wrote, "the play will do good: it's not interesting enough to turn off theater-goers and its archetypal sentimentalities cannot help but move them—as they did me."

Ouch! Though I still feel the same about the play, I was also venting a bit: years earlier I'd blasted Larry's novel *Faggots* in the *New Republic*, and understandably miffed, he'd been taking occasional potshots at me (unfairly, of course!) in the gay press. When New American Library decided to publish *The Normal Heart* Arnold Dolin asked me to write an introduction to it. He said he thought it was "a lousy play, but should be in print—to call attention to AIDS." I told him that I agreed with him on both counts but didn't want to be associated with a work that "ruthlessly denigrates the good work of GMHC," which for all its short-comings had stepped into the breach when the heterosexual world had for the most part turned its back, and had done heroic work in providing support for those suffering with AIDS. Larry and I eventually had a vague sort of reconciliation, but our relationship has stayed on the level of formalities.

Late in 1985 one of my own plays, *Visions of Kerouac*, was unexpectedly revived at the American Theater for Actors in New York City. Nearly a decade earlier the play had had a riotously successful month-long run at the Lion Theater on Forty-Second Street and gotten some wonderful reviews, including in the *Village Voice* ("that rare thing in today's theater—it's alive. In its gut and its head") and *New York* magazine ("succeeds in capturing honestly and powerfully, a fascinating moment in this country's literary and social history"). A number of producers at the time had expressed interest in moving the production to a larger theater, but then the *Times* critic, Mel Gussow, weighed in with a negative review that accused me of suggesting "that if Kerouac had admitted to a preference for homosexuality, he would have been healthier, perhaps even a better writer." The homoerotic relationship between Kerouac and Neal Cassady *did* feature centrally in the play and, I remain convinced, in the real-life relationship between the two men. But Gussow couldn't tolerate such a suggestion—and potential producers disappeared from the wings.

The play had met a similar fate in the 1977 L.A. production that had opened soon after my mother's death. The reviews had once again been excellent ("a stunning portrait"; "a classic tragedy")—and once again been undercut by one influential negative. Dan Sullivan in the *Los Angeles Times* described the play as "a sensitive portrait" but then, like Gussow, went on to misinterpret and deplore what he claimed was the play's theme—that "Kerouac would have been happier . . . if he had quit worrying about being thought a 'faggot' and gone with the flow." The play had a decent run in L.A., but the producer canceled his plans for a tour across the country that he'd intended to end with a Broadway opening in New York.

The third try, at the American Theatre for Actors, did not prove the charm. The production was troubled from the start. The producer-director was a longtime fan of the play, but his only background in theater was as an unsuccessful actor. We cast two very fine actors, Victor

Slezak and William Fichtner, to play, respectively, Kerouac and Cody (Cassady), but midway into rehearsals both dropped out to accept better-paying jobs. Their replacements, alas, weren't nearly as gifted. It probably wouldn't have mattered anyway. When the play opened early in February 1986, Walter Goodman, the current *Times* critic, proved to be yet another of Gussow's kissing cousins. He too wrote a negative review ("clamorous incoherence"), marked by covertly homophobic overtones. Once again the play died a-borning.

In the years to come, *Kerouac* would have other productions, including one in London, but the "two strikes and you're out" adage has held true in regard to New York City down to the present day. The failure hurt. My repeated near-misses in writing for the theater felt akin to going over and over again into a hardware store to buy doughnuts. The success of my very first play, *In White America*, way back in 1963, had primed me to expect one triumph after another to follow like the night the day; at the time I remember saying to a friend, only half in jest, "Why does everybody keep complaining about how 'hard' the theater is? I wrote my first play in three months, it opened seven weeks later, and was a hit—what's the big deal?"

It was a big enough deal in 1986 to have me doubling up on meetings and scurrying back to Dr. Kleiman's office seeking some sort of comfort. But neither psychotherapy nor AA could rearrange reality: the play had irreducibly failed—again. My job was to white-knuckle it and wait out the pain without doping. To avoid excess brooding I forced myself out of my apartment, took walks, went to meetings, did errands, swam, visited a friend in the hospital, and told myself nobody can simultaneously announce himself an outsider and win mainstream applause.

A friend recommended that I consult the "marvelous" Koji, who had "saved" her life. And I did. He put me on a diet of seaweed and brown rice—with a touch of kuzu for special occasions (like constipation). Why not? I needed *some* form of extremism in my life. After two weeks Koji introduced me to acupuncture, and to the very newest technique, invented in Japan over the past decade, of keeping the needles in for two days. "Trust me," I thought, "never having done acupuncture, to land in the hands of somebody with an experimental technique." I tried it. The effect? More, not less, depression as the days passed. "I've lost the rhythm of my routines," I wrote in my diary, and decided I was having trouble rebounding because Walter Goodman's negative review felt, in its abruptness and finality, reminiscent of the way Chris had left me. Yes, that old scar was still capable of throbbing.

Within three or four weeks the pain ebbed and my days became pleasantly regularized again. I summarized my renewed routine in a diary entry: "5–7 hours on Robeson, interspersed with meetings, exercise, teaching, shiatsu massage, then most evenings (5 out of 7) movie/theater/dinner with friends." Occasionally I said yes to a party because the guest list sounded enticing; publicly critical of our "celebrity-fixated" culture, privately I wasn't above hobnobbing with a few of them now and then. (I had to enliven my diary somehow.)

At one such gathering I ran into a number of people I'd briefly known before. The actor Harris Yulin and I had once toyed with the idea of doing a film; this time around I found him "infinitely more mellow." Bob Lifton and I had been jailed together after being arrested at an antiwar protest in D.C.; the psychiatrist and author seemed much the same: a "boyish pontificator." Gay Talese and I had crossed paths somewhere or other; he seemed "still more than ever self-absorbed." The composer Ned Rorem and I had been borderline friendly, though he'd written me up in one of his published diaries as having had *two* heart attacks; that night Ned seemed "downright serene." I could find nothing to carp about in my diary regarding Judy Collins (also jailed after the D.C. protest); she was simply "glowing and lovely."

A friend who was on the board of Paul Taylor's dance company took me along to his house to celebrate the last performance of the season at another celebrity-choked party. Much later I would interview Taylor for my biography of Lincoln Kirstein, cofounder of the New York City Ballet, but I'd long been a fan of both his choreography and his company and was delighted that night to find my two favorite dancers, Kate Johnson and David Parsons, as winning in their street clothes as in costume. My longest talk of the evening was with Harold Brodkey, the long-touted literary "genius" (Harold Bloom called him "an American Proust") whose much anticipated masterpiece, *The Runaway Soul*, when finally published a few years later, would get a mediocre reception. Brodkey died of AIDS but always insisted he wasn't gay.

As I described our talk that night in my diary, Brodkey "initially startled me with effusive compliments. Then he shifted to an opaque, almost interior monologue about the disastrous American Culture (something about our refusal to build Paul Taylor his own theater, interspersed with a high-sounding lament for a Lost Audience—all half-whispered in an impishly cultivated voice). As soon as I responded—mostly to express uncertainty about whether I'd heard him correctly—he shifted from provocation back to ingratiation, complimenting me again 'for always writing on topics near the cutting edge.'" I reminded him that my first book was on C. F. Adams and my second on J. R. Lowell—those exemplars of the newness!

I spent another, less glamour-soaked evening with my old friend Bill (John William) Ward; we'd both been young history instructors at Princeton in the sixties and had kept in touch over the years. After Bill became president of Amherst in the early seventies, he invited me up to give a talk on what was then the daring topic of "the gay movement"; not only that, but he made a point of walking me down the long auditorium aisle to the podium and providing a warm-hearted introduction. In those years that was a gesture all but unique from someone so well placed—and a brave one, at the start of his presidency.

I'd never forgotten his generosity of spirit, and when he invited me to dinner in the late summer of 1985 (by then he'd resigned as Amherst's president) at the Century Club, I looked forward to seeing him again. It was a high-spirited evening, Bill full of his trademark charm and wit; the only down note was when he told me that he and his wife, Barbara, were separating after many years. Otherwise we had another of our animated, upbeat dinners, full of lively gossip and shared complaint; we were both in great good humor when we said goodnight.

The following day I was stunned to learn that Bill had killed himself after returning to his hotel room. I was still in shock when a close friend of his phoned to tell me that I was the last person to see him alive and to ask how he seemed. "Just fine," I said, still nonplussed. "I never would have guessed that he was troubled—though he did mention that he and Barbara were divorcing." The friend said that after leaving me Bill had called Barbara at 3:00 a.m., "drunk and incoherent." He added that Bill had "a deeply concealed history of depression, with suicidal episodes triggered by alcohol," that the pending divorce had been painful, and that Bill felt he'd never fulfilled his promise as a historian. Was any of that enough to account for a suicide? Who could ever say with confidence? How could I not have picked up some clue of his despair during our evening together? So much for my powers of perception— and for Bill's outsized gift for covering over pain with banter. "What fathomless pits we all are," I wrote in my diary. For years I felt recurring sadness, along with a sense of fragility, over what Bill had done to himself.

Aftermaths: 1985–1988

I remained celibate for about two and half years. Then, mysteriously, without a scintilla of inner struggle, I decided one night that it was time to drop in on Rounds. Yes, it was still going strong, and I was barely in the door when a stereotypical young Italian—my type, dead center— accosted me, whispered passionate promises of transcendent sex in my ear, and whisked me off into a cab. The sex was as rapid as the court- ship: instant disrobing, instant jerk-off, instant departure. Net result: penitent remorse.

That lasted for another month. Then it was back up to Rounds— just like that, without any precipitating event or particular turmoil— and directly into the arms of another humpy Italian, this time with a very different outcome. Mike had no hang-ups about his enjoyment of sex—which promptly brought out all of mine. What was safe? Was anything? I seemed to recall that GMHC's guidelines put sucking on the "safe" side of the scoreboard—but didn't they add "only sucking the shaft, not the head"? How was that supposed to be managed? Never mind, we sucked each other, shaft and head. Was deep kissing allowed? If there were guidelines, we didn't know them; we deep-kissed.

AIDS anxiety aside, I felt acutely uncomfortable with presenting my decidedly less-than-perfect body for fondling. My sobriety indulgence in candy bars and cookies had taken their toll; I felt ashamed of my new paunch, my limp (drug-free) cock, my self-conscious awkwardness. If I'd ever been assertively confident about sex—and if memory holds, I definitely was when younger (and without the buffers of cocaine, grass, and poppers)—a few years from sixty I certainly wasn't self-assured any longer. It *was* nice to be held again and to feel sexually desired, but not nice enough to overcome the feelings of discomfort and vulnerability.

I didn't ask Mike for his number, nor offer mine, but for days af- terward I mulled over the experience. The feelings of inadequacy it aroused in me, in combination with the inhibitions built into gay male sex in the age of AIDS, produced a jumble of feelings—including frustrated defiance. If I was going to start having sex again I wanted to *have* it—in the old uninhibited way, not smothered in terrified calculations about safety. I checked around and discovered that GMHC *did* advise against blow jobs and even warned against deep kissing as a "gray area."

So what did that leave? A peck on the cheek and mutual masturbation. Which was better than nothing, I supposed, but I wasn't convinced. What would happen if, heated up from the preliminaries (supposedly end points), I let my defiance overrule my caution, decided the hell with it, and ended up having *un*safe sex. AIDS anxiety was bound to follow in abundance, and to dull it, I might well pick up a drink or snort a line to steady my nerves. I decided a therapy appointment with Kleiman was in order, someone to mull with me. When I mentioned how moved I'd been at Mike's tenderness and affection, I found myself holding back tears. Kleiman couldn't have been more pleased. "You see," he said, "how easily your need and capacity for affectionate connection is uncorked—even after two and a half years of smothering all signs of it to the point where you've managed to convince most people that you have no emotional needs at all." I nearly cried again. In response Kleiman softly said, "Your vulnerability has brought you so much pain in the past that you've learned how to conceal it." Choking up, I made a dash for irony: "Isn't that the standard alcoholic's self-image: the misunderstood fount of human kindness?" Kleiman's only response was to point out that brittle repartee wasn't a helpful approach to resolving the difficult issue of sex.

Approaching my fifty-seventh birthday, I felt like a case of arrested development. True, the AIDS epidemic had many gay men reassessing their sexual needs, but the virus aside, *I* was still trying to figure out what if anything I wanted to do in bed, with whom, and for what set of expressive needs. This is the Gordian knot teenagers dwell on; forty years later I was still hacking away at it. I'd always been mystified by people whose sexual desires become concentrated on a single activity—who *only* want to fuck teenage boys, or get plowed by studs, or suck cock after cock at an anonymous glory hole. Single-minded in much else, I'd become *more* diffuse in my sexual fantasies the older I got. Which, I realize, could be viewed as an advantage—even a countercultural sign of "growth" (fulfillment of the dream of "polymorphous perversity"). The trouble is, my varied impulses were usually simultaneous, not sequential: I wanted to suck, fuck, kiss, and more, all at the same time. (I think that's called greedy.) To boot, I wasn't much good at the actual execution of any of them, maybe because I couldn't focus on one desire long enough. My partners, I suspected, often mistook my intellectual forcefulness for sexual assurance; they thought I *did* know what I wanted and tended to view my jumbled hesitations as some form of mind-fuck or power ploy.

I finally decided, feeling vaguely idiotic, that at least for now I didn't trust my truant impulses to stay within the safe-sex guidelines, especially since there was still no consensus among the experts as to which activities were or weren't risky. And so, after much mulling, I decided once again to take the veil. I put it this way in my diary: "If it's true that 'no one gets it all,' then maybe sex is what I'm not going to get—the odds against my working it out safely seem too high. If so, it isn't pathetic. I have a life that in many ways does 'work,' if not in all ways. If I never again get to live intensely in my body, I'm once again able to live intensely in my head. Emotional health doesn't hinge on sexual—or even masturbatory—release."

Okay, so I wasn't going to have sex for the foreseeable future, but that didn't mean I had to stop speculating about it. ("Those who can, do; those who can't, theorize.") Reading at the time a great deal about the ancient world in line with my course on "the history of sexual behavior," I came upon one authority's illuminating notion that the accepted norm for adult male citizens back then was to have sex *on* someone rather than *with* someone. The male citizen in Periclean Athens didn't solicit consent nor concern himself with his partner's pleasure; the other person might enjoy the transaction, but that wasn't its purpose. Sex was asymmetrical and polarized, not shared and unifying.

It struck me that today, too, many powerful men use their partners in a comparable way, making their own pleasure the sole goal of erotic contact, ignoring their partner's needs as inconvenient distractions. Those less autonomous, I speculated, had learned to discipline their selfish instincts and find comfort in the reigning ideology that privileged "mutuality." Less bound by social conventions, some gay men—though not situated among the powerful—had (before AIDS) been indulging their version of the ancient world's paradigm for sex as *on* not *with* others in the anonymous sex orgies of the bathhouses, piers, and backroom bars. Avoiding standard social preludes to seduction, they focused solely on satisfying their own fantasies, downplaying or discarding the need to accommodate anyone else's. Was this the true kernel of the sexual revolution, the deviant path that led away from the claustrophobic chambers of bourgeois romance—thus earning the enmity and fear of those more encumbered by conventional commitments? (This revolution, like most, far from being spanking new, in fact led back to behavior commonplace two thousand years ago.)

Next conundrum: Does nonmutual sex preclude intimacy? It depends on how you define intimacy's properties and estimate its value. The dominant cultural presumption is that one's capacity for intimacy and one's maturity are coequal. Some of my therapists over the years had darkly hinted that I had an undernourished capacity, though none, alas, ever paused to define what precise qualities were deficient or absent. From what I could make out, it seemed to have something to do with an inability to form long-lasting relationships—that is, those that conform to the standard model: a lifetime commitment of steadfast emotional closeness in combination with unwavering sexual arousal (monogamously expressed, of course).

Something didn't sit right. First of all, I'd *had* long-term relationships; the longest, it's true, was "only" for five years and for the last two not monogamous. "Ah!" the therapeutic police would cry, "so they didn't *last!*" Right—not for a lifetime. Which proves what? The commitments were deeply affectionate, close, and caring. Since when has longevity become the best measure of superior worth? (Is every eighty-year-old man ipso facto more valuable than any twenty-year-old?) As for monogamy, a case can be made—and often has—for erotic zest in a relationship being of short duration, no matter how loving the two people are; long-lasting couples stay together because they've found a soul mate, not a porn star. Hunting in Rounds for a soul mate, of course, was probably (not certainly) counterproductive.

In sobriety—and further abetted by AIDS anxiety—my libido had notably shriveled, as had my trips to Rounds. Maybe my bottom-line truth was that if I ever had been looking for a mate, I no longer was; the deepest impulse in my personality, perhaps, was the desire to be left alone, to isolate myself in my mostly satisfying routines—with occasional forays out for conversation and sex. The routines of togetherness that traditional coupledom implied simply weren't intrinsic to my makeup. I didn't need merged lives, steady company, regularized cuddling. And none of that amounts to a character failure. It's simply a definition of who I am. It didn't automatically follow—as my (destructive) therapists believed—that I was incapable of closeness and terrified of intimacy. Even several of my therapists agreed that I was an affectionate, empathic person with a large capacity for honest communication, for telling the truth about my own heart and being able to listen to someone else's truth (sometimes *despite* their words).

Besides, why do we so readily assume that sex in a backroom bar necessarily fails—purportedly because of its "depersonalized," transient nature—to qualify as intimate? Who's setting up these standards and making these definitions? Are they mere conventions, or do they embody some sort of universal truth? Let's take a guy—we'll call him Joe—and put him in a backroom bar. Joe spots a guy across the room with pronounced biceps, say, or dimpled cheeks (either face or ass will do), and for reasons Joe couldn't begin to itemize, nor care to if he could, those muscles or dimples trigger a set of fantasies that may originate from any point in his history—from his mother's dimpled smile in his early childhood to the tight jeans the office boy was wearing today—and Joe starts to feel horny. The guy catches Joe's stare, walks right up to him, and grabs his balls; clearly he's bold and forceful, and Joe isn't into "pretty" or "passive."

It's a match. They go at it hot and heavy, licking and tasting, touching and smelling—picking up in the process considerable information about each other. Their bodies interlock like machine-made parts, like finding one's other half—though no names have been exchanged, no standard information about current employment, past origins, future goals. They already know more about each other's personhood than a banal exchange of words could possibly supply. "Anonymous" sex has allowed for the safe projection of some of their most personal, cherished, and deeply buried fantasies—a decidedly intimate phenomenon. If we want to talk about impersonal sex, the best example might be not an orgy bar but what commonly transpires between a married couple of, say, twenty years when the husband is busily fantasizing about that woman in the elevator in order to produce the erection that will qualify the couple as "successful" partners.

BY 1986 IT HAD BECOME CLEAR to me that enough new scholarship about the gay experience had emerged to begin thinking about institutionalizing gay studies on the university level. The time had come, I felt, to attempt the establishment of a center devoted to lesbian and gay studies at the CUNY Graduate School, where I taught. My aim was political as well as intellectual: I felt that LGBTQ scholars had much to tell the mainstream world about gender and sexuality and that their findings needed to be widely disseminated, not least as a way to contest right-wing propaganda about homosexuality as degenerate and criminal.

I wanted to encourage an activist scholarship that would be scrupulous in its methodology yet productive of the kinds of insight that would challenge a host of rusty assumptions ("Homosexuality is a mistake of nature"; "People become homosexual because of faulty genes"; etc.). I believed LGBTQ scholarship held the potential to become a major engine for social change, a kind of Trojan horse whose hidden force, once led inside the gates of traditional academia, would vanquish stereotypic views on gender and sexuality. I wanted to change hearts, minds— and laws.

The organization, in my view, had to exemplify in its own structure, the kind of change it hoped to foster in the culture at large; accordingly I emphasized from the start that what became the Center for Lesbian and Gay Studies (CLAGS) must be based on the principles of gender parity and must represent diverse racial and ethnic concerns, as well as a range of disciplines and communities—including independent scholars without university affiliations. I hoped further that although queer theory was then in its infancy, its dense language wouldn't prevent us from recognizing that its message was of critical importance: namely, that gender and sexuality should not necessarily be viewed, as was then (and still is) commonly the case, as fixed entities but treated as potentially fluid, malleable, and unstable. Which was not to deny, on the other hand, that the current gender and sexual reality of some— perhaps many—individuals brought down on their heads real, not imagined, brutality and violence.

In order to form and build a political movement, LGBTQ people did need to emphasize a shared relationship to the dominant white male patriarchy, to heteronormativity, if you like—an emphasis that allows for a sense of common values and goals and potentially leads us into alliance with other oppressed groups. Yet as soon as we factor in diverse ethnic, class, and racial loyalties, we necessarily complicate the picture—along with better appreciating the difficulty many individuals have in establishing a hierarchy of obligations and allegiances. Though I believe identity politics is an essential conceptual tool, I remain troubled at the inability of overarching categories or labels like "black," "female," or "gay" to represent accurately the multiple, often overlapping identities that characterize individual lives. Some of us are no less uncomfortable about referring to *the* gay community" as if it's one homogeneous unit rather than a hothouse of contradictions; we're concerned too about the inadequacy of our efforts to date to create bridges that would connect marginalized constituencies to each other, thereby increasing the impact of our combined strength.

A full decade later, issues relating to identity continued to bother me. In 1996, when I stepped down after ten years as CLAGS's executive director, I again tried to summarize my views:

> One holds on to a group identity, despite its insufficiencies, because for most non-mainstream people it's the closest we've ever gotten to having a political home—and voice. Yes, identity politics reduces and simplifies. Yes, it's a kind of prison. But it's also, paradoxically, a haven. It is at once confining *and* empowering. And in the absence of alternative havens, group identity will for many continue to be the appropriate site of resistance and the main source of comfort.
>
> Straight critics of identity politics employ high-flown, hectoring rhetoric about the need to transcend our "parochial" allegiances and unite behind Enlightenment "rationalism," to become "universal human beings with universal rights." But to me the injunction rings hollow and hypocritical. It's difficult to march into the sunset as a "civil community" with a "common culture" when the legitimacy of our differentness as minorities has not yet been more than superficially acknowledged—let alone safeguarded. You cannot link arms under a universalist banner when you can't

find your own name on it. A minority identity may be contingent or incomplete, but that doesn't make it fabricated or needless. And cultural unity cannot—must not—be purchased at the cost of cultural erasure.

THE OFFICIAL RECOGNITION of CLAGS as a center at the CUNY Graduate School in 1991 is usually taken as the date of its birth. But in fact it took five years, from 1986 to 1991—years of constant, hard-fought battles, both internal and with the CUNY hierarchy—for CLAGS to reach that point of arrival, to finally win accreditation. During those five years our organizing committee, as we called ourselves, fluctuated wildly, never included more than two dozen people, and struggled mightily against difficult odds—the struggle marked periodically by bitter infighting among ourselves, usually replicating those same divisions of gender, race, and class that agitated the larger society. Since I recount that part of the story in considerable detail in my memoir *Waiting to Land*, I won't repeat it here.

But it's worth saying a bit more about the long string of painful encounters during 1986–91 with entrenched institutional homophobia at the Graduate School—especially since our comparative success in those battles meant that since 1991 CLAGS has been able to enjoy a much more cordial relationship with CUNY administrators and staff.

In the five-year struggle to establish CLAGS, we were fortunate that Harold Proshansky and Frances Degen Horowitz, the two consecutive presidents of the Graduate School, proved unwavering allies from the start. Still others in the CUNY hierarchy were well-disposed, especially Steve Gorelick, Alan Gartner, and Stephen Brier. Alas, they were in a minority. A well-placed number of deans and department chairs seemed determined, discreetly, to throw obstacles in our path. Even after our formal establishment in 1991, it took ten months before we were assigned office space.

I vividly remember the angry confrontation I had with one CUNY vice president over the issue of assigning CLAGS an office—or at least the approximation of one. As he lounged in his Eames chair, blew cigar smoke in my face, and kept unconvincingly assuring me that the Graduate School was simply bursting at the seams and had no available space, I got progressively angrier. I told him we didn't expect the kind of resplendent digs, replete with Eames chair, that marked his own office suite, but a center *did* need to have an address, couldn't float unanchored in space. It was only after I got him to admit that we were the only center at the Graduate School without a physical home that he finally, reluctantly managed to assign us some semblance of an office.

And what a space it was! It more closely resembled a dungeon than an office. Dark and forbidding, it had a single window so thick with soot we could barely make out the brick wall it faced on. Only two or three of the fluorescent bulbs in the ceiling were working; electric wires (not live, happily) lay scattered over the torn and ratty rug; and furniture, in its entirety, consisted of one desk, one chair, and two rickety file cabinets.

In those first years of its formal establishment, 1991–96, the executive director (me) got no course release, had no interns, only belatedly got a part-time graduate assistant, and was given no direct financial support. We got in-kind support only—like that wonderful office—not, as is currently the case, 20 percent of our budget. To find even meager funding for the multiple activities we soon launched, we had to rely on a low-yield membership drive and to literally pass the hat at the public events we organized.

A few—a very few—wealthy gay donors would occasionally send us a sizable check, which in our poverty meant more than $100. But though I tried buttering up any number of them at lunch or dinner, the yield was negligible. In those years, of course, AIDS was rightly regarded as the primary emergency, but in addition the nonscholarly gay world simply didn't get it, didn't understand that the production and dissemination of reliable scholarship was an essential form of activism, that it provided the needed reservoir of information with which to challenge discriminatory attitudes and laws. I repeatedly used the analogy of the *Brown v. Board* decision, underscoring the fact that Thurgood Marshall's successful argument before the Court had relied heavily on recent scholarship regarding race. The looks I got mostly ranged from blankness to disbelief.

Nor, in the beginning, did we have much luck with the foundation world. Even the liberal organizations, we soon discovered, scoffed at the notion that gay studies was a legitimate field of scholarly inquiry, and our applications for financial support got short shrift. Only a few gay funding agencies then existed, and only one, the Paul Rapoport

Foundation, considered us worthy of support; the $10,000 annual grants they awarded us for a number of years provided a memorable lifeline.

During my tenure we did ultimately have two major break-throughs—the first gay group to do so—with both the Ford and Rockefeller foundations. Rockefeller awarded us its prestigious Humanities Fellowships, and then, unprecedentedly, *renewed* the award, thus allowing us to offer two $35,000 grants to gay scholars for a number of years; the Rockefeller imprimatur went a long way toward assuring CLAGS's viability as an institution. By the early nineties we had enough of a financial toehold to be offering research grants that ranged from $5,000 to $35,000 in a field that had previously generated next to no financial support for scholarly research.

Though the work was difficult, time-consuming, and contentious, all was not tedium, dreary squabbling, and relentless chores. Far from it. The ten years I spent as director of CLAGS were filled with far more excitement than contention, and our sense of accomplishment grew more pronounced with the years. Against heavy odds we did more than survive—we flourished. We got Alice Walker and Adrienne Rich to cochair our inaugural benefit in 1991, which drew some five hundred people and raised $26,000—for us, a fortune. Subsequent fund-raisers were chaired by Gore Vidal, Kate Millett, Paul Monette, and Allen Ginsberg, and a gala reading to raise money for CLAGS featured Terrence McNally, Stephen Sondheim, Danitra Vance, Gloria Naylor, and Grace Paley.

We also produced a regular newsletter, compiled a scholarly directory that tied together gay researchers around the globe, and carried off a series of colloquia, panel discussions, and packed conferences, some lasting two or three days and all open to the public free of charge. Those events were often galvanizing; they brought together scholars previously working in isolation and disseminated innovative, sometimes pathbreaking research. A panel on butch/femme roles drew a sea of five hundred women eager to hear debate on such questions as "To what extent do such roles ape and parody patriarchal models?" and "Can a sexuality not based on mutual pleasuring be considered egalitarian?" Among our longer conferences was an explosive two-day event, "The Brain and Homosexuality," that dissected—that's the word—Simon LeVay's recent, much-heralded work (including on the front page of the *New York Times*) claiming that he'd incontrovertibly proved that homosexuality was biological—a claim the CLAGS panelists furiously (and to my mind, successfully) rebutted.

A wide variety of other standing-room-only conferences included "Homo-Economics," "Feminism and Lesbianism," "Homosexuality and Hollywood," "Queer Theory," "Black Nations/Queer Nations," "AIDS and Public Policy," and "Trans/Forming Knowledge." The events draw scholars from around the country (and occasionally from overseas), and the best of them produced lengthy, contested discussion, in the process reformulating long-standing assumptions and reconfiguring what had seemed firmly drawn boundaries and static definitions.

The existence of CLAGS also led to a gradual proliferation at the Graduate Center of course offerings with gay-themed material, as well as the arrival of a substantial number of graduate students drawn to CUNY as a gay-friendly environment—a fair proportion of whom ended up choosing to write their doctoral theses on gay-related subjects. I myself offered a seminar titled Reclaiming Gay/Lesbian History, Politics and Culture that was so oversubscribed I had to turn it into *two* seminars; the course's popularity sent a strong message about the rapidly burgeoning interest in gay studies as a legitimate field of scholarly interest.

There was a toll for all this. The ideal of a disinterested, loving community of scholars gave way all too often to an academic version of gang warfare. Scholars in general—and gay scholars proved no different—proudly disdain as beneath them such mundane tasks as rounding up potential donors, serving on administrative committees, or getting out a newsletter. Yet they can be quick to invent slights, accuse others of failing to do their share, and, with inflated posturing, engage in petty backbiting. I did sometimes weary of what seemed an endless parade of prima donnas whose résumés were thin, who'd been "activists" as of that year, and who often announced themselves "too busy" to follow through on tasks they'd volunteered to complete, yet felt no hesitation in harshly criticizing other CLAGS board members who'd been doing exemplary work on both counts. I tried hard—sometimes unsuccessfully—to swallow my occasional exasperation at having constantly to pick up a dropped ball, telling myself that, as Big Daddy, a fifty-eight-year-old Privileged White Man, I was a sitting target for resentment, a convenient receptacle for dumping pent-up grievances.

I wasn't, by any stretch, a natural for the nuts-and-bolts work of building an organization—and I loathed fund-raising. Fortunately my pronounced obsessiveness served me well at detail work and follow-up, even though my temperamental bottom line has always been "Please leave me alone so I can do my own work." At several points over the years I came close to throwing in the towel, and at least twice begged the board to find a genius or two at organization building to replace me as director.

When I wearily told all this one day to Tim Sweeney, who'd headed up several LGBTQ organizations, he smiled and told me that it was part of the job description—definitely par for the course. Every director of every lesbian/gay organization, Tim said, feels puzzlement and hurt at various points in their tenure when a simple mistake is treated as a cosmic crime.

That made me feel better, but there was still many a day when I longed for the solace of a Valium—or a monastery. At one point in 1988, when in-fighting on the board happened to coincide with a particularly nasty attack on me by Paul Robeson Jr., I was melodramatically feeling like the arrow-ridden body of St. Sebastian, and I came within a hair of resigning—with or without a replacement. I'm awfully glad I didn't. Now, thirty years later, CLAGS continues to exist and continues to generate the production and exchange of critically important new scholarship.

AH YES—PAUL JR. We've arrived at the denouement of that extended tale. By late 1987 I'd completed a draft of the Robeson biography, and Bobbie—my superb editor, Barbara Bristol—and I began, on a nearly daily basis, a laborious, invaluable process of revision. Simultaneously I gave a copy of the manuscript to Paul. Contractually I wholly controlled the book's content, but I'd agreed to let him read the manuscript for possible factual errors, which I felt more than happy to correct. The difference between a fact and an interpretation—aside from, say, a mistaken date or a misspelled name—has long been one of the more bedeviling issues that attend historical writing. It wasn't an issue that concerned Paul. He made it clear that he felt entitled to treat the entire manuscript as fair game for his critique, took it as his prerogative to comment on every word—and contract restrictions be damned. I braced myself for a major assault.

So I was surprised when Frances phoned about a week after Paul got the manuscript to tell me he'd called her to say that he'd read the first eleven chapters and "was not disappointed in any way." I should have known better than to feel pleased. Two days later he again called Frances, this time to say he "hated the book in every way." That was more like it. That was the Paul I knew. As I wrote in my diary, "At the least, I suspect, he will now formally distance himself from the book and probably denounce it publicly."

I assured myself, with fake bravado, that should his public denunciation be abusive, or should he attempt a lawsuit to halt publication, I'd add to the book the full truth about his father's active dislike of him. I'd now had that testimony from a dozen people—along with their stated conviction that Paul Jr. was certifiably disturbed—though I'd refrained from suggesting as much in the book, had given him somewhat more than his due as a confidant to his father, delicately and decently (I told myself) refraining from inflicting needless pain. I never did, I'm glad to report, give vent to my largely rhetorical pugnacity, though Paul did become harshly and publicly denunciatory and did attempt to stop publication; I let my kindlier version of his relationship with his father stand. Postcocaine, I wrote in my diary, "I've lost some of my taste for turmoil."

The choice, it turned out, wasn't mine. Paul sent Knopf seven hundred (!) pages of "commentary" on the manuscript that disputed something on nearly every page and rippled with wild charges—"Duberman is a racist red-baiter"; Essie Robeson lacked "political sophistication"; "Helen Rosen was given to "profound bad judgment"—and insisted that Knopf reject the manuscript and cancel the book contract.

In a real sense I was ready for him. I'd spent years mulling over the puzzle of why he had come to me, an openly gay, Jewish, white man, in the first place, and why he had continued to strew my path with false clues about his father's sexuality and his mother's "perfidy." Thanks to the information I'd gotten over the years from many of those who'd been closest to his father, pieces of the puzzle had gradually come together.

As early as 1985 my agent, Frances Goldin—who'd also been Paul's agent and had known him for many years—phoned one day after having lunch with him. She said—and I recorded her words in my diary—that "she 'loves him' but came away from the lunch convinced that he's 'nuts—beset with demons.' And 'dangerously homophobic.'" Among other bizarre claims, Paul had told her that Vanessa Redgrave had "trapped" Susan, his daughter, into an affair. He'd also reiterated—yet again—that I was "out to destroy his father by revealing [not 'inventing,' note] his 'gay side.'"

As I wrote in my diary, "I begin to think Paul—on a level not available to him—is the one bent on 'destroying' his father. *He* invited a gay man to do the biography. *He* first raised the issue—on our initial meeting—of his father's 'bisexuality,' compelling me to look for evidence. Having found none for an affair with Eisenstein—and having *told* Paul I'd found none—he'd then dropped a new bombshell on Frances: 'my father had an ongoing affair with Marc Blitzstein' "! I'd also tracked down that claim by talking with Blitzstein's biographer, among others, and found no corroboration for it.

According to Frances, "Paul Jr. thinks the worst thing you can say about somebody is that they're gay." Yet he ends up choosing me as his father's biographer. The unavoidable conclusion, it seems to me, is that Paul hoped I'd prove eager to believe his Eisenstein/Blitzstein stories and would proceed to claim his father for gay (or bisexual) liberation—thus compromising his "heroic" stature, bringing him down to earth, and, not incidentally, getting back at him for the distance he'd maintained between them. (By my standards, the revelation of Robeson's bisexuality, had the evidence confirmed it, would have, if anything, enhanced his stature.) I don't believe for a minute that any of this was conscious on Paul's part; I didn't see him as introspective enough to have gotten fully in touch with his father's indifference to him, nor to plot his revenge. Paul was certainly in touch with his anger, but I think it's unlikely that he consciously attributed much of it to the lousy parenting he'd had. He had to have sensed—and probably made haste to bury—the deeply painful, indigestible awareness that his father had been disinterested in him when young and had little use for him as an adult.

Unhappily for Paul, he couldn't allow himself fully to feel (or directly express) the anger toward his father to which he was certainly entitled; it was easier, emotionally, to join those who worshipped the great man. Yet his anger needed an outlet, and as I see it, he dumped a fair amount of it onto his mother—who was, ironically, the more attentive parent. Over the years Paul had "casually" told me that Essie had been a CIA agent or a "double agent," that at one point she'd put speed in his father's heart medication, and that in her later years she'd turned lesbian; Paul—so he told me—had made the decision to burn Essie's "love letters" to and from other women. He was never consistent in portraying his mother as an evil bitch; to some people he denounced my book as too *pro*-Essie, to others (including Helen Rosen's daughter Judy) as too *anti*-Essie.

I had refused the assignment of portraying his father as bisexual— refused on any grounds to act as Paul's surrogate in getting even with him by reducing his stature; left with his resentment of his father un- expressed, Paul redirected at least some of that resentment onto the manuscript that presented his father as one of the giants of African American—which is to say, American—history.

This entire scenario may sound far-fetched, but not to those (like Helen Rosen and Frances Goldin) who'd been exposed for any length of time to Paul's wrenching emotional turmoil, or to the pitiable history of his inability to win his father's interest and regard. The least I could have done, Paul must have felt, was to have confirmed the role he'd long claimed as his father's closest confidant. I could not. When his father had a severe breakdown in London, the person Essie asked to rush to England was Helen Rosen, not Paul Jr. Essie even failed to notify her son of his father's condition—afraid, according to Helen, that Paul's "instability" might make the situation still more difficult.

In fact I handle Paul as gently in the book as I could, short of distort- ing the evidence outright; he may have made my life miserable now and then, but I did feel compassion for him. I did not repeat in the book the shockingly encompassing assessments that Freda Diamond and Helen Rosen—the two women, along with Essie, closest to Paul Sr. over a considerable period of time—had told me about the relationship be- tween father and son. Freda, Robeson's longtime lover before Helen arrived on the scene in the mid-1940s, had gone so far as to insist that his father simply "didn't like him."

Helen's testimony was, if possible, more damning still. After our friendship solidified, she let me read Paul Sr.'s many letters to her, and when the book came out she suggested we make one final tape "to set the record straight for posterity." On that tape she dropped all reticence and spoke bluntly about a number of matters. One of them was the re- lationship of father and son: "He never cared about Pauli [Paul's child- hood nickname] or trusted him or wanted him. . . . He was an unwanted child. And as an adult . . . his father did not like him. . . . I don't think Pauli was ever a confidant. . . . I don't think I ever heard him [Paul Sr.] say anything directly, terribly derogatory about Pauli, but it was perfectly obvious that there was no love."

In regard to Paul's accusation that the biography was excessively pro-Essie, I asked Helen for her frank assessment of the accusation: "Was I too easy on Essie?"

"No, I don't think so at all," she said. "I thought you were very polite and very accurate. . . . She was a very difficult and a very devious lady, and I have to hand it to her, because I think Paul was an impossible husband. . . . I think Paul liked me because I was the only woman who didn't want to marry him."

"What about Freda's denial to me that she wanted to marry him?"

"Oh please," Helen responded with amusement. "He told me story after story about that."

"Finally," I asked, "what about Paul's insistence that his father was never clinically depressed?"

"Oh, my god! . . . He was awfully sick. . . . When I got there [London] that morning, he was curled up like a baby on the bed, in the . . . what they call the fetal position."

WHEN I COMPLETED the manuscript, I sent Helen a copy as well as Paul Jr. She called me a few days later from her vacation home in Key West to tell me that she'd stayed up all night with the manuscript and wanted me to know that she considered it "a triumph—you've captured the man I knew." The next day she called again to say that she'd just been on the phone for an hour with Paul. She'd phoned him to offer congratulations on the book and run straight into what she characterized as an unstoppable "rant."

During their hour-long conversation, according to Helen, Paul complained bitterly, yet again, that the book was too "pro-Essie" and that (yet again) I'd refused to acknowledge his father's six *black* female lovers—"Duberman has that list and is suppressing it." As I'd already said several times over, if such a list existed, Paul had never given it to me. The only black lovers he'd ever mentioned as his father's sexual partners were Fredi Washington, Nina Mae McKinney, and Ethel Waters. In the book I *did* describe both Washington and McKinney as Robeson's lovers for a brief time. (Neither—unlike Freda Diamond, Helen, and several other white women, including Uta Hagen—were in his life for very long.)

In regard to Lena Horne—who Paul had also once mentioned as one of his father's lovers—I included Revels Cayton's remark to me that Robeson had told him that relationship ended when he refused to marry her, though when I asked her directly if they'd been lovers, she replied, "It would never have occurred to me to be physical with him—he was too mythic." As for Ethel Waters, she's widely thought to have preferred women, and in any case I was unable to find a scintilla of evidence that she was even one of Robeson's casual, one-night stands. As Helen said to me on the phone, "Big Paul himself told me he didn't like going to bed with black women because they were too ladylike." She advised me, in the face of Paul's onslaught, to "try and stay cool and calm. You are dealing with an unstable man."

A short time later I happened to be in Helen's apartment one evening when Paul phoned. Guessing at what was coming, Helen signaled me to pick up the other receiver. That night I recorded some of Paul's twenty-minute diatribe in my diary: "Duberman's manuscript is a disaster; he's a racist and a red-baiter and has had a hidden agenda all along to destroy my father; I don't intend to let him get away with it." The rage in his voice chilled me; perhaps overdramatizing, I felt actually frightened, felt Paul was capable of anything—a lawsuit being the least of it.

If nothing else, Paul was tenacious. Furious at Helen's favorable reaction to the manuscript, he turned his energy to blocking the book's publication. The bulky "commentary" he sent to Knopf reeked of fury. Deciding to take no chances, I responded *in writing* to every single one of his comments, most so outrageous that Helen's advice to remain "cool and calm" proved unattainable. A few samples from Paul's commentary, along with my responses, will capture the flavor of the whole.

His father once told him, Paul wrote, that "he was literally afraid to divorce Essie; 'she'd cut my throat if I did.'" The comment is symptomatic of Paul's venom toward his mother. Time and again in his commentary, he attempted to disparage her, criticizing me for not expanding more on her villainy. "There is a failure here," he wrote in the margin of one page, "to note Essie's gross insensitivity. . . . Many people close to both Paul and Essie can confirm Essie's 'suffocating' quality." At other points in the commentary Paul declared his mother "not a consistently reliable source of accurate information," referred to her "obtuseness," accused her of lacking in "political sophistication" and of being "very subjective in her attitudes towards his father." ("Unlike *who*?" I jotted in the margin.) The implication was that I'd taken every word in Essie's diary and correspondence at face value, whereas in fact I'd consistently challenged them, pointing out various discrepancies in her account of events. Besides, in comparison with her son, Essie was a paragon of accurate reporting. Unable psychologically to express anger at his father, Paul may well have transposed it on to Essie. The one became a depository for all the virtues, the other for all the derelictions.

As for his father's sexuality, Paul specifically denied in his commentary that he'd ever heard a rumor about an affair with either Eisenstein or Blitzstein—though he was the one who had initiated both rumors. In regard to Robeson's robust heterosexual history, Paul insisted that his father "did not separate his romantic and sexual relationships. . . . [He was] definitely not a person who engaged in 'one-night stands.'" Yet Revels Cayton, Robeson's closest black male friend, had told me that when they were young men they'd often gone "whoring" in the Village. Freda Diamond amplified: Robeson, she told me, sometimes had simultaneous affairs going on and sometimes slept with several different women in a single night—and told her about it.

Displeased with Uta Hagen for having revealed to me the details of her affair with his father, Paul tried hard in his commentary to discredit her, insisting that she was a heavy drinker who sometimes became "abusive and incoherent" and who "attempted suicide" when his father terminated their affair. He even made the bizarre claim that his father was "disinterested" in Hagen sexually, and demanded that the whole purported affair be deleted from the book as in "poor taste." He insisted that Hagen's "reliability [was] questionable," though he presented no evidence to confirm that view and though I had found her an admirably forthright witness whose testimony always checked out when matched against the accounts of others.

Another set of Paul's accusations revolved around what he called my "anti–Old Left bias." If he meant that I wasn't a fan of Stalin nor a defender of the 1930s show trials, I plead guilty. But with a qualifier: for five years Paul had told me that his father *agreed* with the Soviet purge trials; in his commentary he amends that statement for the first time, belatedly claiming that his father found the accusations against at least one old friend (Ivan Kazakov) "absurd." (Essie, according to Paul, "not only believed them [the accusations] literally but even embellished them.") Further, Paul insisted that his father "signaled to the [Soviet] authorities that he would go along *in public* with their charade" but "warned" them not to harm two of his other friends, Itzik Feffer and Solomon Mikhoels. Since the authorities proceeded to kill both men, one might be justified in deducing that Robeson had no influence with the Soviet leadership—which Paul would of course deny. In any case, he presented no shred of evidence to back up his father's purported warning to the Soviet authorities—nor had he ever mentioned any such statement during five years' worth of conversations with me. Instead he accused me of describing his father as "disillusioned with the Soviet Union." But I never make any such claim in the book; I emphasize instead Robeson's belief that the Soviet experiment would weather Stalin's misrule and in the end triumph.

Paul also denied in his commentary that his father ever suffered from bipolar disorder—which not only contradicts an enormous amount of medical evidence but is tantamount to denying that the government's persecution and denunciation had any effect on him, that he was immune to mistreatment (as gods are wont to be). I preferred to think of Robeson as human and describe him in the book during the terrible years of his ostracism, denunciation, and decline as, like all human beings, vulnerable "to disappointment, weariness, despondency"—a view Paul denounced as "simply ludicrous." Yet at one point in his written remarks he did actually acknowledge—for the first time anywhere!— that his father "could be, at times, impatient, unreasonable, exacting, inaccessible, and suspicious," even as he flat-out denied that such moods could have been related to any extent to a depressive disorder. Bizarrely Paul entirely rejected the notion—documented to the hilt—that his father's breakdown in 1956 was any such thing; gods and heroes do not have clinical depressions. In his commentary he did acknowledge that at least once his father had an "extreme attack of anxiety," but he never defined how that differed from depression.

Not even the Soviet doctors who treated Robeson denied the extremity of his illness; on his chart, a copy of which I had, they wrote "depressive paranoid psychosis." His sympathetic American psychiatrist, Ari Kiev, told me that Robeson suffered from "clinical depression, not merely from a passing instance of 'anxiety syndrome.'" Another of his American doctors described his condition as "dementia" (though he wouldn't let me quote him, for fear, he said, that Paul would sue). Weirdly Paul elsewhere in his commentary described his father as "extremely paranoid" but ascribed it to living again with Essie!

Weirdly too Paul did acknowledge his father's suicide attempt in 1961, though he insisted that the London doctors—at the suggestion, he claims, of the U.S. government—were malignantly wrong in deciding that ECT treatments were the sole remaining recourse for a man suffering terribly and unresponsive to the limited medications then available. Paul denied that such treatments *had* been necessary and blamed—who else?—Essie and Helen. They were "amateurs," according to Paul, and Essie acted out of "her great need to be able to exert control over" his father. Helen, for her part, employed "profound bad judgment" and "wrongly chose to ignore the Soviet doctors' admonition against the use of shock treatment."

First of all, Helen played no role at all in the decision to use ECT; it was made before she arrived in London. As for Soviet medicine in those years, it was hardly on a par with England's, and even today—and even in the United States—ECT remains the recommended treatment for patients unresponsive and in extremis, as Robeson was (which I recount in considerable detail in the book). Paul tried hard in his commentary to discredit Helen, but didn't come close to succeeding. She remains, unimpeachably, among the most reliable witnesses I encountered.

Denounced by our government as a traitor during the cold war, abandoned by most of the black leadership, his passport lifted, his singing and acting careers destroyed—who would *not* have become despondent (or downright disabled if, as was the case with Robeson, an underlying manic-depressive tendency had long been dormant)? But in his commentary Paul claimed to know better, claimed that he and Lloyd Brown (an old Robeson friend) served as "Robeson's inner 'secretariat.' . . . I handled artistic affairs, relations with Party leaders, and relations with the Soviet Union. . . . Brown and I were the only persons other than Rockmore [Robeson's lawyer] who were authorized by Robeson to speak on his behalf. . . . We (separately and together) could serve as his alter ego(s) when necessary."

Alas, poor Paul, those closest to Robeson—Revels Cayton, Freda Diamond in the early years, and Helen Rosen in the later ones—tell a very different story. Paul's gross, and poignant, inflation of his role as trusted confidant can probably best be read as compensation—the obverse side of the coin of rejection. Paul accused me in his commentary of setting up "a false 'tragic Robeson.'" No, the facts do that—just as they sadly testify to Paul's *lack* of influence and standing in his father's eyes.

KNOPF'S LEGAL STAFF closely vetted both Paul's commentary and my written response to it and concluded that there was no sound factual basis for his various charges. No one at Knopf believed the manuscript was a "racist, red-baiting harangue" nor a "subtle, hostile" attack on his father. Knopf was also aware that Paul had no legal grounds for demanding changes in the manuscript. Nonetheless Sonny Mehta, Knopf's editor in chief, suggested a meeting in his office between the three of us, plus my agent Frances and Bobbie Bristol, the book's editor. There Paul announced that he was a "revolutionary, with worldwide commitments" in regard to the book, and *would be heard*. After Paul left, Sonny said, his tone one of disbelief, "What a piece of work!"

We tried to come up with some sort of compromise, to go the extra mile, that would allow Paul to save face. We settled on the idea of letting him name any third party he chose to read the manuscript and give their opinion of its merit. Paul chose Angus Cameron, a legendary figure in the publishing world, who'd suffered mightily for his own uncompromising left-wing views. Cameron, who was turning eighty at the time, had long been a fierce noncommunist critic of America's interventionist foreign policy; during the witch hunts of the late 1940s through the mid-1950s he'd been fired as editor in chief of Little, Brown and had spent a decade in the wilderness.

A few weeks later Frances called to report Cameron's verdict. "The book is spectacular," Cameron wrote Mehta. "Duberman has written a marvelously balanced portrait of what is now for the first time clear was this country's greatest black figure." Cameron added that he didn't know how I'd "managed to pull it off," and he planned to write Paul a "careful" letter which he hoped would "bring him to his senses." I was thrilled and relieved, of course, to have Cameron's good opinion. But I knew that the odds of bringing Paul around were close to nil—though perhaps, I wrote in my diary, "Cameron's opinion will at least modify the ranting a bit."

It didn't. Nor did the favorable reception the book got when published early in 1989 from many of the leading black scholars in the country, including David Levering Lewis, Arnold Rampersad, Nathan Huggins, and Nell Painter. The *New York Times* gave the book to the neoconservative historian John Patrick Diggins, who praised it highly but spent most of his review red-baiting Robeson all over again (and praising Essie!). With Paul denouncing the book as *anti*-Soviet and Diggins denouncing Robeson as *pro*-Soviet, I was tempted to say—if I didn't disapprove of the golden mean—that I must be doing something right. Paul certainly didn't think so. In the box interview that accompanied the *Times* review, the interviewer misquoted me as saying that Paul had chosen me because of my political activism in the gay movement! If Paul had any gaskets left intact at that point, the last one would surely have blown.

ENTER ELI—CONFOUNDING all expectation and a fair share of my prior speculations and fatalistic acceptance of a "mate-free" life. We met in 1987 at the first-anniversary party for the ACLU's Gay Rights Project. It was an instant case of what the French call "hooked atoms." A diary entry I made two months later captures the texture of what followed:

> Eli was here for 12 hours yesterday. The plan was for me to work, for him to sunbathe and read. I don't think we managed more than a 10 minute stretch without one of us *having* to see/touch the other. Even when we weren't patting and cooing, I sat stuporized in the study, not caring if Robeson was a man or a cheese. Finally I gave up the pretense to work and we stretched out for one of our marathon cuddles, breaking for a two hour movie (during which I cried profusely at any reference to love or mortality); me of the well-defined margins is rapidly liquefying. I've spent the last two hours chopping onions, tomato and chicken for dinner, and wondering if I should go to the corner again to see if any cranshaw melons have arrived. At last a daily agenda that comports with the rest of the world!

The atoms have stayed hooked—we've passed our thirtieth year together—but over time those marathon cuddles have alternated with a fair amount of mutual torment, fierce accusation, and near dissolution. As I said: like the rest of the world. But we've stuck it out and we've worked on it, knowing on a deep level that we are far better off together than apart. The details don't matter, aren't part of this story. Suffice it to say that the relationship has long since become impregnable and our routinized life an immense comfort.

THE COMPLETION OF the Robeson biography, along with starting up the Center for Lesbian and Gay Studies, marked the contented close of the least contented decade in my memory. In jumping to the end of the eighties, I've passed over much of what preceded in the years 1986–88, since most of it was satisfyingly ordinary. Suffice it to say that I continued to stay sober and that my relationship with Eli continued to develop, its multiple, necessary highs and lows the stuff of private memory.

Most of the everyday happenings of those three years isn't worth the retelling. I pretty much returned to the routines—barring Rounds and drugs—that antedated my rocky descent of the previous period. In 1986 I went back to my old stomping grounds, the Integral Yoga Institute; along with swimming, a healthy diet (Snickers bars *verboten*), and occasional massage and acupuncture, I was back to taking good care of myself physically—though a few new habits refused to take: hot water and lemon on retiring, "Thanks" whispered softly to a non-anthropomorphic ceiling on arising.

In continuing to work for the formal recognition of CLAGS as an official center of the CUNY Graduate School—which happened in 1991—I was also again committing considerable amounts of time to movement work (or my version thereof). My writing too, in output and vigor, fully returned to pre–Payne Whitney levels: post–*Paul Robeson* I've written some dozen books. In truth my greatest pleasure *is* writing. Compulsion is surely involved, part of the process—an undeniable ingredient in all my activity. The bottom line is that I find more contentment and satisfaction when at work on a book than when doing most anything else. This, I've learned, is a standing affront to those who self-describe as writers but loathe the actual process.

From time to time my lifelong ambivalence about a life primarily devoted to scholarship has continued to chaff, though in recent years I've gravitated to a nontraditional form, something close to what others have called "the nonfiction novel." Now and then I still think of traditional scholarship as "a life of invalid chores" (as I once called it) and have belittled in particular the professional historian's bottom-line effort "to fix fluidity" as an "essentially anti-life process." Discontent, though, is an ingrained element in my personality, and the scholarly life, as I've long known, is in fact well suited to my temperament. I have the three personality traits most congenial to it: a large appetite for solitude, a compulsive need to hunt down *every last detail*, and a well-developed sense of fairness.

HERE AND THERE in the scattered diary entries I continued to write during the late eighties, I've come across several stabs I made at summarizing the unhappy period preceding, as if to remind myself, now and then, of that low point in my life—a stay against repetition. A few of those jottings still strike me with force.

One is the entry I made about my last therapy session with Dr. Kleiman. I asked him to tell me how I'd initially struck him when I sought his help in the mid-eighties, since my own memory had become dim. I wrote down what he said pretty much verbatim: "You were physically exhausted. You walked like a man who had no reserves of energy left, and not a lot of hope. You didn't see how you could get through the first few months without drugs. Your sleep was shattered, you were unable to read, let alone work. You were frightened of having to go back to teaching. Your days were almost as bad as your nights. You were tortured, fragile. But you kept going to meetings, though you usually didn't like them. You still had the will to survive." Yes, I thought, that mysterious will to survive—the ultimate gift for which we can claim no credit.

"Today," Kleiman went on, "the shift has been remarkable—but not magical: you've worked hard for the ground gained. The one thing that hasn't yielded is your blocked emotional memory. Perhaps you still need that for protection against the pain of the past, though it does make you vulnerable to needlessly repeating experiences that, if you were more aware, you'd avoid from the start as unprofitable."

Afterward, pondering what Kleiman had said, I drew up my own inventory in a diary entry of 1988:

> Emotionally, I still carry around a certain base level of low anxiety
> that I feel will for me always be temperamentally "normal." In the

same way, I'll always have an attraction to dramatic amplitude, though these days I'm much more likely to flee turmoil than to seek it out. Yet I'm never going to make it as a cosmic muffin, or even a daffodil, despite my serene new vocabulary, my regularized dips in the pool and my diet of Greek yogurt, hummus, and organic peanuts. Though perhaps . . . perhaps aerobic dance, and the substitution of kiwi juice and kale chips for—no, no, no!

And then, of course, there's Eli—a relationship of solidity and comfort that's a far cry from my previous pursuit of unaware, unavailable men like Chris. "There's a downside to the 'ordinary, sensible' world I've come to inhabit," I wrote in my diary in 1987. "There'll always be—for someone of my temperament—a downside." No more the fireworks, the conflagration of coked-up sex with dreamboat hustlers. No more the narcotized sleep and the speeded-up writing. No more the insistent pursuit of the unobtainable person or goal. No more excessive self-blame; I can now actually share some of it. No more mainstream fantasies of idyllic vacations in the country—no more bloody trips to bloody Maine! "Most people," I wrote, "seem to dislike their daily routine and the pattern of their lives so intensely that any escape from it is welcome. These days I *like* my routine, even while recognizing that it's circumscribed—and it's okay to go on liking it twelve months a year."

I did sometimes wonder, though, how close my new reality was to the certified model. What do most people consider "appropriate" behavior for a fifty-eight-year-old—in terms, say, of productivity, sleep, erotic arousal, exercise? Was it okay to have a spreading waistline, unreliable erections, low-grade anxiety, muscle pain, moods? One part of me wanted to hear that I was doing just fine by "normal" measurements (not that I'd believe it). Another part of me didn't care what others thought was "appropriate" for someone approaching sixty. Had I ever been "appropriate"? Well, yes, in many ways I had. I'd followed a traditional career route, fought strenuously for "credentials," rarely been outlandish in public, presented myself for therapeutic correction, dreamed of a home and comrade to share it. Yet for most of my life I'd also harbored a smoldering defiance that stubbornly insisted on my own way of doing things. I once described myself as "pliably intransigent"—I questioned authority and rose up against it.

At the end of the eighties I'd very much learned to count my many blessings, though, as I wrote one day in my diary, "I loathe the ungrateful bastard in me who manages so continually to lose sight of them. Maybe this irreducible discontent is the best I can do (as AA might put it: 'try not to be so hard on yourself. You're just one more imperfect, struggling human being—and only your grandiosity keeps you from acknowledging that')."

When I spoke at a Cocaine Anonymous meeting on my fourth anniversary of being "clean and sober," I talked about the *comfort*—not the supercharged excitement I'd earlier pursued—of my relationship with Eli. I choked up and had to stop for a few seconds. As I later wrote in my diary, "I've had little comfort (as opposed to acclaim) in my life—and feel so grateful to have it at last. I feel haunted with gratitude, surrounded by so much suffering in the world."

Acknowledgments

I'm greatly indebted to the staff at Duke University Press for their un-
common and multiple skills in helping me to bring this book into its
final form. In particular, I want to thank Liz Smith for her advice on nu-
merous issues relating to production; Olivia Polk for her many cheerful
interventions; Amy Buchanan for calmly putting up with my sudden
alarms; Judith Hoover for her superb copyediting; and Mark A. Mas-
tromarino for his equally superb index. Above all I'm grateful to my
skilled editor, Ken Wissoker, for his sensitive response to the material
and to my complicated set of needs. Michael Bronski and John Howard read the manuscript in its entirety, and I'm hugely grateful to them;
their cogent comments have been indispensable. My partner, Eli Zal,
was as always steadfast in his support and wise in his insights.

Index

Belfrage, Cedric, 125
Bell, Alan, *Homosexualities*, 136
Bell, Arthur, *Village Voice* and, 53, 75
Berkowitz, Richard, "We Know Who We
  Are," 120
Bersani, Leo, 74, 80, 141; as friend of
  MD, 34, 41, 55, 151; as queer
  theorist, 41
Bettelheim, Bruno, *Children of the
  Dream*, 111
bioenergetics, MD and, 13–14, 34, 168
bisexuality, bisexuals, 17, 24, 140; Robesons
  and, 87–89, 129–30, 209, 210–11, 214
Black, Hillel, 83
Black Panthers, 120
blacks, 55, 72, 91, 126, 129, 216; Black Power
  and, 109–10; in Communist Party, 87,
  131, 132–33, 144; as gays, 76, 77, 99, 100;
  In White America, 85–86; liberals' and
  middle-class whites' views of, 72, 176–77;
  slavery and, 23, 26; stereotypes of, 177;
  struggles of, 85, 124, 133
Blake, Eubie, *Shuffle Along*, 126
Blau, Herbert, "Disseminating Sodom,"
  139–40
Bledsoe, Geraldine ("Gerry") Maimie
  Neale, 126–27, 182
Bleser, Carol, 23
Blitzstein, Marc, 130, 210, 214
Bloom, Harold, 194
Boggan, Cary, 97
Boudin, Kathy, 126
Boudin, Leonard, 125, 126
Bowers v. Hardwick, 186–87
Bowman, Parke, 100
Boyers, Robert, 135, 141, 143
Brad, as MD's love interest, 28, 30, 37
Bram, Christopher, 100
Brier, Stephen, 204
Briggs, John, 44; Briggs amendment
  and, 142
Brill, Ernie, 57
Bristol, Barbara ("Bobbie"), as MD's editor
  at Knopf, 90, 208, 217

Broadway, 12; off-, 11, 12, 85; Robeson in
  Othello on, 127–28; *Visions of Kerouac*
  and, 192
Broderick, Vincent, 184
Brodkey, Harold, 194–95; *The Runaway
  Soul*, 194
Brodsky, Joseph, 83
Browder, Earl, 132
Brown, David, 156; cocaine and, 83, 84,
  154–55, 156
Brown, Dee, *Bury My Heart at Wounded
  Knee*, 79
Brown, Howard, 28–29
Brown, Lloyd, 216
Brown, Oscar, Sr., 126
Brown, Rita Mae, 69; *Rubyfruit Jungle*, 100
Brownmiller, Susan, 41, 64, 66
Brown v. Board of Education, 205
Bryant, Anita, "Save Our Children"
  campaign, 46, 142
Buckley, Dick, 72, 128
Bunch, Charlotte, 76
Burger, Warren, 186
Burroughs, William, 99
Bush, George W., 141
Bush, Larry, 75
BWMT (Black and White Men Together),
  70–71

CA (Cocaine Anonymous), 168, 169, 171,
  175–76, 222; MD and, 177–79
Cabaret, 153
California, 142, 154, 157; MD in, 91, 92.
  See also Los Angeles; San Francisco
Callen, Michael ("Mike"): bathhouse scene
  tour of, 148–49; as gay activist, 109–11,
  119–20, 148–49; sexual revolution and,
  117–18; "We Know Who We Are," 120
Cameron, Angus, 217
cancer, 153, 181; of MD's mother, 1, 2, 3, 5–6
Carter, Jimmy, 45, 55
Cassady, Neal, 40; Kerouac and, 12, 192–93
Catholics, 11, 30, 32, 37, 71, 112, 116; seminar-
  ians, 30–31, 33, 48

Anonymous); alcohol, alcoholism; CA (Cocaine Anonymous); cocaine; DA (Drugs Anonymous)

Duberman, Josephine Bauml (MD's mother): business of, 1; character of, 1–2; death and funeral of, 8, 9, 31, 39, 192; final illness of, 1–8; as influence in MD's youth, 11; marriage of, 5; MD's grief and anguish over loss of, 9–10, 14, 48, 49, 93–94; MD's homosexuality and, 2–3; MD's relationship with, 2, 3, 4, 49; physical appearance of, 9–10; pride of, in MD, 2; unconditional love for MD, 165

Duberman, Joseph M. (MD's father), 5, 9, 49, 176

Duberman, Lucile (MD's sister): children of, 5; MD's heart attack and, 50; MD's relationship with, 9, 50; mother and, 1, 5

Duberman, Martin (MD): name change of, 35. See also character traits of MD; childhood and adolescence of MD; cocaine, MD and; depression, MD's; detoxification, supervised, MD's; diaries and journals of MD; drugs, illegal and prescribed, MD and; exercise, MD's physical; finances of MD; friends of MD; health, mental and emotional, of MD; health, physical, of MD; heart attack, MD's; homosexuality of MD; *Paul Robeson* (Knopf 1989); Payne Whitney Psychiatric Clinic, MD's detox at; physical appearance, MD's; political activity, MD's; psychotherapy, psychotherapists, MD's; scholarly career of MD; sex and love life, MD's; social life, MD's; teaching by MD; writing, MD and; *and entries on MD's writings*

Duberman family: conflict in, 9, 10; mother's final illness and death and, 1–2, 4, 5–6, 9

Dunkell, Dr., 172, 173–74

Durang, Christopher, *The Marriage of Bette and Boo*, 191

East Berlin: gays in, 185, 186; MD in, 182, 183–86; Pergamon Museum, 185

Eastern Europe, gays in, 186

East Germany (German Democratic Republic; GDR): Communist Party in, 185; gays in, 185–86; MD's travels in, 90, 182–86

Echols, Alice, 46

ECT (electroconvulsive therapy), Robeson and, 183–85, 216

Eggan, Fred, 17

Eisenstein, Sergei, 214; Robeson and, 129–30, 210

El Salvador, 149

Elshtain, Jean Bethke, 139, 143; "Homosexual Politics: The Paradox of Gay Liberation," 141–42

Enlow, Roger, 154

Enzensberger, Hans Magnus, 44

Everard Baths, 118, 138

exercise, MD's physical, 190; aerobic dance, 221; health club, 191; Nautilus workouts, 52, 93; post–heart attack, 51; resumption of, 80, 93; squash playing, 52; stationary bike, 51, 80; swimming, 191, 193, 219; Trevor recommends, 157; walking, 193; yoga, 219

Falwell, Jerry, 55, 115

family: cultural conservatives on, 113; homosexuality as assault on, 141–42; monogamy and, 111, 113, 117, 136, 141, 142, 149; radical gay critique of, 110

Farrar, Straus, 67, 89

FBI (Federal Bureau of Investigation): MD sues under FOI Act, 159, 184; Robeson and, 129, 132

Feffer, Itzik, 215

fellatio: AIDS and, 149, 197, 198; in Pueblo culture, 16. See also oral sex

feminism, feminists, 27, 67, 114; Alpert and, 39–40; ERA and, 55; history of, 123; Lasch denounces, 107–8, 112; lesbians as, 70, 136; pornography and, 61–62; prostitution

feminism, feminists (continued)
and, 61–63; proto-, 56; second-wave, 54; *Signs* and, 16; Weisstein and, 54
Ferrer, José, 12, 128–29
Fichtner, William, 193
finances of MD, 84, 89–90, 92, 94
Fink, Dr. Max, 184
Fire Island, 151, 178
Fisher, Rudolph, *The Walls of Jericho*, 181
flogging and flagellation, 33; in Pueblo culture, 16, 17
Flory, Ishmael, 131–32, 133
Ford Foundation, supports CLAGS, 206
Foucault, Michel, 135
Freedom of Information (FOI) Act, 159, 184
Free Soil Party, 123
Friedman, Dr., 81–83
friends of MD, 98, 151; abandonment by, 58–60, 152, 171, 174; Barbara Hart Weiss, 4–5, 53, 80, 159–61, 164, 166, 170, 188, 189; Bersani, 34, 41, 55, 74, 80, 141, 151; cared for by, 80; Chaikin, 79; Collins, 160, 161; criticism of, 102–3; criticisms by, 77; Dawson, 53; Gornick, 80; Harris, 100; Higgins, 53; Hunter, 70; Kimmel, 153–54, 160, 161, 164, 166, 170; Lemisch, 53–54; lost to AIDS, 179; MD visits in hospital, 193; Penny, 81, 151–52, 153, 160, 167, 171, 174; Poirier, 36–38, 58–60, 152, 174; Ron Gold, 70–72; Rosen, 127; Stoddard, 53, 72, 186, 190; Ward, 195–96; Weisstein, 53–54; Whitney, 53

Gail, as MD's fellow patient at Payne Whitney, 166
Gandhi, Indira, 125–26, 159
Garden, Nancy, *Annie on My Mind*, 100
Garson, Barbara, *MacBird!*, 56
Gartner, Alan, 204
Gary, as editorial assistant, 174, 187
Gates, John, 132–33
Gauchan, Bhim Prasad, 34
gay activism, activists, 114, 117, 191, 207; AIDS crisis and, 119–21, 123; leftist allies of, 68,

203; MD as, 68–77, 87; new generation of, 53, 70, 75, 121, 123–24; scholarship and, 205. *See also* Stonewall riots
Gay Activists Alliance (GAA), 46, 68, 76–77, 121, 123
gay bars and clubs, 94, 113, 137, 158, 200; Anvil, 118; Dallas, 94, 95; Eagle's Nest, 118; Gilded Grape, 29; Haymarket, 39, 40, 94; as middle class, 95–96; Mineshaft, 118; The Saint, 118; S/M, 118; Spike, 118. *See also* Rounds
gay culture: attacks on, 107; countercultural élan of, 68, 142, 199; democratization in, 148; erotic magazines and, 73–74; flowering of, 100; gay identity and, 69, 203–4; global, 99; macho in, 53, 66; mainstream, 73, 74, 76; recreational sex in, 117; safe sex and, 118, 119, 148–49, 150, 198, 199. *See also* differentness and gay culture; gay press
gay history and gay studies, 15–27; at AHA, 190; institutionalization of, 202; legitimization of, 207; primary sources of, 15, 19–25, 26. *See also* CLAGS (Center for Lesbian and Gay Studies); writings of MD, on gays
Gay Liberation Front (GLF), 46, 68, 76–77, 120–21, 123
Gaylord, Jim, 71
Gaylord v. Tacoma, 70–71
Gay Men's Chorus, 190
gay political movement, 67, 75, 139; ACT-UP and, 119, 120–21, 142; AIDS and, 100, 113, 116, 119, 120, 121; allies of, 72; alternatives to, 157–58; assimilationists in, 142, 143; birth of, 76, 77, 116, 120, 142; conformism and liberalism in, 76, 100, 102, 142, 158; counterculture and, 142; current, 70; division in, 121–24; events of, 73–75, 76; intersectionality and, 68–69; "just folks" view and, 121, 122, 135–36; lesbians in, 100, 136; male sexism in, 69, 76; MD and, 3, 10, 124, 158, 195, 219; 1987 March on Washington and, 187; radical minority in, 121–24, 136, 141, 143; reformism and civil rights in,

Haring, Keith, 100
Harrington, Ollie, 185
Harris, Bertha, 73, 75; *Lovers*, 41, 100
Hart, Barbara. *See* Weiss, Barbara Hart
Hart, Gary, 101
Hart-Davis, Rupert, 125
Harvard University, 112; Countway Medical
    Library, 15, 24; MD at, 136
Hawley, Dr., St. Vincent's Hospital, 50–51
Healey, Dorothy, 132
health, mental and emotional, of MD, 199;
    addictive personality, 155, 174; anger
    issues, 168; anxiety, 49, 82, 84, 88, 151, 157,
    162, 163, 165, 169, 174, 220, 221; avoidance
    mechanisms and, 52; blocked emotional
    memory, 220; breakdown, 159–60, 165;
    Chris and, 30–33, 36, 37, 38, 48, 49, 51, 52,
    78, 194; companionable love and, 78, 84,
    198; dreams and nightmares, 175, 176, 179;
    feelings toward mother and, 9–10, 14,
    48, 49, 51, 93–94, 165; fragility, 156, 196,
    220; homosexuality and, 3, 10, 49, 161,
    189; hopelessness, 220; humiliation, 49;
    intimacy, 52, 93; lethargy, 157; loneli-
    ness, 150, 156, 172; mood swings, 188, 221;
    need for dramatic amplitude, 64, 67, 172,
    177, 189, 221; panic attacks, 77, 161, 179;
    penchant for excess, 82; recurring need
    for excitement or variation, 67, 78, 79, 189;
    resilience of, 164; routine and, 13, 193, 194,
    219, 221; self-blame, 63, 77, 168; self-doubt,
    63; self-indulgence, 107, 162; self-pity, 37;
    self-sabotage, 78; solitude and, 152, 153,
    200–201; territoriality, 78, 80; vulner-
    ability, 28, 52, 57, 158, 197, 198, 220; will to
    survive, 220. *See also* depression, MD's;
    detoxification, supervised, MD's; psycho-
    therapy, psychotherapists, MD's
health, physical, of MD: acupuncture, 193;
    amoebiasis, 119; appetite, 80, 150, 159;
    bowel movements, 154, 156, 157, 160, 170,
    193; breakdown, 159–60, 165; cavities, 171;
    dizziness, 157; energy level, 94, 150, 155;
    exhaustion, 220; food choices, 173, 189,

193, 197, 218–19, 221; hepatitis, 79–80, 102,
    119, 156; insomnia and sleep problems,
    150, 166–68, 169, 171, 172–74, 179, 220; liver
    problems, 102, 165; nausea, 157; physicians
    of, 50–51, 79–83, 102, 162; shakes, 77, 167;
    spasms, 169; stress and, 51, 80; sweats,
    77, 157, 159; weight, 150, 173, 197. *See also*
    detoxification, supervised, MD's; exer-
    cise, MD's physical; heart attack, MD's;
    physical appearance, MD's
heart attack, MD's, 50, 93, 124, 174, 194;
    angina and, 102, 150; arrhythmia and,
    79–82, 102, 162, 164; chest pains and, 50,
    150, 162; Poirier and, 58–60, 152; recovery
    from, 50–52
Heep, Uriah, 144
Hellman, Lillian, 43
Helms, Jesse, 55, 61
Hemphill, Essex, 100
heterosexuality, heterosexuals, 19, 27, 122,
    140; fantasies and, 201–2; heteronorma-
    tivity and, 203; heterosexist dictatorship
    and, 142; as mainstream culture, 73, 74;
    Salmagundi and, 139; power relations in,
    61; sex and, 71, 139
Higgins, Rosalyn, 53
Hill, Joe, 74
Hispanics, 29, 121, 148
Hiss, Alger, 128
history of sexuality, 15, 24, 27; sources of, 16.
    See also gay history and gay studies
Hocquenghem, Guy, *Homosexual Desire*, 75
Holleran, Andrew, *Dancer from the
    Dance*, 100
Hollibaugh, Amber, 101
homophobia, homophobes, 24, 114, 120, 178,
    186; AIDS and, 115, 116, 186; during MD's
    adolescence, 49, 59; at CUNY, 164, 204;
    internalization of, 137, 165; liberals and,
    72; mainstream publishers and, 67–68,
    99; NYCLU and, 72; Paul Robeson Jr. and,
    209–10; in reviews of *Visions of Kerouac*,
    192–93; *Salmagundi* special issue and,
    139–43

homosexuality: in ancient Greece, 64, 199; anonymous sex and, 201–2; biological basis of, 206–7; challenging assumptions about, 202; cross-dressing and, 17; "cures" for, 185–86; God and, 140–41; history and, 15, 20–27; Kerouac and, 192; laws against speaking about, 71; in mainstream journals, 135, 139–43; Native Americans and, 16, 17; opposed by right wing, 55; oppressive social climate for in 1950s, 137–39; orgies and, 118, 138, 200; pederasty and, 64–66; public opinion of, 149; recategorized by APA, 68; scholars on, 113, 140–42; spread of AIDS and, 115; as threat to family and society, 113. *See also* bisexuality, bisexuals; lesbians; LGBTQs; *and gay entries*

homosexuality of MD, 35, 61, 189; "comes out," 3, 99; diary and, 10; guilt and negative feelings over, 3, 10, 49, 165; informs mother of, 2

Homosexuals (Whitney documentary), 53

Hoover, J. Edgar, 111

Horne, Lena, Robeson and, 213

Horowitz, Dr. James, as MD's physician, 51

Horowitz, Frances Degen, 204

Horowitz, Vladimir, at Rounds, 38

Houghton Mifflin, 89

House Un-American Activities Committee, 86

Housing and Urban Development Act, 71

Howard, Richard, 73, 75

Huggins, Nathan, 218

Hughes, Richard, 108

Human Rights Campaign Fund, 121, 124; annual dinner in 1982, 121–22

Hunter, Nan, 70

hustling, hustlers, 62; MD and, 64, 67, 94, 98, 119, 156, 221. *See also* Rounds

Illinois, Communist Party in, 131

Indiana University: Kinsey Institute, 15, 24; Lilly Library, 15

inequality, 45; economic, 56, 69, 108; structural, 68

Integral Yoga Institute, 219

Iran, 153

Ireland, Doug, 101, 116

Irene, from East Berlin, 185

Irving, Jules, 12

Ishtar Gate, Pergamon Museum, 185

Israel, 153, 191

Jackson, Esther, 131

Jackson, James, 131

Jackson, Yolande, 125

Japanese Americans, World War II internment of, 149

Jeff, as MD's roommate at Payne Whitney, 163, 167

Jenner, Bruce (Caitlyn), 154

Jew, Jews: cemeteries of, 185; MD as, 87; Orthodox, 107, 163, 167

John Birch Society, 11

Johnson, Ellsworth ("Bumpy"), 129

Johnson, Howard ("Stretch"), 131

Johnson, Kate, 194

Joint Committee of Historians and Archivists, 25

Journal of Homosexuality, 18, 26

Jung, Carl, 15

Jurrist, Charles, 117

Kalstone, David, as neighbor, 57–58

Kameny, Frank, 69, 117

Kapff, Sixt, 24–25

Kaplan, Helen Singer, 149

Katzenstein, Dr. Alfred, and Robeson, 182–85

Kazakov, Ivan, 215

Kenan, Randall, 100

Kennedy, Flo, 41

Kennedy Center, Washington, DC, 12

Kent, Sherman, 112

Kerouac, Jack, 39, 40; Cassady and, 12, 192–93

Khrushchev, Nikita, 133

social life, MD's: alternating with binges, 159; attends parties, 61–63, 64–66, 118, 128, 185, 194, 218; attends plays, 191–92; attends premiere of *Before Stonewall*, 190–91; birthdays, 1, 4, 61, 80, 198; celebrities and, 194; Christmas, 53, 54, 179; dinners, 42, 43, 44, 48, 50, 63, 101, 118, 128, 176–77, 181, 190, 194, 195; family dinners, 1, 2; hosts campaign fundraiser, 181; meets Eli at party, 218; moderation in, 63–64; resumption of, 53; return to normalcy of, 171; vacations in Maine, 151–54, 156. *See also* friends of MD

sodomy, 140; laws against, 68, 71

Sondheim, Stephen, 206

Sontag, Susan, 135

South Africa, 191

South Carolina College, 22

South Caroliniana Library (Columbia, SC), 21, 24, 25–26

Soviet Union, 133; Hiss and, 128; KGB and, 146; Moscow, 90, 129; Paul Robeson Jr. and, 144, 146; Robeson and, 86, 131, 132–34, 144, 214–16

Spender, Stephen, 135

Stalin, Joseph, 133, 214, 215

Steiner, George, 135, 137

Sterne, Hedda, 128

Sterner, Anita, 125

Stevens, Roger, 12

Stimpson, Catharine, 16, 42

St. Martin's Press, gays at, 99

Stoddard, Tom, 72, 186, 190; as MD's friend, 53

Stonewall riots, 75, 191; aftermath of, 68, 76, 116, 120, 121, 142

Stowe, Harriet Beecher, *Uncle Tom's Cabin*, 75

Strasberg, Lee, 11

Straus, Roger, 67, 89

St. Vincent's Hospital, 81; MD's heart attack and, 50–51

Sullivan, Dan, 192

SUNY, Stony Brook, 184

Sweeney, Tim, 208

Swinton, Pat ("Shoshana Ryan"), 42

Tabernacle Missionary Baptist Church, 132

Talese, Gay, 194

Talese, Nan, 89

Taylor, Paul, 194, 195

teaching by MD: at CUNY, 48, 104–6, 190; fear of returning to, 220; "History of Radical Protest in the U.S.," 104, 181; "History of Sexual Behavior," 104, 181, 199; in Ivy League, 96, 104; at Princeton, 195; "Reclaiming Gay/Lesbian History, Politics, and Culture," 207

Ted, as brother of "Sean," 95–96

teenagers, sex and, 65–66, 142, 172, 198

television, 77; rights to *Paul Robeson* on, 90; writing for, 12

Thatcher, Margaret, 116

theater: MD returns to, 10–13; MD sees Durang's *The Marriage of Bette and Boo*, 191; MD sees Kramer's *The Normal Heart*, 191; MD sees Rabe's *Hurlyburly*, 158. *See also* writings of MD, plays

Thom, Bill, 105

Thompson, Hunter, 85

Tibet, 35

Tiffen, Gregge, reads MD's circadian chart, 34–36, 79

Times Literary Supplement, 143

Times of Harvey Milk, The (1984 film), 53

Tom, as guard at Payne Whitney, 164, 166

Tom, as literary editor of *Christopher Street*, 101

Toronto, 73

transcendental meditation, 34

Transparent (Web TV show), 29

Treasures and Trifles, mother's resale shop, 1

Trevor, Bill, 156, 160; during MD's breakdown, 160–61; as non-doctrinaire psychotherapist, 52; on risks, 83, 84; sessions with, 77–79, 81

Tripp, C. A., 25; *The Homosexual Matrix*, 24, 25

writings of MD, essays, 67; *Hidden from History: Reclaiming the Gay and Lesbian Past* (with Vicinus and Chauncey Jr., 1989), 91; *The Uncompleted Past* (1969), 85

writings of MD, on gays: "About Time" (column), 18, 21, 23; *About Time: Exploring the Gay Past*, 25, 35, 155, 156, 171, 174, 188; on gay history, 15–27; *Hidden from History: Reclaiming the Gay and Lesbian Past* (with Vicinus and Chauncey Jr., 1989), 35, 91, 180; in *New York Native*, 121–22; "On Being Gay: A Modern Appraisal" for NAL, 84, 91, 171, 180; "Sexual Deviance: Historical and Contemporary" (seminar), 84

writings of MD, memoirs: *Cures*, 52; *Midlife Queer*, 13, 51; *Waiting to Land* (2009), 54, 204. *See also* diaries and journals of MD

writings of MD, plays, 68, 83–84; awards for, 85; for *Christopher Street*, 101; on Goodman, 171; *In White America*, 10, 12, 85–86, 193; *The Memory Bank*, 11–12; *Mother Earth*, 12; *Visions of Kerouac*, 9, 12, 192–93

writings of MD, reviews, 2, 10, 48, 112; of Bell and Weinberg, *Homosexualities*, 136; of Genovese, *The Political Economy of Slavery*, 108–9; of Kramer, *Faggots*, 191; of Lasch, *The Agony of the American Left*, 109–10

writings of MD, scholarship, 14; as activism, 124, 202; on black history, 85, 124; *Charles Francis Adams* (1961), 85, 195; on gay history, 15–27; *Hidden from History: Reclaiming the Gay and Lesbian Past* (with Vicinus and Chauncey Jr., 1989), 35; on history of sexual behavior, 104; *James Russell Lowell* (1966), 85, 195; Lincoln Kirstein biography, 194; *Paul Robeson*, 35, 85–92, 125–34, 144–47, 175, 181–89, 208–19. *See also* Goldin, Frances; *Paul Robeson* (Knopf 1989)

Yale University, 112
Young, Allen, 114
Young, Marilyn, 42
Young Lords, 120
Yulin, Harris, 194

Zal, Eli, as MD's companion, 218–19, 221, 222
zaps, by gay and lesbian activists, 68, 69